Your Workplace Rights

Your Workplace Rights

and How to Make the Most of Them

An Employee's Guide

ROBERT J. GREGORY

AMACOM

American Management Association
New York • Atlanta • Boston • Chicago • Kansas City • San Francisco • Washington, D.C.
Brussels • Mexico City • Tokyo • Toronto

This publication is designed to provide accurate and authoritative information in regard to the subject matter covered. It is sold with the understanding that the publisher is not engaged in rendering legal, accounting, or other professional service. If legal advice or other expert assistance is required, the services of a competent professional person should be sought.

Library of Congress Cataloging-in-Publication Data

Gregory, Robert J.
    Your workplace rights and how to make the most
of them / Robert J. Gregory
        p.   cm.
    Includes index.
    ISBN 0-8144-7991-X
    1. Employee rights–United States. 2. Labor laws and
legislation–United States–Popular works.
    I. Title.
    KF3455.Z9G74   1999
    344.7301–dc21
                                                99–13182
                                                CIP

Printing number

10 9 8 7 6 5 4 3 2 1

CONTENTS

Introduction   vii

Part I   The Law of the Workplace   1

Chapter 1. Race Discrimination   3

Chapter 2. Sex Discrimination   25

Chapter 3. National Origin Discrimination   45

Chapter 4. Religious Discrimination   55

Chapter 5. Age Discrimination   68

Chapter 6. Disability Discrimination   84

Chapter 7. Fair Labor Standards   107

Chapter 8. Employee Benefits   126

Chapter 9. Family and Medical Leave   144

Chapter 10. Wrongful Discharge   160

Part II   Workplace Rights in Practice   173

Chapter 11. Do I Have a Claim?   175

Chapter 12. Should I Pursue a Claim?   194

Chapter 13. The Pre-Suit Procedures   212

Chapter 14. Litigation   236

Part III   Some Major Workplace Issues   **253**

    Chapter 15. Sexual Harassment   **257**

    Chapter 16. Down(Sized) but Not Out   **283**

    Chapter 17. The Disability Dilemma   **304**

Index   **319**

INTRODUCTION

For most of its history, the American workplace was governed by a single principle: employment-at-will. An employer could hire the employee of its choice. The employee hired served at the will of the employer. If the employer wanted to terminate an individual's employment, it could do so at its complete discretion. While an employee could, theoretically, protect his or her rights by private contract, such agreements, between employee and employer, were rare. For the most part, the employee had no legal rights and no legal recourse against the employer, no matter how unfair the employer's actions.

The last several decades have seen a profound change in the nature of the employer-employee relationship. At the federal level, Congress has enacted numerous statutes that proscribe various employment practices and provide individual rights-of-action to aggrieved individuals. State legislatures have enacted similar laws, sometimes expanding protection beyond that provided under federal law. State courts have taken the matter a step further, using the doctrines of implied contract and public policy to circumscribe the employer's ability to terminate employees. The employment-at-will doctrine, if technically alive, is surely on life support, as the unfettered discretion of employers gives way to a more regulated work environment.

For employees, these developments, while favorable, do not come without a price. An employer that has unfettered discretion to fire an employee might well do so. That employer, however, might also be willing to cultivate a long-term relationship of trust with its employees—one secured not by the threat of a lawsuit, but by mutual need and benefit. Once the law begins to regulate the workplace, the employer's approach, by necessity, becomes more legalistic. Employers are increasingly sophisticated in their under-standings of the legal environment surrounding the employer-employee realtionship. Employers, moreover, appear more than willing to rid themselves of employees, sometimes in droves, as long as they "do it by the book," thereby avoiding legal liability. The regulated work environment, for all its protections, is not a panacea. It still leaves employees at risk of being cashiered, albeit on terms that, on the surface, appear to comport with legal stan-dards. It also imposes upon employees the burden of being suffi-ciently schooled in their basic rights to navigate the complexities of the modern workplace. If information is truly power, the employer, while losing its complete discretion to deal with its employees as it wishes, may well have retained the upper hand.

This book, as its name implies, seeks to fill this information gap by providing employees with a basic guide to their rights in the workplace. The matters covered in this book are hardly novel. There are numerous books that deal with the legalities of the employer-employee relationship. Many of these books, however, are written from the management perspective. Others have as their target audience lawyers. This book is not a legal treatise. The book provides a descriptive list of the rights at issue but places these rights in the context of real-world situations. The book is written, unabashedly, from the employee's perspective, with one goal in mind—to provide the average worker with some practical under-standing of the law's operation.

The book is divided into three Parts. Part I provides a panoramic view of the legal rights of individual employees. The first six chapters focus on the protections against discrimination, including the federal and state prohibitions against discrimination on the basis of race, sex, age, and disability. The middle chapters address a variety of labor-related issues, including fair labor stan-dards, protection of employee benefits, and family and medical leave. Part I's final chapter discusses, in general terms, the other possible encroachments upon the employment-at-will doctrine, principally the rights created under the doctrines of implied con-tract and public policy.

Part II of the book shifts the focus from the abstract legal principles to a real-world situation. In this part, the book posits a hypothetical employee who suffers some adverse action at the hands of an employer, giving rise to a potential legal claim. The book first explores the decision whether to initiate legal proceedings, balancing the merits of the claim against the real-world implications of bringing a formal complaint. In succeeding chapters, the book literally takes the hypothetical employee through the stages of the legal process, discussing the potential procedural pitfalls and the factors that may influence the decision to settle a potential claim. This part concludes with an explanation of the nature of litigation, with particular focus on the real-world impact of litigation on the individual.

Finally, in Part III, the book explores several discrete areas of employment law that are of fundamental importance to the workplace of the 1990s. These include: (1) the evolving law on sexual harassment; (2) the downsizing phenomenon, particularly as it affects the older worker; and (3) the overlapping (and potentially conflicting) statutory protections for disabled workers.

While I intend this book to be as comprehensive (and helpful) as possible, there are limits on the utility of any book of this nature. First, no book can cover it all. This book addresses a broad range of legal protections under federal and state law. The book's primary focus, however, is on the employee's right to be free from employment actions that unfairly impact the terms and conditions of employment. The book omits any detailed discussion of such specialized fields as workers' compensation and workplace safety. The book does not deal with the protections secured by collective bargaining agreements or, in general, with the issue of collective rights under the National Labor Relations Act. The book's discussion of state law is necessarily truncated, since legal doctrines vary in many respects from state to state.

Further, it should go without saying that this book does not substitute for the advice of a lawyer. I am a lawyer and have practiced in the employment field for a number of years. As noted previously, however, this is not a legal treatise. The book aims to provide useful, real-world advice to lay individuals. By necessity (and design), the book simplifies what are, in some cases, highly complex legal doctrines. The book provides a handy workplace reference for the employee. It does not constitute legal advice.

Finally, a book of this nature suffers from an inherent limitation. The employer's role in the workplace is largely proactive. An employer dictates the terms of the employment relationship and, with proper advice, can take steps to protect itself against a possible lawsuit. Employees, by contrast, are almost invariably placed in a reactive posture. Employees can take protective steps to enhance their legal position, once they are confronted with an adverse employment action. It is the rare case, however, where an employee can take steps in advance to head off a legal confrontation with the employer. This book can be of assistance to an employee once the axe has fallen, but whether the axe falls in the first instance is largely the prerogative of the employer.

Still, for all of these limits, there is an important role for a book of this nature. An employee, when confronted with an adverse employment decision, can always retain a lawyer. That lawyer, in turn, can file suit on the employee's behalf. Many employment disputes, however, can be resolved without litigation. The chances of this occurring are enhanced to the extent the employee is aware of his or her legal rights and can assert those rights intelligently before the parties have locked themselves into an intractable litigation posture.

There are other reasons, moreover, why employees should have some basic knowledge of the governing legal principles. First, there are consequences to any decision to pursue a legal claim. The law, for example, permits an employee to file a charge of discrimination with the Equal Employment Opportunity Commission (EEOC). The law also protects the employee from being retaliated against for filing a charge. Despite this legal protection, employers sometimes retaliate. By no means should an employee with a viable claim be intimidated by the threat of retaliation. By the same token, an employee should not, on a whim (and at some risk to the employee), conjure the scarce resources of government agencies and courts. An employee with some understanding of the legal framework can act responsibly in deciding whether to turn a potential claim into a federal case.

By the simple act of filing a charge, or even retaining a lawyer, an individual cedes away at least some control over the case. Once a charge is filed, government agencies can pursue enforcement actions on behalf of the employee. This is true even if the employee has second thoughts and no longer wishes to pursue the claim. A private lawyer, of course, cannot act against the wishes of the client, but the lawyer's interests do not always coincide with those of the employee. This book does not substitute for the advice of a lawyer, but it can provide a basis for meaningfully assessing such advice.

Too often, the regulatory culture encourages an assumption that if the legal right exists, it must be exercised. This is a common complaint of employers and their conservative allies, but employees themselves can be hurt by falling prey to this assumption. Not every adverse employment action is unlawful. Not every possible claim, even viable ones, should be litigated. A central theme of this book, Part II in particular, is that pursuing contentious litigation is not always in the best interest of the employee.

It should be apparent from this discussion that in saying this book is written from the employee's perspective, I mean just that. This is not a book written for the plaintiff's bar (i.e., those attorneys who represent employees). Nor is it written for the enforcement community (i.e., the EEOC and other government agencies and civil rights groups). The interests of these groups generally coincide with those of the employee, but not always. An employee must navigate an extremely complex legal environment, one comprising not only his or her natural adversary—the employer—but also the seemingly sympathetic institutional actors that come to the employee's aid. In this book, I seek, in a small way, to assist the employee in that journey.

Part I

The Law
of the Workplace

Part I of this book delineates the basic legal rights of employees. In keeping with my promise not to turn this into a legal treatise, I have tried, as much as possible, to avoid overly technical language and formal legalese. When making reference to a particular legal standard, I have attempted to use language that will be useful to the reader, while still doing justice to the complexities of the legal principle at issue. Part I is not organized by the statute or law in question. Instead, the focus is on the nature of the employment action or right involved. Nevertheless, since employee rights are largely a creature of statute, the reader must have some understanding of the underlying statutory framework. Where appropriate, I refer to specific laws or statutes by name, although I do not provide legal citations for the individual statutory provisions (or cases) that I discuss.

The federal prohibitions against discrimination in the workplace are contained in a number of statutes. The principal federal statute is Title VII of the Civil Rights Act of 1964 (Title VII), which prohibits discrimination on the basis of race, color, sex, national origin, or religion. Age discrimination is prohibited by the Age Discrimination in Employment Act of 1967, while disability discrimination is covered by the Americans With Disabilities Act of 1990 and the Rehabilitation Act of 1973 (which applies to the claims of federal employees). Other civil rights statutes provide overlapping protections, particularly 42

U.S.C. 1981, which was recently amended by Congress to prohibit most forms of race discrimination in the employment relationship.

Most states have laws prohibiting employment discrimination. While these laws mirror, to a large degree, the federal protections, there are differences. Some state laws have a broader reach, covering forms of discrimination not proscribed by federal statute. Some state laws provide for additional forms of relief and extend the protections of the law to employees of small employers not otherwise covered under federal law. Despite these distinctions, courts, for the most part, apply the same legal standards in analyzing claims of discrimination under federal and state law.

There are also a number of federal and state laws that regulate, in general, the employment relationship. The principal federal statutes include the Fair Labor Standards Act, which establishes wage and hour protections, the Employee Retirement Income Security Act, which protects employee benefits, and the Family and Medical Leave Act of 1993, which guarantees a minimum period of unpaid leave for family and medical reasons.

While comprehensive in scope, there are limits to the reach of some of the individual statutes. Title VII, for example, covers only those employers with fifteen or more employees. Title VII does not reach discrimination against independent contractors, nor does it apply to the employment decisions of Indian tribes or certain private membership clubs. Still, when the various federal and state laws are considered together, the gaps in coverage are relatively slight. Taken as a whole, these laws embrace the vast majority of employees, public and private, working in the United States.

Finally, it must be remembered that when statutes create rights, they also create procedures under which those rights are to be exercised. In the case of the federal antidiscrimination statutes, these procedures are complex, involving not simply the filing of a lawsuit but the filing of administrative charges with the appropriate state and/or federal agency. No matter how compelling the legal claim, that claim will be lost if the employee fails to comply with the procedural dictates of the pertinent statute. These procedural issues are discussed at some length in Part II of the book.

CHAPTER 1

Race Discrimination

For several reasons, it is appropriate to begin with a discussion of race discrimination. Race, of course, has been at the center of this nation's history. When Congress first acted to prohibit discrimination in the workplace, it was motivated chiefly by the specter of race. Race discrimination has been and continues to be pervasive. Because of its central role, race has been the driving force behind the law's approach, in general, to eradicate discrimination. Many of the legal principles adopted in the racial context have equal applicability to other forms of workplace discrimination.

The basic prohibition is easy to state. It is unlawful for an employer to discriminate against an employee on the basis of race with respect to any term or condition of employment. In this chapter, I deal with each of the component parts of this prohibition.

What Is Race?

If it is unlawful for an employer to discriminate on the basis of race, the first question is obvious: What is race? At one level, this is a complex (and sensitive) question. Race can be defined in biological terms. Race can also be seen as a sociopolitical concept, defined by culture as much as biology. In a heterogeneous society such as ours, the boundaries of race and ethnicity are particularly difficult to define. How does one classify, in racial terms, an individual who has a mixture of white, black, and Hispanic ancestors? Is this individual a racial minority? If so, to which racial or ethnic minority does the individual belong? Is the individual primarily African American? Is the individual primarily Hispanic? Or is the individual's minority status defined by reference to both his or her African and Hispanic lineage?

Fortunately, the law, in this context, does not require a precise definition of race. The laws against race discrimination exist to equalize the position of all employees, regardless of their particular racial background. The laws, for the most part, address the societal perception (or misperception) that there are differences in ability and merit among members of different racial groups. An individual who is perceived by society to be African American can claim the protection of these laws when, as a result of that perception, the individual is treated less favorably in the workplace. The individual need not provide specific proof of his African lineage. Further, since federal law prohibits discrimination on the basis of race or color, the law extends to any person of color regardless of the racial classification to which that individual might be assigned. In most cases, there is little controversy concerning the protected status of an individual asserting a claim of race discrimination.

There are, of course, cases on the fringe. An employee may claim that he was discriminated against because of his status as a racial minority. In biological terms, the employee's status as a racial minority may be in doubt. The employee, moreover, may hold himself out as a member of the dominant racial group. On the other hand, the employer may regard the employee as a racial or ethnic minority due to some physical or behavioral characteristic. One might argue that the employee, in these circumstances, cannot claim the status of a racial minority. A strong argument can also be made, however, that because the employer perceives the employee as a racial minority, the employee should be allowed to pursue a claim of race discrimination if, as a result of that perception, the employee suffers an adverse employment action.

EXAMPLE: An employee claims that he was fired from his job because of his status as a Native American. There is evidence that he possesses only a small amount (1/16) of Native American blood. The evidence also shows that he is not a member of a tribe and does not live in a Native American community. On the other hand, there is evidence that the employee has the physical appearance of a Native American and that the employer believes him to be a Native American. The employee should be allowed to pursue his claim of race discrimination.

While the threshold definition of "race" rarely presents a problem, there is a more fundamental point raised by the "What is race?" question. There is a perception that the legal prohibition against race discrimination applies only to racial or ethnic *minorities*. Thus, it is unlawful for an employer to terminate a black employee because of that employee's race. It is not unlawful, however, for the employer to terminate a white employee because of that employee's race. This perception, although widespread, could not be more wrong. Antidiscrimination statutes, for the most part, do not target specific racial or ethnic groups. They prohibit an employer from taking an adverse employment action against *any individual* because of that individual's race. The U.S. Supreme Court has long held that all Americans, black and white alike, are protected against race discrimination. Because each of us is a member of at least one racial group, all of us are protected against discrimination on the basis of a racial characteristic.

EXAMPLE: A company decides to reduce its workforce. The company president believes that, as a general matter, blacks make better employees and, accordingly, instructs the company's managers to make sure that only white employees are terminated. Several white employees are let go. The decision is made solely on the basis of race. The white employees have a claim of race discrimination.

Historically, of course, most claims of race discrimination have been brought by racial minorities. The reason for this is obvious. In a society infused with racism and dominated by a white power-elite, the victim of discrimination typically has been a member of a minority racial group. As more minorities move into positions of power, the picture becomes more complex. Laws against unlawful discrimination largely address the pervasive societal discrimination against racial minorities. The genius of these laws, however, is that they apply with equal force to any form of race-based decision making, whether the victim of that decision making be white or black.

The one caveat to all of this is affirmative action. Under some circumstances, an employer can voluntarily adopt programs that grant preferences to racial minorities. To pass legal muster, however, these programs must comport with the strict standards established by the Supreme Court. First, voluntary affirmative action is permissible only if the employer can establish the necessary factual predicate for the preference program. That factual predicate is met if the program is necessary to remedy the identified effects of its own discrimination. It might also be met, at least in the case of private employers, by proof of a manifest imbalance between minority employees and the applicable labor market. Even if the factual predicate for affirmative action is established, there are still limits on the scope of the preference program. As a general rule, programs that create an absolute bar to the employment or advancement of nonminority employees are highly suspect. So too are programs that result in the termination or layoff of nonminorities.

In recent years, the Supreme Court has cast an increasingly critical eye toward affirmative action. It remains to be seen how far the retrenchment will go, but the important point, for our purposes, is that affirmative action is an exception to the basic rule. Unless the standards for affirmative action are met, an employer cannot take race into account in making an employment decision. This is true no matter how benign the motivation or how justified the decision might appear to be.

EXAMPLE: A company takes over a retail outlet in a predominantly minority area. It decides that it would help generate goodwill with the customer base to employ a black manager. The company fires the white manager and replaces her with an African American. The company does not have an established affirmative action plan and cannot justify its decision under the Supreme Court's affirmative action standards. The company's decision is unlawful.

What Is Discrimination?

In most cases, there is no controversy concerning the threshold question of an individual's membership in a protected racial group. The dispute lies in whether the individual has been discriminated against because of the individual's racial status. The concept of discrimination is the foundation of modern employment law. The principles discussed here apply, in large part, to the other forms of discrimination discussed in the succeeding chapters.

There are two types of discrimination: disparate treatment and disparate impact. **Disparate treatment,** or intentional discrimination, involves an employer taking race into account in making an employment decision. This can occur because the employer acts out of discriminatory bias in a particular case. It can also occur because the employer adopts a policy that, on its face, makes distinctions on the basis of race. **Disparate impact** involves employment policies that are neutral in form but which have an adverse impact on members of a racial group. Because disparate treatment is the more common form of discrimination, I begin my discussion there.

The first (and most important) point to make is that disparate treatment discrimination is a relative concept. The laws against discrimination are not designed to protect only the exceptional worker. They are designed to ensure that an employer treats its employees in an evenhanded manner. An employer has the right to rid itself of employees who do not meet performance standards. In doing so, however, the employer must act in a nondiscriminatory fashion. It cannot terminate a black employee for violating a company rule if it would not terminate a similarly situated white employee for violating the same rule. It cannot reject a black applicant, based on what might appear to be a legitimate qualifications standard, if the same qualifications standard is not applied to its white applicants. It is not enough that an employer has a legitimate reason for taking an adverse employment action. That reason must be one that the employer applies in a nondiscriminatory fashion.

> **EXAMPLE: A black employee shows up late for work. The manager fires him on the spot, citing his tardiness. There is evidence that white employees are frequently late for work. None of these employees has been fired. The employer cannot cite any legitimate ground for distinguishing the disparate treatment of the black employee and his white co-workers. The manager's action in firing the black employee is unlawful.**

It should be clear from this discussion that, to be actionable, discrimination need not be the sole reason for the adverse employment action. There may be cases in which an employer is motivated solely by racial bias in making an employment decision. In many cases, however, the employer will have legitimate concerns with the performance of the employee. The discrimination occurs because the employer responds differently to those concerns when the employee is a racial or ethnic minority than it does when the employee is white. If an employer takes an adverse employment action against an individual that it would not have taken but for the individual's race, the employer engages in unlawful discrimination even if there are other legitimate reasons that also motivated the employer's conduct.

Taken together, these points underscore a critical feature of discrimination law. When the laws against discrimination were passed, discrimination occurred in the most open and vile sense.

In that context, even the exceptional minority candidate could be irrationally excluded from employment. Increasingly, discrimination has taken on a more subtle guise. Most employers do not categorically exclude minority applicants from consideration. Indeed, an increasing number of discrimination suits involve claims of unlawful termination brought by racial or ethnic minorities who have occupied positions within the company. Some of these claimants may not be model employees. This may also be true, however, of their white co-workers who, for reasons of race, do not find themselves on the chopping block. In many respects, the law now exists to protect the marginal employee of the disfavored racial group from being treated differently from the marginal employee of the favored group.

There are two other aspects of disparate treatment discrimination that need to be stressed. First, it is not necessary for an individual claiming intentional discrimination to prove that the employer, or one of its managers, was subjectively motivated by racial hostility. The law prohibits an employer from taking an adverse action against an individual because of that individual's race. An action is considered race-based if race is a motivating or determining factor in the decision. For race to be such a factor, it is not necessary that the employer be acting from a racist urge. All that is required is that the employer takes race into account in some fashion, resulting in negative job consequences for the individual.

Second, it is wrong to assume that intentional discrimination occurs only when a member of one racial group rejects a member of a different racial group. Discrimination is often the product of subtle stereotyping. Racial stereotypes permeate our society and can manifest themselves in a variety of ways. Blacks can discriminate against other blacks, just as women can discriminate against other women. To cite just one example (outside the employment context), there is evidence that, in many large urban areas, black men have difficulty hailing a taxi cab. Yet, many of the cab drivers in these areas are also black. The discrimination that occurs in this context may not be the product of pure racism (i.e., a feeling of racial superiority on the part of the dominant racial group). The discrimination still exists, however, and may be just as offensive for the individual denied the cab ride.

Similarly, discrimination can occur even when the employer chooses between members of the same racial group. An employer may have no problem with hiring minority employees; however, it may base its employment decisions on impermissible racial stereotypes. For example, it may hire only certain "types" of blacks, thus discriminating against those black candidates not willing to conform their behavior to the employer's stereotypical assumptions. Such intragroup discrimination is actionable even if the employer chooses between or among two or more black applicants in making the employment decision.

> **EXAMPLE: A black male applies for a job. He is rejected in favor of another black applicant. There is evidence that the company screens out those black males who are perceived as threatening or untrustworthy because they do not assume the submissive, "step and fetch it" posture favored by the employer. There is no evidence that the employer applies any similar standard to its white applicants. The rejected black applicant has a viable claim of race discrimination if he can prove that he was rejected due to an impermissible racial stereotype.**

The second category of discrimination, **disparate impact discrimination**, involves different considerations. In a disparate impact case, an employer is not acting on the basis of race, as such. Indeed, the employer's practice is, on its face, entirely neutral. The problem is that the practice has an adverse impact on racial minorities, leading to the exclusion of large numbers of minority candidates. In some cases, such an impact can give rise to a claim of unlawful discrimination.

There are two critical features of disparate impact theory. First, as a threshold matter, an individual must show that the employer's practice or policy disproportionately excludes members of the individual's protected class. The quantum of proof necessary to make this showing has not been definitively established. It depends largely on complex statistical models, the precise contours of which are beyond the purview of this book. The basic standard is that the statistical disparity be sufficiently large to make it unlikely that the disparate impact occurred as a random act.

Even if the individual can meet the threshold showing, there is a second step to the analysis. The employer can justify the disparate effect of its practice or policy by demonstrating that the practice or policy is job related and consistent with business necessity. *Business necessity* is not a precise term. Generally speaking, however, it means something of a compelling nature, a job standard which, at a minimum, is manifestly related to job performance. It is not enough that the practice might, in some general sense, further the employer's interests, nor is it sufficient that the employer might legitimately impose the practice if not for the adverse impact upon a racial group. The less connected the practice or policy to job performance, the less likely a court will find the practice or policy to be justified.

> **EXAMPLE: The employer, a retail pizza company, maintains a no-beard policy. A black individual with a beard applies for a job as a pizza delivery person. The employer rejects the individual pursuant to its no-beard policy. There is evidence that African Americans suffer disproportionately from pseudofolliculitis barbae (PFB), a condition that makes it extremely painful to shave. The black applicant in this case has PFB. The employer's only justification for its no-beard policy is that it furthers the company's clean-cut image. The employer cannot show that being clean-shaven affects, in a direct way, an individual's ability to deliver pizza. It is unlikely that a court will find the no-beard policy to be a business necessity.**

One area where employers have been successful in asserting business necessity defenses is where the practice or policy can be tied to safety concerns. Obviously, an employer cannot be required to eliminate a performance standard, no matter how severe its impact on a protected racial group, if the standard is necessary to protect the safety of the public or the employee. If the employer can make a credible showing that its policy has safety implications, it is likely that a court will uphold the policy unless the individual can demonstrate with highly persuasive evidence that there are ways to reduce the adverse impact of the employer's policy while preserving the employer's safety concerns.

> EXAMPLE: Same no-beard policy as in the previous example. In this case, however, the black individual with PFB is applying for a position as a firefighter. The employer claims that being clean-shaven is necessary to the safe performance of the job, because individuals with facial hair cannot safely utilize respirators. A court is likely to find that the employer's no-beard policy is justified as a business necessity.

One final point about discrimination theory. For the most part, the law in this area focuses on the treatment of the individual. The Supreme Court has repeatedly made clear that there is no absolute bottom-line defense to a claim of either disparate treatment or disparate impact discrimination. An individual who suffers race discrimination at the hands of an employer can assert a claim of discrimination even if the employer otherwise hires or retains a significant number of individuals of the same protected group.

> EXAMPLE: A black employee is fired from her job. There is irrefutable evidence that the manager terminated the employee because of her race. The employer presents evidence that the manager's decision was an aberration. The employer shows that it hires significant numbers of black employees and that blacks occupy positions at all levels of the company. The employer specifically proves that blacks occupy a majority of positions in the same department as the terminated employee. None of this provides a legal defense to the employee's suit. Because she can show that she was discrimi-

nated against because of her race, she can prove unlawful discrimination.

The Terms and Conditions of Employment

Even where race discrimination exists, not all events that occur in the workplace fall within the reach of the antidiscrimination laws. To be covered under these laws, the employer's conduct must generally affect the terms and conditions of employment. In most cases, this is not a difficult standard to meet. If an individual suffers a tangible job detriment (i.e., is fired from his or her job, denied a promotion, compensated at a lower wage, demoted, or refused employment as an initial matter), the terms and conditions of employment are obviously implicated. There are circumstances, however, where the employment action does not have such a tangible impact on the employee's job status. When can an employee, in such cases, assert a viable claim of discrimination?

One way in which an employer can affect the terms and conditions of employment without imposing a tangible job loss is by creating or maintaining a hostile working environment. The hostile environment theory is often associated exclusively with sexual harassment. The theory, however, actually had its origins in claims of racial harassment. Because I address the hostile environment theory at some length in a later chapter dealing with issues of sexual harassment, I leave for that chapter a detailed examination of the theory. There are a few points, however, to be covered here.

The first point is obvious—to constitute unlawful race-based discrimination, the hostile environment created by the harassment must differentiate along racial lines. This occurs, most obviously, when the harassment takes the form of racist epithets or other derogatory comments that specifically refer to race. The harassment can also be race-based, even if neutral on its face, if there is evidence that the harassment is directed exclusively at members of the disfavored racial group. Harassment that does not meet these proof standards is not actionable as race discrimination, no matter how pervasive the harassment.

Even if the harassment is race-based, it must be sufficiently pervasive or severe to alter the terms and conditions of employment. Not every racial comment or off-color joke gives rise to an unlawful act. The harassing behavior must interfere in some fashion with a reasonable person's work performance. This typically requires either proof of repeated incidents of harassing behavior or proof of conduct that is so severe in its own right that, even in isolation, it alters an employee's working conditions.

Finally, the fact that a hostile working environment exists does not impose automatic liability on the employer. Where the harassment is perpetrated by co-workers, the employer is liable only if it knew or should have known of the harassment and failed to take appropriate remedial action. Where the harassment comes at the hands of management-level officials or employees, the employer can be held liable, without regard to its knowledge of the harassment, based on the legal principle of "vicarious liability" (discussed at some length in Chapter 15).

Courts, for the most part, have shown heightened sensitivity to claims of racial harassment. They have condemned, in no uncertain terms, the use of racial epithets and slurs. They have found actionable discrimination even where the harassing behavior is relatively isolated. In many respects, those asserting claims of racial harassment have fared better than their employee counterparts asserting claims of sexual harassment.

EXAMPLE: A black employee finds a noose hanging over his workstation. The next day, the employee encounters KKK graffiti in the bathroom. The employee complains to management. Management expresses sympathy but fails to take any action. The employee has a strong claim of hostile environment discrimination. The noose and graffiti are likely to be seen as race-based harassment. The incidents, while few in number, are so severe that a reasonable person's work performance could be affected. The employer's response, moreover, is clearly inadequate. A court may well find the

employer liable for maintaining a racially discriminatory hostile working environment.

Aside from the hostile environment theory, disputes over the terms-and-conditions issue typically arise when the employer takes personnel actions that fall short of constituting what might be deemed a final employment action or that, while final, do not materially alter the employee's job status. An employer, for example, might give a negative evaluation to an employee. That evaluation, although placed in the employee's file, has no immediate impact on his or her job status. An employer might also assign an employee to new job duties. Although the employee perceives the reassignment as a demotion, the employee continues to work the same hours and receive the same pay.

There is an argument that these actions are sufficient to implicate the protections of the antidiscrimination laws, assuming that the employer has acted for a discriminatory reason. After all, the employer has taken an action that either alters the terms of the job or has the potential of doing so. Recently, however, some courts have shown a reluctance to extend the antidiscrimination laws to personnel actions of this nature. Without some materially adverse job consequence, and assuming that the standards for a claim of hostile environment discrimination are not met, an employee in these cases may be without legal recourse under the antidiscrimination statutes.

The Problem of Proof

Up to this point, the discussion (I hope) has been straightforward. It is relatively easy to describe and to come to terms with the basic principles underlying the concept of race discrimination. What complicates the matter, and what has caused courts a considerable amount of angst, is the problem of proof—precisely how does an individual prove that, in fact, an adverse employment decision was the product of race discrimination? In the case of the disparate impact theory, the inquiry is based largely on statistical models. While complex, these proofs can be reduced to some objective standard. In the case of disparate treatment discrimination, the focus is on the more elusive issue of discriminatory intent. That issue largely defies objective quantification, requiring an inquiry on a case-by-case basis into the motivation for an employment decision. To understand fully the concept of race discrimination, one must understand the basic standards for proving claims of disparate treatment discrimination.

It is obvious that an employee can establish unlawful discrimination by pointing to smoking gun evidence of discrimination (e.g., a document indicating that the employee was fired because of his race). It is equally obvious, however, that such smoking gun evidence is rarely available. This is particularly true in recent years, as employers have become more sophisticated in justifying their personnel decisions and covering up any paper trail of discrimination. Because there is rarely an eyewitness to employer motivation, the Supreme Court has constructed a method of proof that permits an employee to prove intentional discrimination by indirect means. This proof scheme is known as the *McDonnell Douglas* standard.

The *McDonnell Douglas* standard establishes a three-step process for analyzing disparate treatment claims. At step one, the employee must produce evidence that supports an inference of discrimination—what the law refers to as a prima facie case. If a prima facie case is established, the employer must rebut it by articulating a legitimate nondiscriminatory explanation for its decision. Finally, the employee must prove that the legitimate reason proffered by the employer is a pretext for discrimination.

The employee's burden, at the prima facie stage, is not onerous. In the typical refusal-to-hire case, the employee must show: (1) that he is a member of a protected group; (2) that he applied for the position and was rejected; (3) that he meets the minimal qualification standards for the position; and (4) that the company continued to seek individuals of similar qualifications to fill the position. The purpose of the prima facie case is to eliminate the most common nondiscriminatory explanations for the employment decision (e.g., lack of qualifications and the absence of a vacant position).

It is important to stress that the prima facie case, under the *McDonnell Douglas* standard, is a flexible construct. An employee can make out a prima facie case by pointing to any combination of proof that supports an inference of unlawful discrimination. The elements of the prima facie case are merely guideposts, not necessary elements to every discrimination claim.

> **EXAMPLE: An individual applies for a job. The employer screens him out without considering his qualifications. The individual files suit, alleging race discrimination. He is not required to establish his qualifications to make out a prima facie case. Since the employer did not consider the individual's qualifications in rejecting him, lack of qualifications could not have provided the basis for the decision. The purpose of the prima facie case is not served by permitting the employer to rely upon a factor that did not, in fact, motivate the decision. If the employee is truly unqualified, he will be limited in his ability to recover full relief for any discrimination that occurred. His lack of qualifications, however, does not defeat his claim at the prima facie stage.**

Once the prima facie case is established, as step two, the employer must come forward with some explanation for its decision. The employer's burden is slight. The employer is required merely to articulate some legitimate nondiscriminatory explanation for its decision, not to prove that its decision was justified. In wrongful discharge cases, employers typically cite poor performance or misconduct on the part of the employee. Employers may also claim that the employee's job was eliminated as part of a reduction in force.

The third and final step of the *McDonnell Douglas* standard is the critical stage. In response to the employer's proffered explanation, the employee must produce evidence that the explanation proffered by the employer is a pretext for discrimination. Pretext proof can include evidence of racial bias on the part of the employer. Again, however, the law assumes that such evidence may be difficult to come by. Thus, an employee can support his claim with any evidence that supports a finding that the employer's explanation is unworthy of credence. The typical pretext proof includes: (1) evidence of shifting explanations on the employer's part; (2) evidence that calls into question the factual bases for the employer's proffered explanation; and (3) comparative evidence (i.e., evidence that the employee was treated more harshly than a similarly situated employee of a different racial group).

Of the various types of pretext evidence, the most persuasive may be evidence that the employer has shifted explanations for its decision. At the time of an adverse employment decision, employers will often provide the employee with an explanation for the decision. Later, after a lawsuit is filed, it will become clear to the employer that its contemporaneous explanation cannot be sustained. The employer will shift to another explanation in an attempt to defend itself against the suit. To catch the employer in this kind of turnabout is a boon for the employee both because it calls into question the credibility of the subsequent explanation and because it raises questions about the employer's veracity. Pretext evidence is most compelling when it tends to support a finding that the employer is lying to cover up a discriminatory act.

> **EXAMPLE: An employee is fired from his job. The employer's official explanation is that he was terminated because the employer was eliminating the position. In fact, the position is left open and a replacement is hired two weeks later. In response to the employee's lawsuit, the employer now claims that it fired him because of performance concerns that were not documented either prior to or at the time of the termination. A court is likely to view the change in the employer's explanation as highly persuasive pretext evidence.**

Evidence that challenges the factual bases of the employer's proffered explanation can also be persuasive. This is particularly true where the employee produces evidence to rebut the specific grounds cited by the employer in support of its decision. On the other hand, general evidence concerning the relative qualifications of the employee is less likely to persuade. Courts recognize that no employer is perfect and that mistakes can be made in assessing the relative qualifications of a pool of qualified candidates.

> **EXAMPLE: An employee applies for a promotion. The promotion is given to another candidate, allegedly because the other candidate is more qualified. The rejected employee produces evidence in support of his claim that he was the more qualified candidate. The employee, however, does not produce evidence that calls into question the specific grounds cited by the employer in support of its decision to favor the other candidate. While it is possible to view the rejected employee as more qualified—in a general sense— the difference in qualifications is not large. It is also clear that the individual receiving the promotion was also qualified for the position. A court is likely to find that the employee's pretext proof is unpersuasive.**

Cases based upon comparative evidence may be the most difficult to prove. Theoretically, these cases should present compelling pretext evidence. If, as a black employee, you can show that you were disciplined more harshly than a similarly situated white employee, you would seem to have a strong claim of race discrimination. The problem lies in showing that the white employee was similarly situated. Employers have proven resourceful in drawing factual distinctions between the two cases being compared, thus supporting an argument that the disparity in treatment was justified. Courts have been receptive to this line of argument. Unless there is a very tight factual fit between the complainant's case and the comparative evidence, an employee's claim of pretext is likely to founder.

EXAMPLE: A black employee is caught stealing an item from the company. The employee is terminated. The employee brings suit, citing the case of a white employee who was also caught stealing but who merely received a suspension. The evidence shows that the item taken by the white employee was of less value to the company. The evidence also shows that different managers were involved in deciding the appropriate punishment in the two incidents. The white employee, moreover, had a clean work record, while the black employee had been cited in the past for workplace infractions. The black employee's pretext evidence is likely to be rejected.

While pretext proof can be critical to an individual's ability to prevail on a discrimination claim, this discussion begs a critical question: Is pretext evidence alone sufficient to establish unlawful discrimination? An affirmative response to this question is supported by the logic of the *McDonnell Douglas* standard, which is designed to permit an individual to prevail on a discrimination claim without specific proof of racial bias. On the other hand, a case can be made that, standing alone, pretext evidence does not compel a finding of discrimination, because the fact that an employer has proffered a false explanation for its decision does not mean automatically that the employer is covering up race discrimination.

Over the years, courts have taken different approaches to the issue. Some courts have ruled that by establishing a prima facie case and discrediting the employer's proffered explanation, the employee is entitled to a finding of unlawful discrimination. Other courts have held that such proof permits a finding of discrimination but does not compel it in all cases. Still other courts have insisted upon additional proof of discrimination, ruling that pretext evidence, by itself, is never sufficient to sustain a finding of unlawful discrimination.

In a recent case, the Supreme Court clarified the law in this area. The Court acknowledged that pretext evidence, together with the employee's prima facie proof, can sustain a finding of unlawful discrimination. The Court rejected the argument, how-

ever, that a finding of pretext *compels*, in all cases, a finding of discrimination. In the Court's view, it is for a jury to decide, in a particular case, whether the employee's pretext evidence, although
sufficient to discredit the employer's proffered explanation, is also
sufficient to support a finding of unlawful discrimination.

There are two observations to make about the Supreme
Court's decision. First, the decision recognizes that employment
decision making is complex. An employer, when put on the spot,
may not be able to articulate a coherent or consistent explanation for its decision. It does not follow, however, that in all such
cases the employer has unlawfully discriminated. The Supreme
Court's decision permits juries to apply their commonsense
understandings in assessing the weight to be accorded an
employee's pretext evidence.

> **EXAMPLE: An employee claims race discrimination. It becomes
> clear at trial that the employer's explanation for the employ-
> ment decision is false. It also becomes clear, however, that
> another nondiscriminatory reason, not articulated by the
> employer, led to the decision. The employer may have chosen
> not to articulate the alternative explanation because it is
> embarrassing to the company for other reasons. The employer
> may have failed to do so because the company is poorly man-
> aged and could not come up with a coherent explanation for
> its actions. A jury could conclude that, despite the pretext
> proof, the employer did not act for a discriminatory reason.**

The Court's decision is also responsive to the changing
nature of discrimination. The *McDonnell Douglas* standard was
adopted by the Supreme Court nearly a quarter of a century ago.
The standard assumes that if a minority employee can satisfy the
minimal requirements of the prima facie case and discredit the
employer's articulated reason for the decision, discrimination
must underlie the employment action. One could argue that this
assumption no longer holds true. Certainly, there are now specific
job contexts in which the simplistic model of white-on-black dis-

crimination does not fit. While pretext evidence has obvious relevance to the inquiry, juries should be free to place that evidence in context in deciding whether to hold the employer liable for unlawful discrimination.

> **EXAMPLE: A black employee files a claim of race discrimination, alleging that she was terminated from her job because of her race. The employer contends that the employee was terminated because of poor performance. The employee presents compelling evidence that the employer's explanation for the decision is false. There is also evidence that the management hierarchy is largely white and that the company hires and retains only a small number of minority employees. If a jury finds that the employer's explanation is unworthy of credence, it is likely to conclude that the employer engaged in unlawful discrimination.**

> **EXAMPLE: Same example as above except that the black employee works for a minority-owned company. The company is dominated by black managers and hires and retains a significant number of minority employees. The employee cannot cite any evidence (e.g., evidence of race stereotyping) that would explain why race discrimination would have occurred in this context. A jury could well find in favor of the employer even if it determines that the employer's explanation for the decision is unworthy of credence.**

So far, the discussion has assumed that the employee is attempting to prove his or her case without any specific evidence of racial bias. While the law permits the employee to do so, the persuasiveness of the employee's case will be enhanced if the employee can cite evidence that is more directly probative of a racial bias. As noted above, an employee will rarely have access to smoking gun evidence. However, employees can come across evidence of racial bias that, while falling short of a smoking gun, is highly probative. If compelling enough, such evidence can by itself establish the employee's case, imposing a heavy burden on the employer to justify its decision. Even if the evidence is not sufficient, in its own right, to carry the employee's case, the evidence can be relevant to the employee's showing of pretext under the *McDonnell Douglas* standard. In some cases, an employee's ability to prevail under the *McDonnell Douglas* standard may well depend on his or her ability to point to other evidence suggestive of a racial bias on the part of company decision makers.

The most common evidence of this type involves the discriminatory statements of company officials or managers. Most companies are savvy enough not to commit to writing a specific statement that an individual was rejected for a racially discriminatory reason. Individual managers, however, will often make statements that are suggestive of a racial bias. These can include specific statements about the employee in question or general remarks of a discriminatory nature.

The weight to be accorded these statements depends on several factors. Discriminatory statements are most probative when linked in some fashion to the decisional process. Statements made by managers involved in the specific decision at issue are highly probative; statements made by non–decision makers are given less weight. Statements made in reference to the specific decision at issue are obviously critical, although general statements of racial bias, made by decision makers, still carry substantial weight. Finally, temporal considerations also come into play. The more remote in time the statement, the less bearing it has on the employer's motivation at the time of the decision.

> **EXAMPLE: A black employee is denied a promotion. The chief decision maker was the employee's supervisor. During the decision-making process, the supervisor made several derogatory comments about the employee. At one point, he referred to the employee as one of those "dumb blacks" who could not do the job. The supervisor's statement is compelling evidence of racial bias sufficient, by itself, to support the employee's case.**

EXAMPLE: Same example as above except, in this case, the supervisor does not make any racially discriminatory statements during the decision-making process. The supervisor, however, was overheard in the past saying that "if it were his company, he wouldn't have any blacks around." The statement was alleged to have been made less than a month before the promotion decision. The supervisor's statement is strong evidence of racial bias. It might be viewed as sufficient, by itself, to support the employee's case. At the very least, it is highly relevant evidence that can, together with other evidence, support the employee's claim.

EXAMPLE: Same example as above except, in this case, no discriminatory statements are attributed to the supervisor. The company president, however, was once overheard using a racial epithet. The president was not involved in the promotion decision at issue. The racial incident, moreover, occurred several years before the decision. The president's remark has only marginal relevance to the employee's claim.

Proving that an employer has intentionally discriminated on the basis of race is a difficult task. The law has developed ways to ease the employee's burden but, even under the most favorable conditions, the burden is still substantial. For all the glowing rhetoric, the effectiveness of the antidiscrimination laws depends to a large degree on the ability of the individual employee, in the trenches, to prove his or her claim.

CHAPTER 2

Sex Discrimination

If race discrimination provides the foundation for modern employment law, sex or gender discrimination is the proverbial late bloomer. The prohibition against sex discrimination was added to the Civil Rights Act of 1964 almost as an afterthought. At that time, the idea that women would be in need of employment protections—that they could compete on equal terms with men in the workplace—seemed to many a curious, even humorous, idea. Some thirty-five years later, the picture could not be more different. Women have entered the workplace in high numbers. Issues of sex discrimination occupy a central place in employment law. Women are no longer second-class citizens, and sex, or gender, as a protected category is at center stage of employment law.

In many respects, the law on sex discrimination closely parallels the law on race discrimination. As in the case of race, sex is a broad category. Women are protected against discrimination on the basis of sex or gender, but so are men. As with race, there are two theories of discrimination: disparate treatment and disparate impact. The law extends to all sex-based employment actions that affect the terms and conditions of employment, including sexual harassment, an issue that I take up in some detail in Part III. Finally, claims of sex discrimination are generally governed by the same legal standards that apply to claims of race discrimination. Thus, the *McDonnell Douglas* standard, discussed in Chapter 1, applies to individual claims of disparate treatment sex discrimination.

Despite these similarities, there are issues that are unique to the field of sex discrimination. In this chapter, I explore the discrete issues surrounding the category of sex discrimination.

The BFOQ Defense

Perhaps the most significant distinction between the categories of race and sex discrimination is that the law, in certain circumstances, permits an employer to rely upon sex in making employment decisions. The prohibition against race discrimination is absolute. The law assumes that there are no inherent differences in abilities between members of different racial groups. An employer cannot justify a race-based decision by arguing that an individual, due to his or her race, is less capable of performing a job.

In the sex context, the law recognizes that there are differences between the genders that might, in a particular case, impact upon an individual's ability to meet the demands of the job. In federal law, this recognition takes the form of a legal doctrine known as the bona fide occupational qualification (BFOQ) defense. The BFOQ defense permits an employer to rely upon sex in making a decision in which the employer can prove that sex is a bona fide occupational qualification.

There are two elements to the BFOQ defense. First, an employer must show that there is a direct relationship between a person's sex and the ability to perform the job. It is not enough that members of one gender group might, as a general matter, be better able to perform a certain job. Nor can an employer categorically exclude members of one gender from consideration based on assumptions about the respective abilities of men and women. The evidence must establish either that all or a substantial number of members of the excluded gender group would be unable to perform the duties of the job or that it is impracticable to determine, on an individual basis, which members of the excluded gender could perform the job.

EXAMPLE: A telephone company needs to hire an individual to work in repair and maintenance. The job involves some heavy lifting and climbing. The company assumes that most women would not be able to perform the job and adopts a policy of hiring only men. A female applicant challenges the policy as discriminatory. The company invokes the BFOQ defense. It is unlikely that the company can prevail on the defense. It may be that some women would be unable to meet the physical demands of the job. However, absent evidence that this is true of virtually all women, the company is required to assess each individual applicant on his or her own merit.

The second element of the BFOQ defense is that the job qualification invoked by the employer must relate to the essence or central mission of the employer's business. Even if the employer can demonstrate a direct relationship between sex and the ability to meet some qualification standard, the employer cannot prevail if the job qualification at issue is tangential to the employer's operations. If an employer is in the business of selling sexual titillation to a largely male clientele, the employer might be able to justify a women-only hiring policy for those individuals providing sex-based entertainment. On the other hand, the fact that an employer might prefer to hire members of one gender as part of its marketing of the business does not justify a gender-specific hiring policy if the primary mission of the employer's business is to provide a service (e.g., air transportation, food) other than sexual titillation.

EXAMPLE: A company runs a club that features exotic dancing. The club caters to a clientele of heterosexual men and, thus, hires only female dancers. A male dancer is denied a position with the club and sues, claiming sex discrimination. The club has a strong BFOQ defense. The club may provide food and drink for its customers, but its central mission is to provide sex-based entertainment. The club can adopt a policy of hiring only female exotic dancers.

EXAMPLE: A restaurant has a policy of hiring only women in waitress positions. The restaurant heavily markets the sexuality of its waitresses, dressing them in sexually provocative outfits. The restaurant, however, is zoned as a family restaurant and essentially provides food and drink to its customers. The waitresses do not provide exotic entertainment. A rejected male applicant sues, claiming sex discrimination. The restaurant will have difficulty defending its women-only policy as a BFOQ. The central mission of the restaurant is to provide food and drink. That the restaurant seeks to gain a niche in the market by promoting the sexuality of its waitresses does not shield its discriminatory hiring policy.

EXAMPLE: Another restaurant example, but this one involves a fine eating establishment that hires only men for the position of waiter. The establishment adopted a male-only policy because of the European tradition of using only male waiters in the finer restaurants. A female applicant is denied a job with the restaurant and sues. The restaurant will have difficulty defending its male-only policy as a BFOQ. The essence of the restaurant's business is to provide food and drink to its customers. The fact that it wishes to adhere to a male-only waiter tradition in order to promote an image of fine dining does not justify its sex-based employment policy.

As the above discussion suggests, the BFOQ defense turns out to be a relatively narrow safe harbor for employers. Courts have generally rejected attempts by employers to justify employment policies that favor the hiring of one gender only. This is particularly true with respect to jobs that involve a certain amount of physical exertion, where the employer simply assumes that women, as a group, are not up to the task. An employer, of course, is free to hold all of its applicants to the same performance standards, assuming that these standards do not have an impermissible disparate impact on members of one gender group. In most cases, however, an employer cannot categorically exclude members of one gender from employment consideration.

It is also important to stress that the BFOQ defense is not a license to indulge paternalistic notions about the proper role or place of women. There may be jobs that pose greater risks for women because of some condition (e.g., pregnancy) unique to women. Assuming, however, that a woman can perform the duties of the job, it is for the female worker, not the employer, to assess whether the job risks are too great. Nor can the employer use the BFOQ defense as a conduit for the biases or prejudices of others. It is not enough that the employer itself does not harbor a discriminatory animus. If the employer permits the discriminatory attitudes of others to infect its employment decisions, it violates the prohibition against sex discrimination.

> **EXAMPLE: An employer operates a gun shop. A qualified female applicant is hired to manage the shop. The woman performs the job well, but several of the shop's male customers complain that a man, not a woman, should be hired for the job. They threaten to take their business elsewhere. Faced with this threat, the employer fires the female manager. The employer's action is unlawful. Customer preference, in this context, does not constitute a valid BFOQ. While the employer itself does not harbor a discriminatory bias, the employer has based its decision on the discriminatory attitudes of its customers and, thus, has engaged in impermissible sex discrimination.**

The one area where employers have had some success with the BFOQ defense is where the job standard invoked by the employer touches upon privacy concerns. This issue has arisen most often in the context of prison guard positions or other work settings where the job involves intimate contact of some kind with customers or other workers. While the BFOQ defense is available in these cases, the mere specter of a threat to privacy is not enough to justify a policy of hiring only members of one gender.

The employer must show that privacy interests are essential to the employer's business and that there is a real threat to the protected privacy interest of another. If there are ways, moreover, to accommodate the privacy interests of others while hiring members of different genders, courts will be reluctant to sustain a categorical bar on the hiring of applicants of one gender.

One final note: The BFOQ defense is a defense to claims of disparate treatment discrimination. In other words, it applies when the employer expressly relies upon sex in making an employment decision. In some cases, an employer may impose a neutral qualifications standard, such as a height or weight requirement, that has the effect of excluding substantial numbers of female applicants. Such a standard is subject to challenge, if at all, only under a disparate impact theory, pursuant to the legal standards discussed in Chapter 1. The employer, in such a case, must justify its policy as a business necessity, not as a BFOQ.

Equal Pay

While women have made substantial inroads into the workplace, there is ample evidence that female workers continue to suffer from a significant disparity in pay. Wage discrimination, of course, is impermissible regardless of whether the basis for the pay disparity is race, sex, or some other prohibited factor. The problem, however, is unique to the sex field if only because of its pervasiveness. Indeed, there are two federal statutes that prohibit sex-based discrimination in pay: Title VII of the Civil Rights Act of 1964 and the Equal Pay Act. These statutes, together with various state laws addressing the issue, provide female workers, in particular, with a substantial web of legal protection against wage or pay discrimination.

Obviously, an employer acts unlawfully when it provides different levels of pay to men and women for performing the same job. There is no justification for sex-based pay discrimination. An employer, for example, cannot argue that a difference in pay is justified because men have historically been paid a higher wage than women. Nor can an employer provide different levels of pay based on the assumption that most women have a second income at home. Pay differentials that are rooted in neutral factors other than sex can be justified. If the employer, however, provides men and women with different pay for the same work, it violates the law.

> **EXAMPLE: A company maintains a position of assistant manager at its retail computer store. Five individuals occupy the position, three men and two women. The company pays the three men $10.00 per hour. The company pays the two women $7.00 per hour. The evidence shows that the five workers perform the same job, with equal responsibilities. The disparity in pay between the male and female assistant managers is unlawful.**

As with so many areas of discrimination law, the problem is in proving the discrimination. These days, most employers are not so bold as to adopt a two-tiered compensation scheme for the same position (as in the above example). Moreover, there is rarely a paper trail demonstrating the employer's intent to discriminate against the female (or male) worker. If a disparity in pay exists, it is often apparent (if at all) only upon a close inspection of the employer's job categories and its compensation structure.

The employee's initial burden, in the typical pay case, is to show that the employee is being paid less than a member of the opposite gender who is working at a job deemed sufficiently similar to justify an inference of discrimination. Where the male and female employees work at the same job at the same office during the same time, the disparity in pay can, by itself, support the claim. Where, however, the jobs are not identical but might be viewed as involving similar responsibilities, the task becomes more difficult. The employee must show that the jobs are performed under similar working conditions and that they involve equal or substantially similar skill, effort, and responsibility.

In determining whether jobs are sufficiently similar to be used for comparative purposes, the law looks beyond the label imposed by the employer. An employer, for example, may hire individuals to perform certain jobs. The employer may assign different labels to the positions. Yet, in practice, the jobs may involve the same skill, effort, and responsibility. If the jobs are, in fact, substantially identical in all critical respects, any sex-based disparity in pay between or among the jobs will give rise to a viable claim of pay discrimination, regardless of the job titles assigned by the employer.

> **EXAMPLE: An employer creates two jobs. One is assigned the title of account manager. The other is assigned the title of assistant account manager. A man occupies the position of account manager. A woman occupies the position of assistant account manager. The man is paid a much higher salary. The evidence shows that the jobs involve equal skill, effort, and responsibility and are performed under similar working conditions. Unless based on a neutral factor other than sex, the difference in pay is not justified.**

By the same token, the mere fact that the jobs are assigned a similar job title is not determinative. Employers may retain individuals who are in the same general job category. Certain employees, however, for reasons other than gender, may work longer hours or take on more difficult assignments. While the jobs do not have to be precisely the same, if, in fact, there are significant differences in the amount of effort expended by the men and women performing the jobs, a difference in pay can be sustained.

In recent years, these principles have been tested in cases involving athletic coaches. Men and women are sometimes hired for parallel positions, where each is responsible for a group of individuals of the same gender. This is particularly true in the education and coaching fields, where men typically coach male teams and women coach female teams. On the surface, there would appear to be a substantial identity between the jobs, particularly if the same sport is involved. In most cases, however, certainly at the intercollegiate level, schools pay their male coaches a higher salary. Schools justify this disparity in pay on the ground that the male programs are greater revenue-producers, thus imposing additional pressure and responsibility on the male team's coach. Courts have been sympathetic to these arguments where there is no other evidence that the disparity in pay is sex-based.

> **EXAMPLE: A university maintains basketball programs for men and women. A woman coaches the women's team; a man coaches the men's team. The female coach is highly successful—more so, in fact, than the male—but is paid a salary that is substantially less than that paid to her male counterpart. She sues, alleging an equal pay violation. The university defends by arguing that the job demands for the male coach are greater, given the higher profile of the men's program. The university cites specifically the additional responsibilities of recruiting and the day-to-day public pressures of the job. A court may well find that these differences justify the disparity in pay between the male and female coach.**

> **EXAMPLE: Same example as above except that the women's team was previously coached by a man. The female coach, who has taken over the women's team, is paid substantially less than her male predecessor. There is nothing to justify the difference in pay between the two coaches. The female coach may not be entitled to the same pay as the coach of the men's team. She has a strong claim, however, that she has been subjected to unlawful pay discrimination based on the comparison between herself and her male predecessor.**

As the above examples suggest, the equal pay requirement, while substantial, has its limits. Differences in pay are sometimes the result of biases deeply embedded in our society. There is evidence, for example, that jobs traditionally associated with women have been systematically devalued by the market. While employers cannot perpetuate historic discrimination by continuing to pay women less for the same work, the law does not require employers to compensate for historic wrongs by deviating from prevailing market rates to boost the cause of female workers. Arguments based on far-reaching comparisons between the relative worth of jobs traditionally held by men and women are not likely to carry the day if, in fact, the jobs are not sufficiently similar to meet the comparative standards of the equal pay principle.

Finally, while the use of job comparisons is the most common way to prove an equal pay violation, an employee can always establish unlawful sex discrimination by proving an intent on the part of the employer to pay women a lesser wage. In some cases, there may be no male comparators in the workplace. Yet, the evidence may show that the employer is intentionally discriminating against a female employee because, for example, the employer believes that women deserve less pay than men. While evidence of this nature may be hard to come by, an employee who can provide such evidence can prevail on a claim of pay discrimination.

Paramour Preference

The use of the term *sex,* in most antidiscrimination statutes, creates some confusion. Sex, as used in these statutes, does not mean sexual intercourse or gratification. It is, instead, a shorthand reference to gender. Of course, gender and sex have an obvious connection, and there are cases (as in the area of sexual harassment) where conduct of a sexual nature is deemed to implicate gender and, thus, to violate the prohibition against sex or gender discrimination. The principal objective of the antidiscrimination statutes, however, is to prohibit discrimination on the basis of gender, not sexual predilection.

This point arises in the so-called "paramour preference" cases. Paramour preference refers to a case in which a decision maker favors the employment of an individual with whom the decision maker is romantically or sexually involved. In the typical

case, the decision maker chooses to promote or hire his paramour, thus rejecting some other candidate who might be considered more qualified for the position. One might argue that this,
by definition, constitutes unlawful sex discrimination, since the
decision is based solely on the sexual relationship between the
decision maker and the successful candidate.

For two reasons, courts have rejected the argument that sexual favoritism of this nature is, as a per se matter, a form of sex
discrimination. First, courts have stressed that sex in this context
means discrimination on the basis of gender. The mere fact that
there is a sexual relationship between the decision maker and the
successful candidate does not, by itself, establish unlawful sex discrimination. Further, courts have recognized that, in many cases
of this nature, the motivation for the action is not gender but the
simple fact that the decision maker prefers someone that he
knows. The decision maker, in other words, favors his paramour
for the same reason that he might favor a relative or a friend.
Such an act of sexual nepotism, whatever else it may be, is not an
act of unlawful sex discrimination.

> **EXAMPLE: A hospital needs to hire a physician's assistant. The
> hospital administrator is in an existing sexual relationship with
> a physician's assistant who works at another hospital. The
> administrator would like to have his sexual partner work at
> the same hospital so that they can drive to work together and
> see each other for lunch. The administrator pulls some strings
> and secures the position for his sexual partner. Without more
> evidence than this, a court is unlikely to find that the adminis-
> trator's actions constitute unlawful sex discrimination.**

While acts of sexual favoritism do not constitute per se violations of the antidiscrimination laws, they can be relevant to a
claim of sex discrimination in at least two ways. First, the fact that
the decision maker has preferred his paramour may reflect his
broader view of the role of women in the workplace. The decision maker may believe that granting sexual favors is part and

parcel of the employment relationship. He may always want a girlfriend or a willing sexual partner to occupy a particular job. He may essentially define the job as having a sexual element and limit his consideration of candidates to individuals who are willing to grant sexual favors. In this context, the granting of job preferences to a paramour can provide strong evidence that the decision maker is engaging in unlawful quid pro quo discrimination by making submission to sexual advances a term or condition of employment.

> EXAMPLE: A man is appointed to the position of court executive. A woman, named Carla, works in the position of assistant to the court executive. Carla has worked in the position for years and is eminently qualified. Shortly after becoming court executive, the man invites Carla into his office and makes an ambiguous sexual pass. Carla rebuffs the advance. He then strikes up a sexual relationship with another female worker. The man fires Carla from the assistant's position and replaces her with the female worker with whom he has become sexually involved. The fact that the court executive has favored his paramour does not, by itself, constitute unlawful sex discrimination. It does, however, provide evidence that he has unlawfully made submission to his sexual advances a condition of employment. The evidence is particularly probative in this case, given the fact that Carla's termination closely followed her rejection of his sexual advance.

Acts of sexual favoritism can also lend support to a claim of hostile environment sexual harassment discrimination. A manager may routinely ask for sexual favors from his female staff. He may also give job benefits to those who are willing to grant sexual favors, boasting about his conquests throughout the workplace. Taken together, these acts may be viewed as both sex-based and sufficiently pervasive or severe to implicate the terms and conditions of employment for those female workers forced to endure the manager's crude behavior.

As always, it should be remembered that the laws against employment discrimination do not ensure absolute fairness in the workplace. Favoring the employment of a sexual partner over a more qualified individual is not the best employment practice and may well violate the employer's own personnel standards. Such favoritism, however, does not in all cases give rise to a claim of unlawful sex discrimination.

Sex Stereotyping

The previous discussion provides a logical transition into what is quickly becoming one of the most important areas of discrimination law—the phenomenon of sex stereotyping. In Chapter 1, I discuss stereotyping in the context of claims of race discrimination. As I point out there, an employer can violate the antidiscrimination laws when it bases an employment decision on an impermissible racial stereotype even if, in so doing, it chooses between or among members of the same racial minority. The phenomenon of impermissible stereotyping can also occur in the gender context. Indeed, if anything, the problem is more acute in this area because of the very pervasiveness of sexist attitudes.

Obviously, an individual does not have to prove the existence of sex stereotyping to establish a claim of sex discrimination. In most cases, the employer will not admit that it relied upon a factor that correlates in any way with a sexist stereotype. The employer, instead, will cite some performance-based deficiency that is entirely sex-neutral. In such a case, the employee must rely upon the same indirect method of proof discussed in Chapter 1 to prove his or her claim.

In some cases, however, the employer may cite factors that appear to reflect a sexual stereotype. Or, the employee may uncover evidence that the employer's decision makers have in fact relied upon such a factor. In such a case, the question becomes whether the employer's reliance on the gender-related stereotype can support a claim of unlawful sex discrimination.

The most common form of sex stereotyping occurs when an employer assumes that members of one gender group are inherently unqualified to perform a job. If the employer makes its reliance on the sex-based stereotype explicit by adopting a policy of not hiring members of one gender, there is no question that the employer's policy constitutes unlawful sex discrimination unless the employer can justify its policy as a valid BFOQ. An employer, however, may take a more subtle approach. The employer, for example, may use code words that correlate in some fashion with certain sex-based stereotypes. In some cases, the use of such code words can support a claim of sex discrimination.

> **EXAMPLE: An employer is considering candidates for a civilian position with the military. Men have traditionally occupied the position. Two female candidates apply for the position; both are highly qualified. The employer chooses a male candidate for the position, describing the female candidates as overly nervous and emotional. The employer's explanation can be reasonably tied to an impermissible sex stereotype (i.e., that women are not fit by temperament to occupy positions of leadership in a military setting). Together with other evidence in the case, the employer's explanation can support a finding of unlawful sex discrimination.**

The list of potential code words is long. An employer, for example, could reject a female candidate because she is too "soft" or not sufficiently tough or aggressive. Standing alone, these characterizations do not translate into a finding of unlawful sex discrimination because it may be that, in the particular case, the female candidate does lack some attribute deemed necessary for the position. In context, however, such characterizations might be probative of a gender bias. This is particularly true if the position at issue is one traditionally occupied by males and the comments of the employer appear to reflect general assumptions about the attributes of members of a particular gender.

A more subtle form of sex stereotyping occurs when the employer applies conduct or qualification standards to members of one gender that it does not apply to members of another. An employer, for example, may value aggressiveness when exhibited by a male. Yet, when a female exhibits the same behavior, the employer may be put off. The employer might also have little concern about the physical appearance of its male employees. Yet, the employer may insist that its female employees dress in an appropriately feminine manner or demean themselves in a way that comports with traditional views of the subordinate or sexually submissive status of women. Evidence that these factors have entered into an employment decision can support a finding of unlawful sex discrimination.

> **EXAMPLE: A woman applies for the position of partner with an accounting firm. Her candidacy is considered by a number of male partners. Several of the men criticize her for being overly aggressive. In some cases, these comments are tied to suggestions that she consider wearing a dress or using more makeup. Others suggest that she enroll in charm school to learn appropriate manners. The woman is rejected for the position. The comments of the male partners can support a claim that the decision to reject the female candidate was influenced by impermissible sex stereotyping on the part of the men.**

Sex stereotyping can also manifest itself in the form of employment practices that are a combination of both discriminatory and nondiscriminatory factors. An employer may be perfectly willing to hire some female candidates. The employer, however, may adopt a policy of not hiring those female candidates who share a certain condition or characteristic. By reason of a sexual stereotype, the employer may choose not to hold similarly situated men to the same standard. The employer's policy is unlawful even if it does not have the effect of excluding all female candidates from consideration.

> EXAMPLE: A company believes that women with young chil-
> dren do not belong in the workplace and adopts a policy of
> not employing women with children under age 5. The com-
> pany does not apply this policy to men with young children.
> The company's policy is unlawful because it discriminates
> between similarly situated men and women. The policy is not
> saved by the fact that some women (those without young
> children) are not adversely affected by the policy.

While employers cannot rely upon sex stereotypes to draw
distinctions between male and female employees, the law does
not outlaw all employment practices that might appear to be the
product of a sexual stereotype. Many employers, for example,
require their employees to meet certain grooming standards.
Often these standards will vary, in some respects, between men
and women. An employer, for example, may insist upon a
grooming requirement for hair that differentiates in length
between men and women. For the most part, courts in these
cases have sided with the employer. An employer cannot impose
an appearance standard on one gender while completely
exempting members of the other gender from any comparable
standard. It can, however, draw reasonable distinctions in imposing appearance or grooming standards that apply to both genders.

Finally, there is one other area where the sex stereotyping
theory has proven ineffective. Gender stereotypes are tied closely
to sexual orientation. One could easily make the case that rejection of an employee because of sexual orientation is a form of
impermissible sex stereotyping. While theoretically sound, this
argument has not carried the day in the courts, which have
rejected attempts to include claims of sexual orientation discrimination within the federal prohibition against sex discrimination.
Some states and municipalities have laws that specifically prohibit
discrimination on the basis of sexual orientation. There have also
been efforts in recent years to pass such legislation at the federal
level. As it now stands, however, federal law does not prohibit an

employer from discriminating against an individual on the basis of sexual orientation.

Pregnancy Discrimination

At first blush, discrimination on the basis of pregnancy would appear to be an obvious case of sex discrimination. Only women, after all, can become pregnant. Yet, it was not until 1978 that Congress made clear that pregnancy discrimination was included within the federal prohibition against sex discrimination. Congress' action followed two U.S. Supreme Court cases that had left the issue in doubt. Congress specifically defined sex discrimination to include discrimination on the basis of pregnancy.

There are two basic issues that arise in the context of pregnancy discrimination. The easiest concerns the case of an employer that takes an employment action against an individual because of her pregnancy. Some employers are hesitant to hire or retain pregnant workers. If an employer takes an adverse action against a female applicant or employee because of her pregnancy, that employer commits an act of unlawful sex discrimination.

It is no defense to a claim of pregnancy discrimination that the employer acted out of a concern for the health or well-being of the pregnant employee. The very purpose of the prohibition against pregnancy discrimination is to eliminate paternalistic attitudes toward pregnant workers. It is for the pregnant worker, not the employer, to weigh any risk associated with her employment.

> **EXAMPLE: A woman applies for a position as a cashier with a retail outlet store. The store manager conducts the interview. The interview is going well until the woman informs the manager that she just learned that she is pregnant. The manager is very understanding but expresses concern that the job might be too tiring for someone who is pregnant. The manager also expresses a fear that she might injure herself or her baby on the job. The manager tells her that she won't be hired for the job but urges her to apply again after she has**

**had her baby. The manager's decision constitutes unlawful
sex discrimination.**

There are jobs for which pregnancy could be a BFOQ. Thus,
courts have upheld mandatory pregnancy leave policies in the
case of flight attendants, where the airline can demonstrate that
the pregnant condition of the worker hampers her ability to meet
the safety demands of the job. As discussed earlier, however, the
BFOQ is a relatively narrow defense. A mandatory leave policy
cannot be based upon general assumptions about the ability of
pregnant employees to work.

The second issue that arises with respect to pregnancy in
the workplace concerns the pregnant worker's entitlement to
leave and benefits. The law assumes that many pregnant
women are able and willing to work during the period leading
up to childbirth. However, the law also recognizes that, as a
result of pregnancy or childbirth, women often need a period of
convalescence, similar in nature to the type of temporary disability for which employers frequently provide a period of paid
or unpaid leave. There is now a federal statute (discussed in
Chapter 9) that guarantees workers a certain amount of unpaid
family and medical leave. The issue here, however, is under
what circumstances the failure to provide voluntary leave (or
benefits) for a pregnant worker constitutes unlawful sex discrimination.

For discrimination purposes, the leave issue turns on
whether the employer provides the same amount of leave and
benefits for pregnant employees as it does for employees with
some other kind of temporary disability. If an employer provides
no disability leave for its employees, its failure to provide such
leave for a pregnant worker does not constitute unlawful sex discrimination. If, however, an employer provides leave or benefits
for individuals with temporary disabilities, its failure to extend
such leave or benefits to a pregnant worker can be unlawful.
Because the law requires that pregnancy be treated the same as
any other disabling condition (of a temporary nature), the

employer cannot categorically exclude the pregnant employee from its disability leave or benefit policy.

> **EXAMPLE: A company has a generous policy of providing paid disability leave to its employees. The company provides two months paid leave for all temporary disabilities. The company does not provide any leave for pregnant workers, even for the period immediately following childbirth. The company is not required to provide paid leave for temporary disabilities. Having done so, however, it cannot exclude pregnant workers from its leave policy.**

In the above example, it is clear that the employer is not providing comparable treatment to the pregnant worker. The comparability issue, however, can become more complicated. An employer, for example, may choose to provide leave or benefits only for certain types of disabling conditions. It may not be clear, under the circumstances, whether pregnancy is more like the type of condition for which the employer provides the leave or benefits or more like the type of condition for which no leave or benefits are provided. Unless the employee can demonstrate that pregnancy is more comparable to the type of condition for which the employer provides the leave or benefits, failure to provide the leave or benefits for the pregnant employee will not constitute unlawful sex discrimination.

> **EXAMPLE: An employer has a generous disability leave policy. However, it makes a distinction between individuals who become disabled due to an on-the-job injury (who receive full pay during a period of disability leave) and those who become disabled for some reason unrelated to the job (who receive only half-pay). Consistent with this distinction, the employer treats pregnancy as a disability unrelated to the job, meaning that a pregnant employee on disability leave receives only half-pay. A court may well find that the employer's policy is nondiscriminatory because it treats pregnancy the same as it does comparable conditions or disabilities.**

Finally, it should be stressed that the federal prohibition against pregnancy discrimination merely forbids an employer from subjecting pregnant employees to less favorable treatment. It does not require an employer to accommodate the pregnant worker by excusing job standards or qualifications that are applied equally to all employees. Nor does it require the employer to provide the pregnant worker with voluntary leave for any period of her pregnancy for which she is not disabled unless it generally provides personal leave to its employees, in which case it must treat the pregnant worker the same as it does all other workers. While the law, in other contexts, might impose affirmative obligations on the employer in its treatment of pregnant workers, in this context a viable claim of discrimination turns (as always) on evidence of disparate treatment.

CHAPTER 3

National Origin Discrimination

N ational origin bears an obvious resemblance to the protected categories of race and color. A person of color from a foreign country who suffers discrimination in the workplace may well have claims of both national origin and race/color discrimination. Indeed, in cases of this nature, the aggrieved employee often asserts multiple claims of discrimination, invoking both national origin and race.

While there is an obvious overlap between the protections against race and national origin discrimination, there are reasons for drawing distinctions between the two protected categories. Title VII of the Civil Rights Act applies to both race and national origin discrimination. Other federal statutes, however, extend only to claims of race discrimination. The remedies available under those statutes may be greater in some respects than those available under Title VII. Further, while there is no bona fide occupational qualification (BFOQ) defense to claims of race discrimination, that defense is available in cases of national origin discrimination. In some cases, distinguishing between race and national origin can have a significant impact on the viability of the employee's claim.

As a protected legal category, national origin has become increasingly important as the controversy surrounding new immigration and the primacy of the English language has intensified.

In the employment context, the debate often centers on attempts by employers to impose English-only rules in the workplace. The degree, if any, to which the law prohibits such rules is a hotly contested point, and one which I address later in this chapter.

What Is National Origin?

It is important, as an initial matter, to define precisely what the law means by national origin. At one level, this is not a difficult question. National origin refers to an individual's place of origin. Typically, this means the country of origin of the individual or the individual's ancestors. An individual is of Hispanic origin if the individual's family comes from, say, Mexico. If the individual is discriminated against because of his Hispanic background, the individual suffers discrimination on the basis of national origin.

National origin can have a broader meaning. National origin is not dictated simply by place of birth or physical ancestry. Often physical, cultural, or linguistic characteristics play a strong role in defining an individual's national identity, quite apart from the individual's place of birth or bloodline. If the individual's outward appearance manifests a connection to the identifying characteristics of a particular national group, the individual may be considered a member of that protected group for discrimination purposes, even though the individual does not have direct ancestral ties to that group.

> EXAMPLE: An applicant claims that he was rejected for a position because of his national origin (Hispanic). The employer claims that the individual is not Hispanic, citing the fact that neither of his parents were of Hispanic descent. The evidence shows that the applicant was born in a country in which the Hispanic culture is dominant. The applicant speaks Spanish and is immersed in the Spanish ways of life. A court may well find that the applicant can assert a claim of national origin discrimination based on his Hispanic identity.

For legal purposes, the more vexing question is not so much what national origin is, but what it is not. An employer violates the prohibition against national origin discrimination when it rejects an individual for employment merely because the individual comes from a country deemed undesirable by the employer. An employer does not violate that prohibition, however, when it adopts a policy of hiring only U.S. citizens. The distinction, while subtle, is critical. Aliens are covered under the employment laws of the United States. Thus, a noncitizen who is discriminated against on the basis of race, sex, or national origin can assert a claim under the nation's antidiscrimination laws. Alienage, however, does not equate with national origin. While a U.S. employer cannot refuse to employ those of a particular national origin, a category that implicates citizens and noncitizens alike, it can adopt a policy of hiring only U.S. citizens without engaging in national origin discrimination.

> **EXAMPLE: An employer maintains a policy of hiring only U.S. citizens for positions in its clothing factory. The evidence shows that the employer applies its policy on a consistent basis. The employer does not differentiate between or among different groups of foreign citizens. The employer, moreover, hires individuals with foreign ancestry as long as they are U.S.citizens. The employer's policy does not constitute unlawful national origin discrimination.**

While discrimination on the basis of citizenship does not equate with discrimination on the basis of national origin, the employer's refusal to hire noncitizens can have legal consequences. First, federal law imposes other restrictions on citizenship requirements. Most notably, the Immigration Reform and Control Act prohibits employers from discriminating on the basis of citizenship, subject to some exceptions (e.g., that an employer can prefer the hiring of U.S. citizens where the citizen and noncitizen are equally qualified). Further, a citizenship policy cannot be used as a pretext for discriminating on the basis of national origin. A policy that is clearly designed to exclude individuals of a particular national origin might well be viewed as unlawful even though purportedly based on a citizenship standard.

> **EXAMPLE: An individual of Mexican ancestry applies for a position with a company located in the United States. The individual, while legally in the country, is not a U.S. citizen. The employer refuses to hire the individual, citing a policy of hiring only U.S. citizens. The evidence shows that the employer has hired individuals who are noncitizens, although none who are citizens of Mexico. The evidence also shows that the employer has no Hispanics in its workforce. The individual has a strong claim of national origin discrimination.**

If national origin does not equate with citizenship, it is also distinct, at least in theory, from the category of race. Discrimination against an individual solely because of his or her nation of origin is not race discrimination. In that case, it is the individual's place of origin, not his or her racial makeup, that leads to the disparate treatment. On the other hand, in many cases the individual's place of origin will be closely intertwined with ethnic characteristics that can be considered racial in nature. Where the disparate treatment is based on the ethnic characteristics of individuals as much as their geographical place of origin, the discrimination will be seen as a form of both race and national origin discrimination.

> **EXAMPLE: An Iranian national applies for a job with a U.S. employer. The employer's manager states that the company does not hire "camel jockeys" and rejects the Iranian's application. The employer's statement can be viewed as a reference to the applicant's national origin. It can also be seen, however, as a pejorative comment on the ethnic characteristics of Arabs in general. The applicant has claims of national origin and race discrimination.**

As discussed previously, the distinction between race and national origin can be legally significant. It is often in the interests of an employee to assert a claim in racial terms even though the discrimination might appear to stem from the individual's national origin. For the most part, courts have permitted the cross-pollination of the two protected categories, broadly defining race to include the types of ethnic characteristics that seem less the product of race than of place of origin. Theoretical distinctions aside, where foreign ancestry is involved there is a significant overlap between the categories of race and national origin.

What Is National Origin Discrimination?

National origin discrimination is similar in nature to discrimination on the basis of other protected traits. An individual seeking to prove a claim of national origin discrimination must rely upon the same methods of proof that exist with respect to race and sex discrimination. In most cases, there will be no smoking gun evidence of discriminatory bias. To prove a claim of intentional discrimination, the employee must cite evidence suggestive of a discriminatory bias while raising questions about the validity of the employer's explanation for its decision. The disparate impact theory (discussed in Chapter 1) is applicable in this context. That theory has often been used in challenging minimum height and weight policies, which may have a disproportionate impact on individuals of certain national origins. If the policy has such an adverse effect and the employer cannot justify the policy as a business necessity, the policy is unlawful.

As suggested earlier, discrimination on the basis of national origin is not limited to cases in which an employer discriminates against an individual because of that individual's specific place or nation of origin. An employer might hold a bias against an individual because of the particular country from which the individual hails, but more typically, an employer will hold a bias against large groups of individuals who share some physical or cultural trait. An employer, in fact, may despise all foreigners and not wish to employ any individual who does not present himself as a "true American." Most courts have ruled that such a general xenophobia falls within the sweep of the prohibition against national origin discrimination. This is true even though there is no particular nation associated with the employer's discriminatory bias.

> **EXAMPLE: A hospital is looking to retain a heart surgeon. The hospital administrator interviews a candidate from Brazil. The administrator writes a letter recommending against the hiring of the Brazilian. In the letter, the administrator expresses concern about the candidate's presentability, stating pejoratively that the candidate looks and speaks like a foreigner. The administrator's comments support a claim of national origin discrimination. This is true even though the comments do not reference a particular place or nation of origin.**

While some employers may harbor a bias against all those with foreign traits, others might exhibit a more selective bias. An employer, for example, may be more than willing to hire an individual who comes from France. The same employer, however, may choose not to hire any individual who comes from Mexico. In a particular case, the employer may favor the hiring of an individual with French ancestry in lieu of an individual with Mexican ancestry.

As discussed in previous chapters, such intragroup discrimination should be viewed as unlawful. Discrimination law is designed to protect the individual. If an employer discriminates against an individual because of the protected characteristic of that individual, the employer's action is not excused merely because the employer does not disfavor every member of the protected group. This point holds particularly true in the context of national origin discrimination, where the potential for selective bias is great given the sheer number of national origin groups. Even where an employer chooses between or among individuals of foreign ancestry in filling a position, the employer engages in national origin discrimination if it harbors a bias against one of the individuals due to that individual's national origin, and acts on that bias in making its decision.

> EXAMPLE: An employer wishes to hire an accountant. The employer's manager conducts interviews and chooses an individual of Japanese ancestry for the position. The manager confides to a co-worker that he hired this individual even though another candidate of Iranian ancestry was more qualified. The manager explains that he rejected the Iranian because "those Middle Eastern guys can't be trusted." A court may well view the manager's comments as direct evidence of national origin discrimination. This is true even though the individual selected for the position is also in the protected class.

The Issue of Language

The protected category of national origin is inextricably tied to the question of language. For all its diversity, the United States continues to be a country dominated by the English language. For some, the concern with language is intertwined with a deep-seated nativism. To be an "American," one must speak fluent English. By the same token, the ability to speak English is an important part of day-to-day American life and is certainly essential to the performance of many jobs. There are two issues that arise with respect to language and national origin: (1) Under what circumstances can an employer base an adverse employment action on the insufficient language skills of an individual of foreign ancestry, and (2) under what circumstances can an employer impose English-only rules upon its employees?

The first issue turns almost entirely on context. Obviously, there are situations in which an employer can take an individual's language skills into account in making an employment decision. There are jobs that demand a high level of communication skills. Even in jobs that are language intensive, the ability to speak at least rudimentary English may be a necessity. If an individual cannot speak fluent English and the individual's inability to do so interferes with his or her ability to perform the job, an employer can rely upon the language deficiency in rejecting the individual for employment. This is true even if the deficiency in language skills ties, in some fashion, to the individual's foreign ancestry.

> **EXAMPLE: A woman applies for a position as a receptionist with a law firm. The position requires the individual to answer phone calls and to greet visitors to the firm. During the interview, it becomes clear that the woman knows very little English. Most of the firm's clientele is English-speaking, meaning that the woman will have to speak fluent English to perform the basic functions of the job. The firm can rely upon her inability to speak fluent English in rejecting her application.**

The problem is that concerns with language skills can too easily be used as a cover for rejecting an individual based on national origin. Some individuals of foreign ancestry speak with an accent, yet these individuals can speak English clearly enough to be understood. Others may know very little English but, given the nature of the job, are able to perform the job with no difficulty. While an employer is free to impose any nondiscriminatory qualifications standard that it desires, the fact that the purported language deficiency does not interfere with the ability to perform the job is strong evidence that the employer's requirement of language skills is, in fact, related to discrimination based on national origin.

> **EXAMPLE: An individual of Mexican ancestry applies for a position as a warehouse worker. A company supervisor conducts an interview with the individual and declares him unfit for the job. The supervisor refers vaguely to the individual's foreign accent. There is evidence that the individual speaks clear enough English to be understood. The job itself is not**

language intensive. The supervisor's comment provides strong support for a claim of national origin discrimination.

The English-only cases present a more complex question. English-only rules are usually imposed, if at all, in those workplaces that have a significant number of bilingual employees. The rules require employees to speak English while they are on the job. Typically, employers justify the rules as necessary to maintain discipline and order in the workplace.

An English-only rule does not, on its face, discriminate on the basis of national origin. While national origin and language fluency have an obvious connection, the two are not synonymous. An employee, nonetheless, can challenge an English-only rule under two theories. First, the employee can argue that the rule, while not facially discriminatory, is being used as a mask for singling out individuals of foreign ancestry for harsher treatment. The employee can also argue that the rule has a disparate impact on such individuals. In the latter case, the rule will be upheld if the employer can justify it as a business necessity.

The legal theories aside, the validity of an English-only rule may well turn upon the employer's ability to link the rule to legitimate workplace concerns. There may be circumstances where it is important for an employer's managers, all of whom are fluent in English only, to monitor the conversations of their subordinates. An English-only rule that is narrowly tailored to such a managerial concern may well pass muster. On the other hand, blanket rules against the use of a foreign language in the workplace may be harder to justify. The less job-related the rule appears to be, the more vulnerable the rule to legal challenge.

EXAMPLE: An employer maintains a bilingual workforce. Tension develops on the production line among certain workers. The tension arises because Hispanic workers appear to be making derogatory comments about their English-speaking co-workers and managers. There is evidence that the Hispanic workers can speak fluent English and typically do so in

the workplace except when they wish to make derogatory comments. To resolve the problem, the employer imposes an English-only rule, narrowly tailored to the production-line problem. A court is likely to uphold the employer's carefully crafted rule.

EXAMPLE: An employer adopts an English-only rule. The rule is not adopted in the context of any complaint by a co-worker or manager. The rule applies to any communication that takes place within the physical environs of the work-place. Two Hispanic workers are fired because they refuse to honor the rule while on break. The employer may have diffi-culty defending the application of its English-only rule in this circumstance.

It should be stressed that employees have not had a great deal of success in challenging English-only rules. Many courts, in fact, have dismissed such claims out of hand, at least where the rule is applied to bilingual employees who have the ability to speak English. These courts have reasoned that speaking the lan-guage of one's choice is not a term or condition of employment and that an employer can freely insist upon adherence to an Eng-lish-only rule absent evidence that the employer is doing so with a clear intent to harass or intimidate workers of a particular national origin. If an English-only rule appears at all reasonable, many courts will defer to the employer's judgment and uphold the rule.

CHAPTER 4

Religious Discrimination

T he United States was founded on the bedrock principle of religious freedom. The U.S. Constitution guarantees the free exercise of religion while, at the same time, prohibiting the "establishment" of religion. Private employers are not subject to the dictates of the Constitution, which applies only to government action. Nonetheless, constitutional concerns are implicated when a statute seeks to proscribe religious discrimination in a way that might infringe upon the free exercise rights of those regulated by the statute.

Federal employment law contains a clear prohibition against discrimination on the basis of an individual's religion. However, because of the potential conflict with the Constitution, the law provides a limited exemption for certain religious organizations. The law also seeks to protect the free exercise rights of employees by requiring employers, in some cases, to accommodate an employee's religious practices. Finally, the law prohibits religious harassment. As it turns out, this prohibition raises it own potential conflict with free exercise values, at least where the alleged harassment takes the form of religious proselytizing on the part of a fellow worker. Just as one man's ceiling is another man's floor, one man's religious harassment may well be another man's religious calling.

The Religious Exemption

It should be apparent that any broad prohibition against religious discrimination raises the potential of seriously infringing upon the free exercise rights of religious institutions. The Catholic Church, for example, permits only males to occupy the position of priest. Can the church be sued for unlawful sex discrimination? The answer, not surprisingly, is no. The reason is that Title VII of the Civil Rights Act contains a limited exemption for religious organizations. That exemption permits those organizations qualifying for the exemption to discriminate on the basis of religion in making employment decisions. It also permits such organizations to discriminate on other grounds (e.g., race or sex) with respect to highly sensitive religious positions.

The threshold issue raised by the religious exemption is whether the organization qualifies for the exemption. In many cases, this is not a difficult issue to resolve. Most churches, for example, would meet the definition of a religious organization. So too would any entity owned, controlled, or managed by the church. This is true even if the activities of that entity are secular in nature. Where an established church carries out its activities through subsidiary companies that are directly controlled by the church, both the church and its subsidiaries qualify for the exemption.

> **EXAMPLE: The Mormon Church operates a number of private businesses; among these is a health club. The club itself does not carry out any religious activities, but it is owned, controlled, and operated by the church. The club maintains a strict policy of hiring only members of the Mormon Church. The club qualifies for the protection of the religious exemption.**

The issue becomes more difficult when the inquiry moves away from organizations that have a direct connection to an established church. There are a number of institutions (e.g., hospitals, schools) that may have a religious affiliation of some kind. If these institutions are controlled or operated by a church, they will merit the protection of the exemption. If, however, they are not owned, controlled, or operated by a church and their activities are essentially secular in nature, they will be treated no differently than any other private employer.

> **EXAMPLE: A private boarding school is established by will. The will provides that the school's teachers are to be members of some Protestant sect. The school, although it requires its students to attend weekly chapel services, is essentially secular in its curriculum. The school, moreover, is managed by a board of trustees, whose members are selected by an outside body with no connection to any Protestant church. There is no requirement that trustees be ministers or hold any position of authority in a Protestant church. Neither the school nor the board is owned, supported, controlled, or managed in any significant way by any Protestant denomination. A court is likely to hold that the school is not protected by the religious exemption.**

While application of the religious exemption can lead to some close cases, it is clear that an employer cannot claim the mantle of the religious exemption merely by proclaiming itself a religious corporation. Some companies are owned by individuals who hold strong religious convictions. These individuals may well desire to create a climate in the workplace that is compatible with their religious views. Despite these religious intentions, the mission of the company may be essentially secular in nature. It is unlikely that the company will qualify for the religious exemption.

> **EXAMPLE: A company manufactures mining equipment. The company is family owned, and the owners are devoutly religious people who believe that God cannot be separated from their daily lives. The company encloses a gospel tract in each piece of outgoing mail, prints Bible verses on all company**

documents, and encourages religious worship on the part of its employees. The company is not, however, affiliated with any organized church or religious institution. A court is likely to find that the company does not qualify for the religious exemption.

A second question raised by the religious exemption is what conduct is encompassed within the protection of the exemption. Clearly, the exemption permits a qualifying organization to favor members of its religion in making employment decisions. Many religious organizations prefer to hire members of their own faith in carrying out the mission of the religion. This, in effect, is a form of religious discrimination otherwise prohibited by law, but the religious exemption provides a safe harbor for this type of religious preference.

It is less clear whether the exemption extends to the religious beliefs of the qualifying organization. By its terms, Title VII of the Civil Rights Act states only that a religious organization is entitled to favor the employment of individuals of a particular religion. This might be interpreted to mean that a religious organization can limit employment to those individuals affiliated with the religion but cannot otherwise condition employment on adherence to the organization's religious precepts. Logic, however, dictates that the exemption be given a broader reading. A religious organization can decide to hire only those individuals who are members of the particular religion. It can also decide, however, to broaden the pool of applicants to nonmembers, while nonetheless insisting upon adherence to its religious precepts among those whom it hires. If a religious organization may lawfully limit its employees to members of a particular faith, there is a strong argument that it should be permitted to hold its employees to a less severe standard of religious adherence (e.g., "We'll hire nonmembers as long as they do not do anything that offends our religious beliefs").

EXAMPLE: A Catholic school qualifies for the religious exemption. The school hires teachers who are not members of the Catholic

Church. The school, however, requires that these individuals not violate certain tenets of the church. A Protestant woman works as a teacher for the school. The woman, who is divorced, remarries in violation of church doctrine. Upon learning of the remarriage, the school terminates the teacher's employment. A court may well find that the decision to discharge the teacher falls within the ambit of the religious exemption.

With one critical exception, the religious exemption does not protect an employer that discriminates on the basis of some ground other than religion. A religious organization is permitted to discriminate on the basis of religion by preferring individuals of its religious liking. It is not entitled, however, to engage in invidious race or sex discrimination. The religious exemption immunizes religious organizations on those matters that are religious in nature. It does not provide an absolute free pass from the provisions of the antidiscrimination statutes.

The one exception to this principle concerns those positions that are deemed to have a highly sensitive religious component. As noted previously, the Catholic Church is not required by federal statute to employ women as priests. This is because the position of priest goes to the heart of the Church's religious mission. Indeed, to subject such a decision to legal regulation would raise serious constitutional concerns. To avoid these concerns, courts have placed employment decisions involving the clergy or other sensitive religious positions outside the reach of the antidiscrimination statutes.

EXAMPLE: A church seeks to hire a janitor. A woman applies for the position. The hiring official rejects the female applicant, stating "this is a man's job." The female sues, alleging sex discrimination. The church's decision is not exempted from the reach of the antidiscrimination statutes.

EXAMPLE: A woman seeks tenure on the faculty of a Catholic university. The woman teaches in the university's canon law

program. The program's mission is to provide religious instruc-
tion. The program is empowered by the Vatican to confer
ecclesiastical degrees in canon law and strictly adheres to the
religious teachings of the Catholic Church. The female is
denied tenure and sues, claiming sex discrimination. A court
may find that the woman's claim falls outside the reach of the
antidiscrimination statutes, given the essentially religious
nature of the position.

Religious Discrimination and the Principle of Reasonable Accommodation

In many respects, religious discrimination is similar in kind to discrimination on the basis of other protected traits. An employer
cannot take an adverse employment action against an individual
because of the religion of that individual. Religion need not be
the sole cause of the action, nor does the individual have to produce smoking gun evidence of the discrimination. An individual
proves religious discrimination under the same indirect methods
of proof applicable to other forms of employment discrimination.

The principle of intragroup discrimination, discussed in prior
chapters, applies with particular force in this context. An
employer may well favor the employment of members of one religious group (e.g., Protestants) while having a strong bias against
members of another (e.g., Catholics). Or an employer could
impermissibly discriminate between or among members of the
same religious sect, favoring, for example, the employment of
Reformed Jews while refusing to hire Orthodox Jews. Unless the
employer qualifies for the religious exemption, it cannot draw
such distinctions in making employment decisions.

Religious discrimination is not limited to discrimination on
the basis of an individual's affiliation with an established church.
In federal law, the prohibition against religious discrimination
extends to all aspects of religious observance and practice, including religious beliefs. An individual can hold religious beliefs even if

the individual is not a member of a religious sect. Indeed, even the belief that God does not exist (atheism) merits the protection of the law. As long as the individual has a sincerely held belief that is fairly tied to religious dogma, an employer cannot discriminate against the individual because of that belief.

> **EXAMPLE: An individual does not drink alcohol and believes that it is against God's will to do so. The individual is not a member of a religious sect that maintains this belief; nonetheless, the belief is religious in nature and sincerely held. An employer cannot refuse to hire the individual merely because the individual holds that religious belief.**

What differentiates religious discrimination from race, sex, or national origin discrimination is the principle of reasonable accommodation. Antidiscrimination laws are typically written in the negative. They prohibit the employer from taking the protected trait into account in making employment decisions. With respect to religious discrimination, federal law goes a step further. It not only imposes a negative limit on employment action, it requires the employer, in some circumstances, to take affirmative steps to accommodate the religious beliefs or practices of an individual employee. If an employer fails to take such steps, its actions may well be unlawful, even if the employer is not targeting the individual for adverse treatment because of the individual's religion.

There are two general categories of accommodation cases. The less common involves cases in which an employer seeks to create a religious atmosphere in its workplace. The employer may seek to require its employees to submit to the employer's religious beliefs by, for example, attending prayer meetings conducted on company premises. If the employer qualifies for the religious exemption, it may insist upon such religious adherence among its employees. If, however, the religious exemption does not apply, the employer may have to accommodate the interests of those who do not share the employer's religious beliefs.

EXAMPLE: A manufacturing company is owned by a born-again Christian. The owner believes that proselytizing is part of his religious obligation. The owner imposes a requirement that all employees attend a daily religious service to be conducted on company premises. Despite the owner's religious pretensions, the company does not qualify for the religious exemption. An employee objects to the forced religious service, claiming that it violates his atheist beliefs. The owner is entitled, within reason, to cultivate a work atmosphere of his own choosing. He is not entitled, however, to force his religious views upon an unwilling employee. The company may well have to accommodate the disgruntled employee by excusing the employee (and others with similar religious objections) from the religious service.

In the second category of accommodation cases (the more common) the employer does not seek to impose its religious views on the employee. Instead, the employer seeks to impose a neutral workplace rule that, as it turns out, infringes upon the religious beliefs or practices of an employee. Employers often maintain rules that, on their face, seem entirely nondiscriminatory. Thus, an employer might require that its employees be available for Saturday work. For most employees, this requirement, while an annoyance, presents no issue of discrimination. For certain individuals, however, Saturday is a day of religious significance that must be observed as a day of rest. The employer's rule, as applied to these individuals, produces a collision with religious belief. To avoid this dilemma, individuals can ask the employer to accommodate their religious belief or practice by excusing them from the Saturday work requirement.

The contours of the accommodation requirement cannot be defined with precision. Some general observations, however, can be made. First, courts have shown a tendency to defer to the employer's management prerogative. An employer is not required to accommodate an employee's religious beliefs or practices if doing so would constitute an undue hardship. Undue hardship, in this context, is defined as anything imposing more than a *de minimis* cost upon the employer. Where granting the accommodation would impair the rights of other workers or produce a measurable burden on the employer's operations, the otherwise neutral employment policy is likely to be sustained.

On the other hand, courts have not rubber-stamped all neutral employment rules that impact religious beliefs. If granting the accommodation does not infringe upon the rights or interests of other employees, a court may well require the employer to provide the accommodation unless the employer can demonstrate some other tangible harm or cost. At bottom, the lawfulness of the employer's actions will turn on the nature of the workplace rule, the reasonableness of the requested accommodation, and the objective content of the employer's objection to the accommodation.

> **EXAMPLE:** An employer has a well-established job assignment system embodied in a collective bargaining agreement between the employer and a union. Under that system, workers with less seniority are required to be available for work on Saturdays. An employee seeks an exemption from the Saturday work requirement citing the dictates of his religion, which require that Saturday be taken as a day of rest. There is evidence that the employer could not grant the accommodation without violating the collective bargaining agreement. There is also evidence that granting the accommodation would either trump the seniority rights of other workers, forcing them to work the Saturday shift, or require the employer to hire substitute or replacement workers to fill the Saturday shift. The employer, in these circumstances, is not required to provide the accommodation.

> **EXAMPLE:** Same Saturday work policy as above except there is no collective bargaining agreement at issue. Nor is there any seniority policy that dictates the Saturday work schedule. The employee seeking the accommodation from the Satur-

day work rule is willing to compensate for his absence on Saturday by working extra hours during the week. There is evidence that, by making minor adjustments in schedules, the employer can provide sufficient Saturday coverage without placing any additional burdens on other workers. A court may well find that the employer is required to accommodate the employee by excusing him from the Saturday work rule.

Of course, a seemingly neutral rule cannot be used as a mask for engaging in intentional discrimination against a religious practitioner. Accommodation analysis applies where an employer maintains a truly neutral workplace rule that, as applied in a particular case, places a burden on an individual's exercise of his or her religion. Where, however, the context suggests that the employer is seizing upon a supposed workplace rule as a pretext for excluding individuals of a particular religion, the employer's conduct is analyzed under traditional disparate treatment analysis. In such a case, the purported workplace rule is subject to challenge without regard to the issues of accommodation or undue hardship.

EXAMPLE: A Jewish individual applies for a job. The individual wears a yarmulke in accordance with the dictates of his religion. The manager conducting the interview informs the individual that the company has a workplace rule that forbids employees from wearing hats or other head coverings. As it turns out, there is no written evidence of the supposed workplace rule. Indeed, individuals in the mailroom often wear baseball-style caps while working in the office. There are other indications that the company, or at least some of its managers, may hold biases against individuals of the Jewish faith. The individual can challenge the refusal to hire as an act of intentional discrimination.

Finally, it is not simply employers that must abide by the antidiscrimination statutes. Labor unions are also subject to these statutes where they discriminate against their members (or employees). Unions often find themselves the subject of claims of religious discrimination brought by individuals who have a religious objection to the union's activities. Typically, these individuals seek to be exempted from the payment of union dues as a reasonable accommodation. Courts have been sympathetic to such claims—to a point. Courts have excused individuals in these cases from paying at least a portion of their union dues with the caveat that the individuals contribute an equivalent amount to a charitable organization. In effect, courts have sought to balance the religious concerns of the individual with the union's need for effective collective action.

Religious Harassment

It is probably fair to say that religious harassment is not as prevalent in the workplace as either racial or sexual harassment. One might theorize that religious harassment is less common because religion does not provoke the same degree of hostility as race or gender. While such a theory has history against it, it is possible that religion is sufficiently homogenized, at least in some pockets of the United States, to mute the parochial differences that mar the nation's grand experiment in religious pluralism. It is also true, however, that for many individuals, religion is an intensely personal matter. A co-worker is likely to know an individual's race or gender but may have no reason to know the religious views of the individual, even if the two work closely together. Religious harassment may occur less frequently simply because the trigger for the harassment—religious affiliation or belief—is less visible.

It is obvious that an employer violates the antidiscrimination laws when it creates or tolerates a work environment in which an individual is subjected to severe or pervasive harassment due to the individual's religion. The classic case of religious harassment occurs when an employee is forced to endure a barrage of derogatory comments about the employee's religious affiliation or beliefs. Co-workers, for example, may disparage a Catholic employee by ridiculing the Pope or Catholic doctrine, or by raising issues of ethnicity that are tied, in some cases, to the Catholic faith. If the employer does not take appropriate steps to remedy the harassment, the individual may well have a claim of unlawful religious discrimination based on a hostile work environment theory.

The difficulty with religious harassment is that the harassment can take the form of religious displays or proselytizing. An individual, for example, may be a born-again Christian. That individual may believe that it is his religious obligation to convert nonbelievers. The individual may have no animosity against individuals who do not share his beliefs. Nevertheless, the individual seeks to convert all those with whom he comes into contact, including his fellow employees. Another employee may well find the actions of the proselytizer to be objectionable, complaining to the employer that it put an end to what this employee views as a form of religious harassment.

For the employer, the dilemma is obvious. If the employer permits the actions of the offending employee to go unabated, it risks a claim of religious harassment by the offended employee. If, on the other hand, it forbids the offending employee from proselytizing, it risks a suit by that employee, who may claim that the employer is violating his religious rights. The problem is most acute for the public (i.e., government) employer, since any action by government directly implicates the protections of the Constitution. Any attempt by the public employer to suppress religious expression risks violating an employee's constitutionally based free exercise rights.

If there is an answer to this conundrum, it is found in the principle of reasonableness that governs almost all legal rules. An employee may feel that it is important to his or her religion to display religious symbols. Thus, the employee may display a crucifix or a picture of Jesus in his or her office. This, standing alone, should not give rise to a claim of religious harassment on the part of another employee offended by the religious displays. An individual should be given the freedom, within reason, to express his or her religious preferences. In this context, the injury, if any, to another employee's religious sensibilities seems slight. To be actionable, hostile environment claims must cross an evidentiary threshold of severity or pervasiveness. The mere display of a religious symbol in the office of a religious practitioner should not be enough to trigger the protection of the antidiscrimination statutes.

The situation changes when the religious activity shifts from mere displays of religious symbols to more active conversion efforts on the part of the religious practitioner. Some individuals may not stop at religious displays. They may feel obliged to press their cause further by subjecting their co-workers to a daily dose of religious advocacy. At this point, the religious practitioner has crossed the line from passive displays of religious symbols to affirmative conduct that, if sufficiently pervasive or severe, can fairly be viewed as harassment. Tolerance is a two-edged sword—it protects the religious advocate from being unfairly suppressed in the exercise of his or her religious beliefs, but it also ensures that, within the closed environment of the workplace, an individual is not held captive to the religious zealotry of a co-worker.

Because of the competing interests at stake, the law must strike a balance between the right of religious expression and the right to be free from expression that rises to the level of harassment. Legal doctrines aside, employers and employees alike can avoid contentious litigation by exercising common sense (and tolerance) to ensure that not every religious dispute turns into a federal case.

CHAPTER 5

Age Discrimination

T he American workforce is an increasingly aging workforce. Americans live longer than ever, and many prefer
to keep working well past the age of "normal" retirement. For employers, this graying of the American workforce
could be viewed as a boon. The employer has at its disposal a
ready supply of seasoned and, in many cases, talented workers. Too often, however, American business has viewed the
aging workforce as a menace, citing, among other things, the
higher cost of employing older workers. The result of this
stingy attitude has been the downsizing phenomenon that has
dominated the American business culture for the past several
years.

The downsizing issue is too complex to be compressed
into a general discussion of age discrimination. I speak to the
legal issues surrounding downsizing or reductions-in-force in a
separate chapter found in Part III of this book. In this chapter, I
address the more basic questions of age discrimination. These
include the evidentiary issues involved with the age 40 cutoff
for statutory protection, the use of age proxies in employment
decisions, the standards for discrimination in employee benefits, and the statutory bona fide occupational qualification
(BFOQ) defense.

Statutory Coverage and the Replacement Issue

The federal statute banning age discrimination in employment was enacted into law in 1967, three years after the passage of Title VII of the Civil Rights Act. Some of the initial legislative proposals prohibiting age discrimination would have made it unlawful for an employer to discriminate on the basis of age, regardless of the age of the individual subjected to the adverse employment action. In other words, just as the 60-year-old could not be discriminated against on the basis of age in favor of the 25-year-old, the 25-year-old could not be discriminated against on the basis of age in favor of the 60-year-old. In the end, Congress chose to limit coverage to individuals age 40 and over. Thus, while the statute broadly prohibits discrimination on the basis of age, the protection of the law extends only to those in the protected age group of age 40 and above.

The use of the age 40 cutoff has created unnecessary confusion concerning the evidentiary standards for resolving age discrimination claims. As discussed in Chapter 1, in proving a claim of intentional discrimination, an individual typically relies upon the *McDonnell Douglas* standard of proof. Under that standard, the claimant must make out a prima facie case. In a case of unlawful discharge, the fourth element of the prima facie case requires a showing that a replacement was hired to fill the claimant's position.

Historically, some courts took the view that, to satisfy the fourth element of the prima facie case, an age claimant was required to show replacement from outside the protected age group. In other words, the claimant had to show that he or she was replaced by an individual under the age of 40. Strictly applied, this meant that a 70-year-old fired from his job and replaced by a 41-year-old could not make out a prima facie case. Unable to rely upon the *McDonnell Douglas* standard, the 70-year-old would be required to produce direct evidence of age bias—no easy task—or else lose his or her claim.

In a recent case, the Supreme Court rejected this view of the replacement issue. The Court reasoned that the purpose of the prima facie case is to raise an inference of discrimination. Whether or not the replacement comes from outside the protected age group is largely irrelevant to that issue. A 40-year-old could be replaced by a 39-year-old, an individual outside the protected age group. That is hardly proof of an age bias. On the other hand, where a worker in her late 60s is replaced by a worker in her early 40s, the difference in age may be suggestive of an age bias even though the replacement worker is herself a member of the protected class. At the very least, replacement by a younger individual, even one from inside the protected class, ought to be sufficient to satisfy the fourth element of the prima facie case.

The Supreme Court's decision is important to the enforcement of the age discrimination law. In an increasingly aging workforce, replacements often come from the over-40 age group. To insist upon replacement by individuals under the age of 40 would make it more difficult for employees in the upper end of the protected age group to establish a claim of unlawful age discrimination. Although not directly at issue in the case, the Court's decision also confirms that intragroup discrimination is actionable under the age discrimination law. An employer may need to reduce its workforce. The employer may be forced to choose between two employees, one who is age 63 and one who is age 42. If the employer terminates the 63-year-old and does so because of the age of that individual, the employer engages in unlawful age discrimination. That is true even though the individual retained is also a member of the protected age group.

> **EXAMPLE: An employee is terminated as part of a reduction-in-force (RIF). The evidence shows that there were fifty employees in the division subject to the RIF. Of those fifty employees, twenty-five were let go. The twenty-five employees discharged were all over age 50. The twenty-five employees retained were all younger, although only a few were under the age of 40 and, thus, outside the protected age group. The evidence is suggestive of an age bias in the RIF**

even though most of the employees retained were also in the protected age group.

In the above example, the employer appears to have engaged in unlawful age discrimination by favoring the employment of younger individuals within the protected age group. What if the employer engages in age discrimination by relying upon age in choosing between two members of the protected age group but, in doing so, favors the employment of the older worker? As noted above, Congress chose to limit coverage under the federal age discrimination law to individuals age 40 or over. In doing so, however, Congress broadly protected those covered individuals from any form of age discrimination. There are strong indications that Congress intended to prohibit any act of age discrimination taken against an individual in the protected age group even if the discriminatory practice favors the employment of an older worker at the expense of a younger worker.

> **EXAMPLE: A company has to reduce its workforce. The company decides that it would prefer to retain its older employees. The company adopts an age 55 cutoff in determining which employees to let go. Those employees age 55 and over are retained. Those employees under age 55 are terminated. A 45-year-old employee, terminated as part of the reduction-in-force, sues, claiming age discrimination. There is a strong argument that the 45-year-old is the victim of unlawful age discrimination.**

Despite the strong statutory support for this position, several courts have expressed skepticism over the use of the age discrimination statute to assert what amounts to a claim of reverse age discrimination. Certainly, this kind of claim cannot be successfully maintained without very compelling evidence of the employer's use of an age criterion, since the normal indicia of ageism—preference for the younger employee—is lacking. On the other hand, it is important to remember that the age 40 cutoff is contained in the *federal* antidiscrimination statute. Many states have their own laws prohibiting age discrimination. Not all of these statutes impose an age cutoff. In those states that make age discrimination unlawful regardless of the age of the aggrieved employee, a claim of reverse discrimination, if supported by the evidence, should be sustainable.

Finally, the age 40 cutoff does not immunize employment policies that use age as a selection criterion, even though the age threshold is under 40. An employer, for example, may adopt a policy of not hiring any individual over the age of 35 for a particular employment position. The employer's policy obviously affects some individuals who have yet to reach the age of 40. On its face, however, it also applies to individuals age 40 and above who might otherwise be qualified for the position. Because the policy is age-based and because it excludes all members of the protected age group from consideration, the policy can be challenged as unlawfully discriminatory.

The Use of Age Proxies

In some respects, age discrimination differs from other forms of workplace discrimination. Race discrimination is rooted in this country's lengthy history of racial hatred and division. Sex discrimination reflects historic attitudes about the subordinate role of women in American society. The discrimination, in these cases, is often perpetrated by a dominant racial or gender group, which seeks to exclude members of a different racial or gender group.

Age discrimination is of a different character. Most of us, if we are lucky, will live past the age of 40. While many hold stereotypical views about the diminished abilities of older individuals, few have an outright animosity toward the elderly. Indeed, those who make employment decisions are often themselves members of the protected age group. Ageism undoubtedly exists, pervasively so, but it manifests itself in more subtle ways.

Because of the subtle nature of age discrimination, claims of age discrimination often center on seemingly benign factors that correlate in some fashion with age. These factors are sometimes referred to as age proxies. A classic age proxy is seniority. Seniority obviously has a connection to age. On the other hand, length of service does not equate with age, since it is possible that a younger employee could have more years of service with a company than an older worker. When an employer purports to base an employment decision on an age proxy, it raises the question of whether the employer's reliance on the age-correlated factor can support a claim of age discrimination.

There are several important points to make about the use of age proxies. First, an employment criterion that correlates in some fashion with age does not, by itself, compel a finding of age discrimination. The age discrimination law prohibits discrimination on the basis of age. It does not make it unlawful for an employer to base employment decisions on a factor that merely correlates with age if, in fact, it is the correlated factor, not age, that drives the employment decision. An employer can rely upon an age-correlated factor (e.g., seniority) without necessarily running afoul of the legal prohibition against age discrimination.

> **EXAMPLE: An employer needs to reduce its workforce. The employer chooses to rely upon seniority in deciding which individuals to select for termination. Individuals with less than ten years of service are exempt from the reduction-in-force. Individuals with ten years of service or more are subject to termination, depending upon the rating they received in their most recent performance evaluation. The employer has chosen a selection criterion for the reduction-in-force that has an obvious connection with age. The use of that criterion might have an adverse impact upon older workers and might otherwise support a claim of intentional age discrimination if it can be shown that the employer used length of service as a pretext to rid the workforce of older workers. Standing alone, however, the employer's use of this criterion does not, as a matter of law, constitute age discrimination.**

While an employer's reliance on a factor that merely corre-lates with age does not necessarily constitute age discrimination, the issue is different where the age proxy itself is defined by age. Employers frequently base employment decisions on an individ-ual's eligibility for pension benefits or retirement. If eligibility is defined solely by years of service or some other factor besides age, the employer does not necessarily engage in age discrimina-tion by basing the decision on the individual's pension or retire-ment status. If, on the other hand, pension or retirement eligibil-ity is defined by age, reliance on pension or retirement status is reliance on age. Where the age proxy itself is defined by age, reliance on the proxy constitutes age discrimination.

> **EXAMPLE: A company fires an employee who has just turned 65. The company admits that it terminated the employee because it wants to rid the workforce of individuals who are pension-eligi-ble. Under the pension plan, an individual is eligible for benefits if the individual has attained the age of 65. In this case, the employer's reliance on the age proxy—eligibility for pension benefits—is itself reliance on the prohibited factor (age). The employer has engaged in unlawful age discrimination.**

In the above example, the employer relied upon a factor that was defined solely by age. More typically, where an employer relies upon a factor such as pension eligibility, the factor relied upon is defined by both years of service and age. This factual wrinkle should not affect the outcome. As discussed in Chapter 1, the prohibited factor does not have to be the sole cause of an employment decision. It is enough that the employment action would not have been taken but for the prohibited factor. If an employer relies upon a factor that is defined, in part, by age, there is a strong argument that the employer's reliance on that factor constitutes age discrimination.

> **EXAMPLE: A company decides to reduce the salaries of all employees who are pension-eligible. Under the company's**

pension plan, an employee is eligible for pension benefits if the employee has at least twenty years of service with the company and has attained the age of 55. The company has based an employment decision on a factor—pension eligibility—that is defined, in part, by age. By definition, all individuals who are adversely affected by the employment decision are in the protected class (age 55 or over). There is a strong argument that the company's reliance on the age-defined factor is age discriminatory.

The remaining question is how to treat age proxies in those cases where the proxy is not defined by age. As noted above, an employer's reliance on an age-correlated factor does not, by itself, constitute age discrimination. That does not mean, however, that the use of such a factor cannot provide evidentiary support for an age claim. In some cases, reliance on an age-correlated factor can support a claim of disparate treatment discrimination. In others, it can provide the basis for a claim that use of the factor has a disparate impact on older workers.

Age proxies can be used as a basis for a claim of disparate treatment discrimination when an employer uses the age-correlated factor as a mask for intentional discrimination. This can occur when the employer purports to rely upon factors that serve as code words for an age bias. An employer, for example, might claim to have fired an older worker because he "costs too much," has been there "too long," or is "nearing retirement anyway." Or, an employer might disparage an older worker for his lack of "versatility," his inability to "adapt" to new methods or technologies, his "lack of energy," or his failure to be a "forward enough thinker." Standing alone, reliance on these factors does not constitute unlawful age discrimination, since a particular employee might, in fact, suffer from one or more of these deficiencies. In context, however, the use of these code words can support a claim that the employer is acting out of a discriminatory bias against older workers.

EXAMPLE: A company decides that it needs to reorganize its operations. The company retains a consultant to review the workforce and to make recommendations on which employees to let go. The consultant is given a list of the employees, with each employee's age, salary, and length of service. The consultant comments that too many people have been there too long and that the more senior employees are paid too much. After one visit to the company, the consultant criticizes the longer-tenured employees for being lethargic and unwilling to adapt to changes. The consultant recommends that the company rid itself of the deadwood and bring in workers who are more state of the art and who have the pace and urgency required for the job. The employer accepts the consultant's recommendations and fires fifteen employees, many of whom are in the protected age group. One of the dismissed employees files suit, alleging age discrimination. The consultant's comments could support a finding that the company acted out of age bias in dismissing the older worker.

The age proxy theory, as an evidentiary device for proving claims of intentional discrimination, has not been fully developed in the law. Nonetheless, there are signs that courts are becoming more receptive to this theory. If there is evidence that an employer has favored the hiring of a younger individual because of a factor that can reasonably be viewed as a code word for age, such evidence, depending on the context, can support a claim of intentional age discrimination.

Even if an employer's reliance on an age proxy does not support a claim of disparate treatment discrimination, use of an age-correlated factor can provide the basis for a disparate impact claim. As discussed in Chapter 1, employers frequently rely upon factors that do not, on their face, discriminate on the basis of a protected trait. Nevertheless, reliance on the factor may lead to an employment practice that has a disproportionate impact upon members of a protected group. Unless the employer can justify its practice as job related and consistent with business necessity, the employer can be held liable for the disparate effect of its practice. In the age context, employers frequently adopt policies that are based on such age-correlated factors as length of service or years of experience. Reliance on such factors can give rise to a viable disparate impact claim.

> **EXAMPLE: A school district decides to develop new hiring criteria for its elementary schoolteachers. The district decides, in particular, not to hire any individual with more than five years of experience. The evidence shows that the effect of the policy is to exclude a disproportionate number of individuals in the protected age group. The school district, moreover, is unable to defend its policy as a business necessity. The district's policy may well be unlawful, as applied to individuals in the protected age group who apply for teaching positions and are rejected as a result of that policy.**

As the above example suggests, the disparate impact theory works best where the employer relies upon an age-related factor that can be objectively measured (i.e., one that is defined by a specific number of years of service or work experience). In cases of that nature, the employment criterion, while related to age, can be readily distinguished from age itself, making it difficult for the employee to prove intentional discrimination under an age proxy theory. On the other hand, by relying upon a factor that is so clearly defined (and measurable), the employer makes it easier for the employee to assess the impact of the claim on members of the protected age group. In sum, the age proxy theory provides an effective whipsaw against age-based employment practices. If the employer relies on the type of subjective or vague age proxy that can be viewed as a code word (or phrase) for age, it exposes itself to a claim of disparate treatment discrimination. If an employer objectifies the proxy (i.e., reduces it to a specific number of years of service or experience), it exposes itself to a strong claim of disparate impact discrimination.

There is one caveat to this—not all courts accept the view that the disparate impact theory is available under the federal age discrimination statute. The age discrimination statute provides that it is not unlawful for an employer to base an employment decision upon a reasonable factor other than age. Some courts hold that this language, which has no parallel in Title VII of the Civil Rights Act, provides an absolute defense to an age-based disparate impact claim. In those courts where the disparate impact theory is not available, the employee cannot prevail under an age proxy theory unless the proxy itself is age-defined or the use of the proxy supports an argument that the employer is fronting the proxy as a mask for intentional age discrimination.

The Bona Fide Benefit Plan Defense

Age discrimination often takes the form of discrimination in employee benefits. Employers frequently provide fringe benefits for their employees. In doing so, employers often make distinctions in eligibility and benefit levels. The prohibition against age discrimination comes into play if those distinctions are age-based.

As originally enacted, the federal age discrimination statute contained a provision permitting employers to make age-based distinctions in employee benefits if those distinctions were made pursuant to the terms of a bona fide employee benefit plan. Most courts assumed that this was a relatively narrow statutory defense that would apply only where the employer could prove that the age-based distinctions were justified by the higher cost of providing the benefit for the older worker. In 1989, the Supreme Court offered a different view of the provision, essentially reading claims of benefit discrimination out of the federal statute.

In 1990, Congress passed a new law, the Older Workers Benefit Protection Act (OWBPA), that amended the age discrimination statute. The amendment essentially restored the law to where it had been prior to the 1989 Supreme Court decision. Under the OWBPA, an employer is prohibited from making an age-based distinction in employee benefits unless it can prove that the distinction is justified by age-related cost considerations. An employer is not required to provide the same amount of benefits to an older worker if it can show that the actual amount of payment made, or cost incurred, on behalf of the older worker is equal to that made or incurred on behalf of a younger worker. Absent such a showing, however, the age-based differential in benefits will fall outside the protection of the bona fide benefit plan defense.

> **EXAMPLE: A company maintains an employee benefit plan that provides retirement benefits for its employees. An employee qualifies for benefits under the plan if the employee has attained the age of 60 and has at least five years of service with the company. An employee also qualifies for benefits if the employee has not yet attained the age of 60 but retires from work due to a disability. The amount of the disability-based retirement benefit is higher than the amount of the benefit paid for ordinary retirement. A 61-year-old worker is forced to retire due to a disability. Because the worker has attained the age of 60, she is eligible only for the ordinary retirement benefit. She is not entitled to the more lucrative disability-based retirement benefit that she would have received had she been under the age of 60. The worker sues, alleging age discrimination in the administration of the benefit plan. The benefit plan makes an age-based distinction in the level of retirement benefits. The employer cannot demonstrate that the distinction is justified by an age-related cost consideration. The benefit plan is unlawful.**

While federal law now provides full protection against age discrimination in employee benefits, there are limits to the change in law brought about by the OWBPA. Specifically, the OWBPA does not apply to any stream of benefit payments that began prior to the Act's date of enactment. If an individual began receiving benefit payments before October 16, 1990, the Act's effective date, the individual cannot challenge the terms of the benefit plan at issue even if the payments continue after the October 16, 1990, effective date. On the other hand, the mere fact that a benefit plan predates the enactment of the Act does not insulate the plan from challenge. If an employer retains a benefit plan that has become unlawful under the OWBPA and an individual begins receiving benefit payments pursuant to that plan after the Act's effective date, the individual can challenge the plan as age discriminatory.

> **EXAMPLE:** An employer establishes a benefit plan in 1985. The plan provides an accidental disability retirement benefit for workers, one with a reduced benefit for those workers with less than ten years of service who became disabled after having attained the age of 55. The employer retains the benefit plan after the enactment of the OWBPA, even though the plan's distinction in the level of disability benefits is unlawful under that Act. Two employees challenge the plan. Employee A began receiving benefits under the plan in 1988. Employee B began receiving benefits in 1995. The claim of Employee A is likely to be dismissed, since Employee A began receiving benefits under the plan prior to the effective date of the Act. Employee B, however, has a viable claim. The employer is liable under the Act if it perpetuates its unlawful benefit plan and initiates new payments under the plan to employees becoming eligible for benefits after the effective date of the OWBPA.

In addition to clarifying the standard for the bona fide employee benefit plan defense, the OWBPA addressed other issues involving employee benefits and the prohibition against age discrimination. Most notably, the Act defined the circumstances under which an employer could adopt age-based distinctions in the administration of an early retirement incentive plan. In a nutshell, such distinctions are valid only if the plan is voluntary and otherwise consistent with the purposes of the age discrimination statute. To be voluntary, the plan must provide the

individual with a reasonable period of time—and sufficient information—to assess the options under the plan. To be consistent
with the purposes of the age discrimination statute, the plan must
avoid arbitrary age-based differentials in the amount of the early
retirement incentive. A plan that offers one early retirement
incentive to individuals between the ages of 55 and 60, say
$20,000, and a much lesser incentive to those over the age of 60,
say $5,000, may well be unlawfully discriminatory.

Finally, the OWBPA established standards for when a waiver
of rights or claims under the age discrimination statute could be
considered knowing and voluntary and, thus, enforceable. This is
an important statutory protection in its own right, one that is
worthy of a more detailed discussion. The waiver provisions of the
OWBPA are examined at some length in Part III of the book, in
the chapter on corporate downsizing.

The BFOQ Defense

For obvious reasons, the federal age discrimination statute contains a defense for age-based employment decisions that are justified as a bona fide occupational qualification (BFOQ). Age discrimination is often based on unfounded stereotypes about the
diminished abilities of older individuals. The age discrimination
statute is designed to combat such ageism by forcing employers
to judge older workers on their merits, not on age-based myths,
prejudices, or stereotypes. There are circumstances, however,
where an individual's age can affect job performance. In some
jobs, particularly those involving public safety, an employer may
be justified in taking age into account in making an employment
decision.

The BFOQ defense for age cases is similar to the BFOQ
defense for cases of sex discrimination (discussed in Chapter 2).
To establish the BFOQ defense, the employer must show that its
age-based policy is reasonably necessary to the essence of the
employer's business. Even if the employer can make that showing, it must still prove that it has no reasonable choice but to rely

upon an age-based criterion. The employer can meet its burden on this point in one of two ways: (1) by showing that it has a substantial basis for believing that all or nearly all of the employees above a particular age lack the qualifications for the job; or (2) by showing that it is highly impractical for the employer to test individually to determine whether each individual possesses the necessary qualifications for the position.

In the age context, the BFOQ defense surfaces most often in cases where an employer, citing safety concerns, imposes a maximum hiring or mandatory retirement age for a particular job or class of jobs. Thus, a police department might establish a policy of not hiring any individual over the age of 45 to serve as a police officer. Or, an airline might establish a mandatory retirement age of 60 for its pilots. It is not enough for the employer to invoke a general assumption about the capabilities of workers over the designated age. The employer must justify its age-based policy with empirical data supportive of its claim that workers above the age in question lack the qualifications for the job. Because of the potential of the BFOQ defense overrunning the statute, the defense is narrowly construed.

> **EXAMPLE: A city adopts a mandatory retirement age of 55 for its firefighters. The city justifies its policy by reference to a federal civil service statute that requires federal firefighters to retire at the age of 55. The city produces no evidence to show that it has independently assessed the validity of its mandatory retirement policy. There are indications, in fact, that the city could adopt one or more physical tests that would measure an individual's fitness for the job. The city's mandatory retirement policy is not justified as a BFOQ.**

Even if an employer's age-based policy is justified as a BFOQ, the employer might still have an obligation to transfer the older worker to another available position. Discrimination law is based on the principle of comparative treatment. An employer might be justified in relying upon an age-based BFOQ to remove an older worker from a position. If the employer, however, grants transfer rights to other employees removed from that position for reasons other than age, it must grant those same transfer rights to the older worker.

> **EXAMPLE: An airline company maintains a policy of disqualifying individuals age 60 or above from serving in the captain's position. That policy can be justified as a BFOQ. The company also has a policy, however, of granting liberal transfer privileges to individuals who are disqualified from the captain's position for reasons other than age. Under that policy, a captain is entitled to transfer to the position of flight engineer, thus "bumping" any flight engineer with less seniority. Since the employer extends such bumping privileges to individuals who are disqualified from the captain's position for reasons other than age, it must extend the same privileges to individuals forced out of the captain's position under the age-based BFOQ.**

Although not part of the BFOQ defense, there are other limits on the reach of the federal age discrimination statute. Most notably, the law permits employers to adopt age 65 mandatory retirement policies with respect to certain bona fide executives and high-ranking, policy-making employees. For this provision to apply, the executive or policy-making employee must have worked in that position for a period of least two years prior to his or her retirement. The employer, moreover, must provide the employee with an immediate retirement benefit of at least $44,000. If these requirements are not met, the forced retirement of the employee is unlawful.

CHAPTER 6

Disability Discrimination

F ew laws entered the books with as much fanfare as the Americans With Disabilities Act. Enacted into law in 1990, the ADA (as it is widely known) outlawed discrimination against the disabled. Title I of the ADA, in particular, made it unlawful for employers to discriminate against individuals with a disability in the terms and conditions of employment. The ADA was designed to transform the American workplace by forcing employers to change the ways jobs are performed and structured, thus breaking down the artificial barriers to employment for persons with disabilities.

It is debatable whether the ADA has lived up to these high expectations. Certainly, the Act has increased sensitivity to the concerns of the disabled population. Employers have educated themselves on their legal obligations under the ADA and, in many cases, taken great strides to open the workplace to disabled individuals. What is less clear is how effective the ADA has been as a litigation tool. Plaintiffs have had their share of victories, but courts have shown a surprising hostility to some of the core principles that underlie the ADA.

The ADA was not the first federal statute to address disability discrimination in the workplace. The Rehabilitation Act of 1973 contained provisions that prohibited disability-based discrimination in the workplace. That Act, however, applied only to the federal government and to certain companies that contracted with the federal government. The ADA was passed to extend to private employment the same basic antidiscrimination principles that have applied for years in federal or federal-funded employment.

In some respects, the ADA is similar to the other antidiscrimination statutes discussed in this book. Like those statutes, the ADA prohibits an employer from basing an employment decision on a protected trait—in this case, disability. Thus, if an employer takes an adverse action against an individual because of a disability-based animosity, the employer's reliance on disability is unlawful. In other key areas, however, the ADA strikes a fundamentally different chord. The Act, for example, contains a definition of "qualified individual with a disability"; that definition is, to be generous, difficult to apply. This has led to extensive litigation over issues of coverage, the kinds of issues that rarely come up under the other antidiscrimination laws. The ADA also contains at least two discrimination principles that are unique to disability law: a prohibition against pre-employment inquiries and a requirement of reasonable accommodation that amounts to an affirmative action provision for the disabled. That latter requirement, in particular, is the linchpin of the ADA and the one principle that most distinguishes disability discrimination from other forms of workplace discrimination.

The Definition of *Disability*

The threshold issue raised by the ADA is whether the individual meets the statute's definition of disability. This issue is critical because in *most* cases (although not all, as we shall see) an individual must have a disability within the meaning of the ADA to be protected under the statute. An individual might well have an impairment of some kind that limits his or her functional capacities to some degree. Yet unless that impairment meets the statutory definition of disability, the individual (in most cases) does not have a claim for disability discrimination under the ADA.

At the outset it must be stressed that, under the ADA's definition of disability, there are no per se disabilities. The ADA does not set forth a laundry list of conditions that qualify as covered disabilities. Instead, the Act focuses on the particular circumstances of each individual's impairment. The same impairment may be sufficiently disabling for some individuals but not for others. To determine whether an individual has a disability within the meaning of the ADA, one must apply to the circumstances of each case the Act's functional definition of disability.

The ADA sets forth a three-pronged definition of disability: (1) An individual has a covered disability if he or she has a physical or mental impairment that substantially limits one or more major life activities; (2) an individual also has a covered disability if he or she has a record of such an impairment even though the impairment does not exist, or is not substantially limiting, at the present time; (3) an individual has a covered disability if he or she is being regarded as having such an impairment.

The first prong of the definition is, by far, the most critical. The "record of impairment" and "regarded as" prongs of the definition, while important, are given a relatively limited reading. In the majority of cases, an individual will meet the definition of disability only if he or she has an actual disability (i.e., a physical or mental impairment that, at the time of the alleged discriminatory event, substantially limits one or more major life activities).

In most cases, there will be no difficulty in determining whether an individual has a mental or physical impairment. An impairment means any physiological disorder or condition, cosmetic disfigurement, or anatomical loss affecting one or more of several body systems. The definition of impairment does not include conditions that are the product of physical, psychological, environmental, cultural, or economic characteristics that are not impairments. Nor does it include common personality traits, such as poor judgment or a short temper, that are not manifestations of a physiological or mental disorder.

EXAMPLE: An employee is having difficulty performing his job. The difficulty stems from the fact that the employee is unable, in the time allotted, to read through the extensive documentation that he must analyze as part of the job. The reasons for his inability to do so are fatigue (due to outside family responsibilities) and his relatively limited educational background. He does not have a physical or mental impairment within the meaning of the ADA.

EXAMPLE: Same example as above except the employee's difficulty in performing the job stems from dyslexia, a physiological condition that affects an individual's ability to read. The individual has an impairment within the meaning of the ADA.

The term *major life activities,* while not defined in the statute, has an established meaning. Major life activities include caring for oneself, performing manual tasks, walking, seeing, hearing, speaking, breathing, learning, and working. Most courts also recognize sitting, standing, and lifting as major life activities within the meaning of the Act.

Some controversy has arisen with respect to the breadth of the category of major life activities. One question that has been the subject of extensive litigation is whether procreation is a major life activity. This is relevant, in particular, to whether infertility or HIV is a covered disability under the ADA. Despite the obvious arguments to the contrary, most courts initially held that procreation is not a major life activity under the ADA's definition of disability. The Supreme Court eventually stepped in to resolve the issue, holding that procreation is a major life activity. This decision extends the protections of the ADA to many individuals who are HIV-positive, even if their condition is asymptomatic.

The language of the ADA might suggest that one looks to the specific circumstances of the individual to determine whether a particular activity is a major life activity. For some individuals, gardening may be central to their existence. For others, outdoor sports like cycling or rugby may occupy a central place in their lives. Individuals in these circumstances could well claim that any condition that limits their ability to perform these activities affects what is, for them, a major life activity. For the most part, courts have rejected this view of the statute. Instead, courts have focused on basic activities that are a central part of the average person's day-to-day existence. An individual who can no longer tend to his or her garden may well have a disability within the meaning of the ADA, because any condition severe enough to prevent the individual from gardening could well restrict such basic activities as standing, lifting, or reaching. The mere fact, however, that the individual is prevented from engaging in a hobby or leisurely activity that is important to him or her may not be enough to bring the impairment within the reach of the statute.

> **EXAMPLE: An individual is an avid soccer player. He competes in amateur leagues, dedicating most of his leisure time to the sport. He injures his back while playing a game. The injury, while permanent, does not significantly restrict him in his ability to walk, lift, or stand. It does, however, prevent him from playing soccer on a competitive basis. The fact that competitive soccer is important to him is not enough to make soccer a major life activity for purposes of the ADA. Since there is no other major life activity for which the injury is *substantially* limiting, the injury does not give rise to a covered disability under the ADA.**

By far, the most complex component of the ADA's definition of disability is the requirement that the impairment substantially limit a major life activity. An individual may have a physical or mental impairment that may involve one or more major life activity. The question, for purposes of the ADA, is whether the major life activity is *substantially* limited by the impairment.

To be substantially limiting, an impairment must be more than the type of temporary, nonchronic condition that affects an individual only for a short period of time. It is not unusual for an individual to suffer from an acute illness or physical injury. In many cases, the illness or injury is, at the time, debilitating. Following a brief period of recovery, however, the individual is once again able to engage in the full range of major life activities. Such a brief or episodic impairment does not generally bring the individual within the protections of the ADA.

> **EXAMPLE: An individual breaks her leg in a skiing accident. During the period of convalescence, which lasts six weeks, she can walk only with the assistance of crutches or needs a wheelchair. At the end of that period, however, she is able to walk with little or no long-term effects. Even though she was incapacitated during her period of recovery, the impairment is too ephemeral to be considered substantially limiting.**

While a purely short-term impairment may fall outside the protection of the Act, an impairment need not be permanent to rise to the level of a covered disability. The fact that an individual is expected, at some point in time, to recover from a debilitating injury does not mean that the impairment cannot qualify as substantially limiting if the impairment significantly restricts the performance of a major life activity and is expected to do so for a period of at least several months. Further, there are some seemingly episodic or temporary impairments that are, in fact, manifestations of an underlying chronic condition. Even if the chronic condition is asymptomatic for substantial periods of time, it might still constitute a substantially limiting impairment during those periods in which it reemerges and significantly restricts the individual's ability to perform one or more major life activities.

> **EXAMPLE: An individual suffers a severe injury to his back and undergoes a surgical procedure known as a disk laminectomy. The individual's back heals, and he returns to work. Eighteen months later, he reinjures his back. He is diagnosed with degenerative disk disease. The physician informs the individ-**

ual that his condition is likely to be permanent, although the periods during which he will be incapacitated, as a result of the underlying condition, will be episodic and relatively brief. There is an argument that, for those periods in which the individual is incapacitated as a result of the degenerative disk disease, he is covered under the ADA. Even though his impairment is substantially limiting only for relatively brief periods of time, the acute condition is an intermittent manifestation of a chronic impairment.

Temporal issues aside, whether an impairment is substantially limiting turns largely on the relative severity of the impairment. Specifically, the question is whether the individual is significantly restricted in the condition, manner, or duration under which he or she can perform the major life activity as compared to the average person in the general population. One of the more common fact patterns that has arisen under the ADA concerns impairments that have an impact on an individual's ability to lift. Lifting is generally considered to be a major life activity under the ADA. The mere fact, however, that an individual has a physical impairment that restricts his or her ability to lift does not bring the individual within the protections of the statute. Often, individuals with a physical impairment are subject to a physician-imposed lifting restriction. Standing alone, such a restriction may not be enough to meet the standard for a substantially limiting impairment. Instead, the individual must point to more specific evidence that compares the individual's lifting capacity to the lifting capacity of the average person in the general population.

EXAMPLE: An individual has a physical impairment that restricts the use of his arms, neck, and back. A physician imposes a 25-pound lifting restriction. The individual brings suit under the ADA, after his employer removes him from the job, citing the limitations imposed by the impairment. In support of his claim, the individual points only to the lifting restriction. A court is likely to find that the impairment is not substantially limiting, and thus, that the individual is not protected under the ADA.

EXAMPLE: Same example as above except the individual is subject to a 15-pound lifting restriction. In support of his claim, he cites the testimony of a rehabilitation expert. The expert states that, as a result of the impairment, the individual has a lifting capacity of approximately 25% of the average person of the same age and gender. The individual also produces evidence showing that the impairment restricts his ability to engage in such day-to-day activities as house cleaning and grocery shopping, thus suggesting that the impairment significantly restricts him as compared to the average person. A court may well find that the individual's impairment constitutes a disability.

There are two issues involving the "substantially limiting" principle that deserve special mention. Many individuals have physical or mental impairments that, left unattended, would clearly be substantially limiting. Thus, for example, an individual with diabetes may lapse into a coma if the diabetic condition is not treated. With medication, however, the individual is able to function without any substantial limitation on a major life activity. The question is whether the issue of disability is analyzed without regard to such mitigating measures as medication or prosthetic devices. There are strong indications that, in passing the ADA, Congress intended for such individuals to be covered under the statute. Nonetheless, some courts have taken the position that if an individual's impairment is fully remediated by a mitigating measure of some kind, he or she does not meet the statutory definition of an individual with a disability. As of the time of this writing, the Supreme Court is poised to decide the issue.

A second issue that merits special mention involves the use of working as a major life activity. It is generally agreed that if an individual cannot establish a disability under any of the other major life activities, an individual may attempt to show that he is substantially limited in the major life activity of working. To meet this standard, the individual must show that he is significantly restricted in the ability to perform either a class of jobs or a broad range of jobs as compared to the average person having comparable job skills and abilities. It is not enough that the individual is significantly restricted in his ability to perform his current job. Nor is the individual required to show, however, that there is no job anywhere that he could perform. By and large, courts have not been overly sympathetic to this method of establishing a covered disability. The problem is that any claim that an individual is substantially limited in his ability to work is in conflict with the underlying assumption of the ADA (i.e., that individuals with disabilities are able to perform work despite the limitations imposed by the disability). For the most part, attempts to establish a disability under the working standard have failed.

The remaining two prongs of the definition of disability focus on conditions that do not constitute actual disabilities within the meaning of the Act. The first of these concerns individuals who have a record of impairment. This prong of the definition applies when an individual no longer has an impairment that substantially limits her in one or more major life activities, but once did. While the individual is not currently limited by any physical or mental impairment, an employer, aware of the individual's record of impairment, takes adverse action against her due, perhaps, to myths or stereotypes about individuals with that condition. In such a case, the individual has a claim that the employer has unlawfully taken action against her because of a disability.

> **EXAMPLE: An individual was diagnosed with tuberculosis as a young child, and the condition was treated successfully. When active, tuberculosis substantially limits one or more major life activities. When inactive, the condition is not substantially limiting. Nor does it pose any danger to other individuals. The individual's tuberculosis in this case has been inactive for thirty years. An employer learns of the individual's medical history, and has an irrational fear that the individual will pass the disease along to somebody else. Thus, he**

terminates her employment. The individual has a claim that she was discriminated against because of a disability.

Finally, the ADA defines disability to include an individual who is regarded as having an impairment that substantially limits one or more major life activities. The "regarded as" prong of the definition essentially protects individuals who are perceived as being disabled even though, in fact, they are not. Employers often respond to stereotypes concerning the employability of individuals with certain conditions. Even if the condition does not rise to the level of an actual disability, the employer's discriminatory attitude imposes a barrier to employment. Because the employer is treating the individual as if he or she were disabled, the protections of the Act come into play.

The "regarded as" component of the ADA's definition of disability has the potential for substantially expanding the class of individuals covered under the statute. For the most part, however, courts have not given the "regarded as" standard an expansive reading. Certainly, the mere fact that an employer regards the individual as unable to perform his or her current job (due to some condition that does not qualify as an actual disability) does not meet the standard for a "regarded as case." That is because there must be evidence that the employer regards the individual as having a covered disability (i.e., as being substantially limited in one or more major life activities). Most employers are too sophisticated to make the mistake of acknowledging that they regard the individual as completely incapacitated from work or otherwise substantially limited in a major life activity. If the evidence shows only that the employer regards the individual as unable to perform the individual's current job, the "regarded as" prong of the definition will not apply.

Who Is a Qualified Individual?

If an individual meets the threshold definition of disability, the individual must still meet the ADA's qualifications standard. In enacting the ADA, Congress was well aware of the fact that, with respect to many individuals in the disability population, the disabling condition will make it impossible for the individual to work. In that sense, the ADA differs from most other antidiscrimination statutes, which generally assume that an individual's protected trait in no way limits his or her ability to perform a job. Congress wanted to level the playing field for individuals with disabilities; however, it did not want to foist upon an employer an individual who, because of a disability, cannot perform the essence of the job. To address this concern, Congress wrote a qualifications standard into the statute. Under that standard, the individual must show that he or she is a qualified individual with a disability (i.e., an individual with a disability who is able to perform the essential functions of the job he or she holds or desires, with or without reasonable accommodation).

There are two critical features of the ADA's qualifications standard. First, an individual must demonstrate an ability to perform only those functions of the job that are deemed essential. There may be a number of minor responsibilities involved with performing a job, and in some cases, an individual's disability may preclude him or her from performing those minor job tasks. Nevertheless, the individual may be fully capable of carrying out the essential functions of the job. If so, he or she is a "qualified individual" under the ADA and, thus, is protected against disability-based discrimination (assuming the individual is also disabled).

Defining what constitutes the essential functions of a job is not an easy task. Obviously, a job function is not essential if the employer does not require individuals in the position to perform the function. The fact that the function is listed in a job description or announcement is not determinative; the employer must, in fact, require the function to be performed. If the employee is called upon to perform the function, whether the function is deemed essential turns on a number of factors. The time spent in performing the function, as a percentage of the individual's typical workday, is relevant. So too is the consequence of an individual's failure to perform the function—a factor that looms large in those cases involving public safety, where the performance of a single task, even on rare occasions, may be critical. Finally, whether a function is considered essential to a job may depend on the number of employees available in the workplace to perform the function. In some workplaces, it may be important that the individual be able to perform even the relatively minor job tasks, given the limited number of workers able to pitch in. In other workplaces, however, a particular job task could be viewed as nonessential given the ease with which job functions can be distributed among employees.

> **EXAMPLE: An individual works on a factory production line. Approximately 95% of her job is comprised of operating a mechanical device that is a part of the production line. Three or four times a day, however, articles that have been gathered from the production line have to be moved in bulk. Historically, she assisted in this task, although it was not necessary that she do so, given the number of employees available to perform the function. Although she becomes disabled, the disability does not affect her ability to operate the mechanical device that is part of the production line. It does, however, prevent her from assisting in the movement of the bulk items. There is a strong argument that her inability to assist in the heavy lifting does not affect her status as a qualified individual. The heavy lifting is a small part of the job that can be performed quite readily without her assistance and, thus, is not an essential function of the job.**

The second feature of the qualifications standard is that the individual meets the standard if he or she is able to perform the essential functions of the job with or without reasonable accommodation. *Reasonable accommodation* is a term of art under the ADA. The concept is discussed in more detail later in this chapter, but for our purposes here, the point is that the ADA permits an individual to invoke possible accommodations by the employer in order to meet the statute's qualifications standard. An individual, due to a disability, may be unable to perform the essential functions of a job without an accommodation. With accommodation, however, the individual can perform the essential functions. If the individual can do the job with accommodation, he or she satisfies the qualifications standard and, thus, comes within the protections of the ADA.

> **EXAMPLE: An individual applies for a job. To be able to perform the essential functions of the job, he must be able to use a personal computer. He has a physical impairment that makes it impossible for him to perform work on a computer, assuming the employer uses the standard computer technology. There is a mechanical device, however, that would permit him to perform work on a computer. The use of such a device could constitute a reasonable accommodation under the ADA. The individual can meet the ADA's qualifications standard even though he cannot perform the essential functions of the job without an accommodation.**

The issue of qualifications has arisen in a number of contexts. The issue has been a particular source of controversy, however, in those cases involving claims of disability discrimination in employee benefits. In the typical ADA case, an individual claims that an employer deprived the individual of a job opportunity because of the individual's disability. Thus, the individual claims that the employer refused to hire him because of a disability. Or, the individual claims that he was terminated from a position or denied a promotion due to a disability. The employer may well respond that it rejected the individual because the individual's disability rendered him unable to perform the job. In such a case, the claim turns on the individual's ability to show that he can perform the essential functions of the job with or without accommodation. If the individual cannot make that showing, his claim fails.

There are other cases, however, where the claim does not focus on the individual's ability to perform the job. An employer, for example, might make employee benefits available to its employees. Those benefits could include long-term disability benefits, health insurance benefits, or pension benefits. In many cases, an individual will not have a need for such benefits until the point at which he, due to a disability, becomes unable to perform the essential functions of the job. Assume that an employer, in providing an employee benefit, discriminates on the basis of disability. Assume as well that an individual who qualified for the benefit (because of his status as an employee) is no longer working for the employer because his disability has become incapacitating. Is such an individual a qualified individual under the ADA and, thus, protected against disability discrimination in the administration of the benefit?

There are two ways to analyze this issue. One could argue that the individual is not covered under the ADA because, at the point at which the individual is in need of the benefits, he is no longer able to perform the essential functions of the job and, strictly speaking, is not a qualified individual. One might also argue, however, that the qualifications standard should not be applied in such a strict sense. Since the individual qualified for the benefits in the first place because of his status as an employee, and since the individual is now in need of the benefits because of his disabling condition, the individual is entitled to the protections of the statute.

At this point, courts have not reached a consensus on this important issue. Most courts have taken the narrow view of the statute, finding that the individual cannot meet the qualifications standard because he is no longer able to perform the essential functions of the job. Other courts have determined that, so long as the individual qualified for the benefit in the first instance because of his status as an employee, the protections of the statute extend to the individual once his disability worsens to the point that he can no longer work and, thus, is in need of the benefit. Whether an individual in these benefit cases will be able to invoke the full protections of the ADA remains to be seen.

It should be stressed that even if an individual in these cases is able to satisfy the qualifications standard, the individual is not home free. For there to be a violation of the statute, the employer must discriminate on the basis of disability. Some distinctions in employee benefits might not be viewed as disability-based. It is not clear, for example, that a long-term disability benefit plan that provides different levels of benefits for those with physical, as opposed to mental, impairments discriminates on the basis of disability. The ADA, moreover, has a defense for benefit and insurance plans. The precise scope of that defense is unclear, but it is possible that a benefit or insurance plan that discriminates on the basis of disability will fall within the defense and, thus, not violate the ADA.

Finally, although not technically a part of the ADA's definition of qualified individual, the ADA imposes an additional limitation on the protective reach of the statute—an employer may refuse to hire an individual with a disability if the individual poses a direct threat to the health or safety of the individual or others. In theory, the direct threat provision applies only where the risk of harm is probable or substantial. The employer, moreover, must rely on objective, factual evidence—not subjective perception. In practice, courts have taken a more generous view of the provision, consistent with the general tendency in the law to defer to employer prerogative in those cases where public safety or health is implicated. If there is a plausible argument that the employment of a disabled individual will pose a genuine threat to the safety or health of others, a court may well find that the direct threat provision applies.

Pre-Employment Inquiries

As the previous sections suggest, the ADA has a complex definition of disability, combined with a specific qualifications standard that differentiates the ADA from the other antidiscrimination statutes. In most cases, an individual cannot claim the protections of the ADA unless the individual is a qualified individual with a disability (i.e., an individual with a covered disability who is able, with or without reasonable accommodation, to perform the essential functions of the position the individual holds or desires). Because employers frequently admit that they have relied on an individual's impairment in making an employment decision, ADA cases often turn almost entirely on whether that impairment rises to the level of disability and whether the individual is a qualified individual as the Act defines that term.

Despite the importance of these threshold requirements, it is not clear that meeting the standard of a qualified individual with a disability is required in all cases. Most provisions of the ADA focus on the treatment (or mistreatment) of persons with a disability. Some provisions, however, are designed to reach a broader range of employer conduct. The focus of these provisions is not on an individual's status as a disabled individual but on employment practices that, if left unchecked, pose a threat to the enforcement goals of the statute. The most important of these provisions is the ADA's limitation on pre-employment inquiries.

The ADA is designed to remove the barriers to employment for disabled individuals. One obstacle to the employment of the disabled is that employers often make assumptions about an individual's ability to perform the job based on information gathered in the interview process about the individual's physical or mental condition. In recognition of this problem, the ADA contains a provision that limits the kinds of questions that employers may ask of job applicants. Specifically, but with certain exceptions, the provision prevents an employer from conducting a medical examination or making inquiries of a job applicant as to whether the applicant has a disability or as to the nature or severity of any such disability.

The first point to make about the pre-employment inquiry provision has already been alluded to—the provision, in a strict sense, is not limited to individuals who meet the statutory definition of disability. The pre-employment inquiry provision limits the kinds of questions that may be asked of a job applicant. The ultimate objective of the provision is to assist in the employment of disabled individuals, but the statute's prohibition is implicated even where the job applicant in question does not technically meet the definition of disability. Although not all courts have agreed, there is a strong argument that an individual can state a claim under the pre-employment inquiry provision even if that individual does not meet the definition of a qualified individual with a disability.

The coverage issue aside, the provision on pre-employment inquiries is divided into two parts: (1) limitations on what an employer may ask (or do) prior to making a conditional offer of employment, and (2) limitations on what an employer may ask (or do) once such an offer is made. The basic rule is that, at the pre-offer stage, an employer may not conduct medical examinations or ask any disability-related questions of the applicant. Thus, an employer may not ask an applicant whether he or she has a particular disability or a history of any physical or mental problems. Nor may the employer conduct a medical examination to test whether an individual has any physical or mental conditions that, in the employer's mind, might preclude the individual from performing the job. If the employer engages in such conduct, the employer violates the ADA.

> **EXAMPLE: An individual with clinical depression applies for a job. The employer is suspicious that she may have a history of mental problems. During the interview, the hiring official asks numerous questions designed to elicit information about a possible disability. The official asks, for example, whether she has ever been hospitalized. The official also asks whether she is taking any medications. The official's questions constitute impermissible pre-employment inquiries.**

While an employer is prohibited from soliciting information that may reveal an individual's disability status, the employer's hands are not tied completely. An employer, for example, may ask whether an individual is able to perform the specific functions of the job at issue. The employer may also ask about the individual's education, work history, and required certifications and licenses, because those matters go to the individual's nonmedical qualifications and skills. Finally, an employer may ask an applicant to demonstrate how the applicant would perform job tasks. This is particularly the case where an individual has a known disability that might reasonably be viewed as limiting his or her ability to do the job. An employer may ask legitimate questions about an individual's ability to perform a job. What it cannot do (lawfully) is ask questions that are likely to elicit information about a disability.

These limitations apply at the pre-offer stage of the hiring process. Once the employer makes a conditional offer of employment, the employer is permitted to ask disability-related questions and conduct medical examinations, subject to two limitations. First, if the employer conducts a medical examination or asks questions about an individual's medical history or physical and mental health, it must subject all putative employees in the same job category to the same treatment. The employer, in other words, cannot target certain individuals for more extensive examination or questioning based on the fact (or assumption) that these individuals are disabled. Second, the employer must keep confidential any medical information uncovered as part of a post-offer examination or inquiry. The confidentiality requirement does not preclude the employer from informing supervisors and managers of necessary restrictions on the work or duties of the employee. The employer may also inform first aid personnel of the individual's condition if the disability might require emergency treatment. Finally, information may be disclosed to government officials investigating compliance with the ADA and to state workers' compensation offices in accordance with workers' compensation laws.

Reasonable Accommodation

Arguably, the most important feature of the ADA is the requirement of reasonable accommodation. The ADA prohibits all forms of workplace discrimination, which can sometimes take the form of adverse employment actions motivated by animus against disabled individuals. Such discrimination is similar in kind to the type of discrimination prohibited under the other antidiscrimination statutes and, thus, is analyzed under the same legal standards that apply under those statutes. The requirement of reasonable accommodation takes the ADA to a different level. The ADA does not simply prohibit an employer from taking adverse action against a disabled individual but holds the employer accountable when it fails to take affirmative steps to accommodate an individual's disability.

At the outset, the principle of reasonable accommodation set forth in the ADA must be distinguished from the principle of reasonable accommodation that applies in the context of religious discrimination (discussed in Chapter 4). In cases of religious discrimination, the employer's burden of accommodation is relatively slight. The employer can escape the accommodation requirement by pointing to evidence that the accommodation imposes more than a *de minimis* cost. The ADA's accommodation requirement is not so easily evaded. The standards for reasonable accommodation, in these two contexts, are not the same.

From the employee's perspective, the critical point is that the employer's duty to accommodate is triggered, to a large degree, by the employee's request for an accommodation. The ADA contemplates an interactive process between the employer and the employee. There may be cases where an individual's disability and need for an accommodation are obvious, thus implicating the duty to accommodate. As a general matter, however, the employer is not required to speculate about an employee's need for accommodation. Instead, the *employee* is required to come forward and put the issue of accommodation on the table. The employee is not required to give a detailed account of every accommodation possible. The employee is required, however, to initiate the interactive process by raising, in general terms, his or her need for an accommodation.

EXAMPLE: An employee has dyslexia, an impairment that can constitute a disability under the ADA. The employee's supervisor is not aware of his impairment. The supervisor

notices, however, that the employee is having difficulty performing the job. The supervisor warns the employee that
unless he improves his job performance, he will be discharged. The employee is unable to improve his performance and, as a result, is fired. The employee never informs
the supervisor, or any other management official, of his disability. Nor does he ask for an accommodation. Nonetheless,
the employee brings suit under the ADA, alleging that his
discharge was unlawful. Even if the evidence shows that the
individual has a disability that could have been reasonably
accommodated by the employer, a court is unlikely to hold
the employer liable. The employee's disability was unknown
to the employer, and the employee failed to raise the issue
of accommodation with the employer.

Once the employer's duty to accommodate is implicated,
and assuming the individual meets the definition of disability, the
question becomes what accommodations the employer is
required to provide. The statute lists several possibilities. These
include making existing facilities used by employees readily acces-
sible to or usable by individuals with disabilities; job restructuring;
part-time or modified work schedules; reassignment to a vacant
position; acquisition or modification of equipment or devices;
appropriate adjustment or modifications of examinations, training materials, or policies; and the provision of qualified readers
and interpreters.

There are two overall limitations on the duty to accommodate. First, the proposed accommodation must be reasonable.
That means, above all else, that the accommodation must be
effective in permitting the individual to perform the essential functions of the job. An employer may be required to restructure a job
by reallocating nonessential job functions to other employees. An
employer, however, is not required to reallocate or eliminate those
job functions deemed essential. If the proposed accommodation
would require the employee to eliminate or reassign an essential
job function, the accommodation is not reasonable.

> EXAMPLE: An individual works on an assembly line. As part
> of the job, he is repeatedly required to lift objects weighing
> more than 50 pounds. He injures his back, causing a perma-
> nent impairment that rises to the level of a disability. He
> requests, as an accommodation, that he be excused from per-
> forming the heavy lifting component of the job. Under these
> circumstances, the heavy lifting task is an essential function
> of his job. Because the requested accommodation would
> require the employer to eliminate an essential job function,
> the accommodation is not reasonable and the employer is
> not required to provide it.

Second, even if there is an available reasonable accommodation, the employer is not required to provide the accommodation if doing so would create an undue hardship for the employer.
Undue hardship, in the ADA context, essentially focuses on
whether the accommodation would be unduly costly. An accommodation might also constitute an undue hardship if it would
fundamentally alter the nature or operation of the employer's
business. In assessing the issue of cost, the law takes into account
the nature and net cost of the accommodation and the financial
resources of the employer being asked to provide the accommodation. The mere fact that an employer is required to incur some
expense in providing an accommodation does not make the
accommodation an undue hardship.

When the ADA was passed, many raised concerns that
employers would be burdened with providing an array of costly
accommodations. There are indications that this has not been the
case. As it turns out, most accommodations involve very little
expense for the employer. The issue is not one of cost but of the
employer's willingness to alter its normal way of doing things to
permit a disabled individual to perform the job. In most cases,
cost alone will not excuse an employer from providing an accommodation that is otherwise reasonable.

There are two accommodations under the ADA that have
been the source of some controversy. First, the ADA has been

interpreted as requiring an employer to provide unpaid leave as a reasonable accommodation. (Paid leave can also be a reasonable accommodation, at least where the employer makes paid leave available to its employees.) The point of this accommodation is to allow the employee to recover from a disabling injury so that he or she can return to work, able to perform the essential functions of the job. This accommodation has proven controversial for an obvious reason—it requires the employer to accommodate an employee by allowing him *not* to work. For the accommodation to apply, the period of leave cannot be indefinite. In addition, there must be plausible reasons to believe that the disability will be accommodated by the leave (i.e., that the individual will be able to return to his or her job following the period of leave).

> **EXAMPLE: An employee is a Vietnam veteran who has been diagnosed with post-traumatic stress disorder (PTSD). The condition has been asymptomatic for a number of years but has recently resurfaced, causing him to lash out at co-workers and supervisors. He is aware of a facility that treats individuals with PTSD. The employee consults a physician who recommends that he be admitted into the program for a period of twelve weeks. The physician believes that, with treatment, the individual can improve to the point that he can return to his job without any incidents of serious violence or anger. The employee requests a twelve-week period of unpaid leave. The employer may well be required to provide the requested leave as a reasonable accommodation.**

> **EXAMPLE: Same example as above except the employee has already taken leave on three occasions. The employee's condition does not appear to have improved. The employee wants to be admitted into a treatment program, but there is no assurance from a physician that the treatment program will be effective. The employee, in essence, asks for a period of indefinite leave. A court is likely to find that the employer is not required to provide the leave as a reasonable accommodation.**

The second accommodation that has proven controversial under the ADA concerns the employer's duty of reassigning a disabled employee to another vacant position. As a general matter, the accommodation requirement focuses on steps that an employer must take to assist an individual in performing the essential functions of the job the individual occupies or is applying for. There may be cases, however, where an employee, due to a disability, becomes unable to perform his current job. In that event, the employee can request, as an accommodation, that he be reassigned to another vacant position with the employer. The reassignment accommodation applies only to existing employees, not job applicants. It is available only when there is a vacant position for which the employee is otherwise qualified. The employer is not required to wait for an indefinite period for a position to become vacant, nor is the employer required to create a new position for the employee where no vacant position exists.

The controversy surrounding the reassignment accommodation stems from two things. First, some courts are uncomfortable with the idea that an employer can be required to place an employee in another position when the employee is no longer able to perform the essential functions of his current job. These courts have found ways to make it more difficult for an employee to invoke the reassignment accommodation. Second, there may be cases where reassigning an employee to a vacant position would conflict with the rights of other workers under a collective bargaining agreement. For example, an employer may have a vacant position, but another employee, with more seniority, may have a superior claim to the position under the terms of a collective bargaining agreement. Where there is direct conflict between the contractual rights of other workers and the reassignment accommodation, courts have tended to favor the interests of the other workers.

CHAPTER 7

Fair Labor Standards

In this chapter, we shift gears. The first six chapters of this book address issues of workplace discrimination. The defining principle in that context is that an employer may not take an adverse employment action against an individual because of a protected trait of that individual. Since all of us have at least two protected traits (race and gender), all of us can potentially claim the protections of the antidiscrimination laws. Those protections come into play, however, only when the employer relies on the protected trait in making an employment decision (or in affecting the terms and conditions of an individual's employment).

While the principle of nondiscrimination dominates employment law, the law does more than simply protect against discrimination. It also regulates the employer-employee relationship, in a more general fashion, to ensure that an employer does not use its superior economic position to subject its employees to unfair working conditions. An employer is generally free to hire the employees of its choice; the employer, however, must not discriminate in doing so. An employer also has substantial leeway in dictating the terms and conditions of the employment relationship; in doing so, however, the employer must comply with certain minimal standards established for the protection of employees.

The principal federal statute that protects the economic rights of workers is the Fair Labor Standards Act (FLSA). The FLSA was passed in 1938 amid evidence of substantial abuses on the part of employers. The FLSA was designed to level the playing field for workers by providing certain wage and hour protections. The Act is premised on the assumption that, if left unchecked, employers will use their superior bargaining power to demand excessive work for limited pay, leading to unjust working conditions and labor unrest.

The basic requirements of the FLSA are not difficult to state. An employer is required to pay a nonexempt employee a minimum wage. The minimum wage, as of January 1, 1999, is $5.15 an hour. An employer is also required to pay overtime for all work in excess of forty hours in a workweek. The overtime rate is generally time and one-half the employee's regular rate of pay.

The FLSA also regulates the use (or misuse) of child labor. The general rule under the FLSA is that an individual is permitted to perform any job for unlimited hours, subject to the Act's requirement of overtime pay. This rule applies to any individual who is age 18 or older. The law also permits unlimited work (subject to overtime pay) for individuals who are age 16 or 17, with the restriction that such individuals may not work in any job classified as hazardous. The employment of individuals under the age of 16 is subject to significant restrictions on the nature and amount of work permitted, with a distinction made between agricultural and nonagricultural jobs. To encourage the hiring of younger workers in summer or temporary jobs, the law establishes a subminimum wage of $4.25 per hour for individuals age 20 or under during the first ninety days of their employment with a particular employer.

Although the basic rules of the FLSA are easy enough to describe, wage and hour law is, in fact, enormously complex. There are two reasons for this. First, the FLSA is the principal *federal* statute addressing wage and hour issues. In this area, perhaps more so than others, the level of workplace protection is subject to the varying approaches of individual states, which have taken an active hand in regulating wage and hour matters. To cite one example, the FLSA does not provide a limit on the amount of hours that an employer can require an adult employee to work in a workweek. An employer must pay an overtime rate for work in excess of forty hours, but it may require the employee to work as many overtime hours as the employer deems proper. The majority of states, however, place a limit of some kind on the amount of hours that an individual is permitted to work. (Out of concerns for safety, federal transportation laws also regulate the hours of those who work as truck drivers, bus drivers, or airline pilots.) Thus, despite the absence of any such limit in the FLSA, an employer may well be subject to a state-imposed limit on the maximum amount of hours worked.

Any comprehensive examination of the various state laws governing wage and hour issues is beyond the purview of this book. It is important to stress, however, that state law is simply a supplement to the federal standards established under the FLSA. A state may provide greater protection for individual workers (e.g., by providing a higher minimum wage than that provided under federal law). It may not, however, provide less protection than that guaranteed under federal law.

The second reason for complexity in this area is more basic. At first glance, it may seem a simple task to establish wage and hour protections. The law simply states that an employer must pay a minimum wage and provide proper compensation for overtime work. The problem is that there are as many employment arrangements as there are workplaces. How does one determine the amount of compensable time? How does one calculate overtime pay? Even if these (and other) issues can be worked out, should every individual fairly characterized as an employee be subject to wage and hour protections? If certain employees are exempt, how does one define the exemption? In theory, wage and hour law is simple enough. In practice, the legal rules are both detailed and complex.

Because of the complexities involved in regulating wage and hour issues, it is impossible to provide a complete description of the myriad of statutory and regulatory rules that govern in this area. Nonetheless, some basic rules can be described and illustrated. In this chapter, I focus on three general matters: (1) the definition of exempt employees; (2) the question of what constitutes compensable time; and (3) the issues surrounding the calculation of pay.

Exempt Employees

The threshold inquiry with respect to the FLSA is who is covered under the statute. In terms of the statutory coverage of employers, the FLSA is extremely broad. The FLSA extends to any enterprise that has annual sales of not less than $500,000. The FLSA also covers public sector employers and any employer, regardless of annual sales, that operates a hospital, medical treatment facility, or educational institution. Even if the employer itself does not meet the definition of a covered enterprise, the FLSA reaches the employees of that employer if those employees are engaged in interstate commerce, a term that, in this context, has been given the broadest reach possible. In most cases, an employer will be subject to the FLSA (as well as any state statute that might impose similar wage and hour protections).

In this context, the critical issues of coverage turn not on the definition of a covered employer, but on the definition of those employees exempted from the Act. The FLSA was passed with an understanding that some workers are not properly brought within the reach of wage and hour protections. This includes, most notably, those individuals whose work is closely aligned with the interests of management. It also includes employees whose jobs, by their very nature, do not implicate the policy concerns underlying the FLSA.

The list of employees exempt from both the minimum wage and overtime pay requirements include: (1) executive, administrative, and professional employees; (2) employees of certain seasonal amusement or recreational establishments; (3) employees of certain small newspapers (those with a circulation of less than 4,000); (4) fishing specialists who catch, harvest, or farm fish and shellfish; (5) farm workers employed by a person who used no more than 500 "man-days" of farm labor in any calendar quarter of the preceding calendar year; and (6) casual babysitters and personal companions.

The list of employees exempt from the Act's overtime pay requirement only include: (1) certain commissioned employees of retail or service establishments; (2) taxi drivers and employees of railroads and air carriers; (3) seamen on American vessels (seamen on foreign vessels are exempt entirely from the Act); and (4) farm workers (who are otherwise subject to the minimum wage requirement).

Arguably, the most controversial of the statutory exemptions is the exemption for executive, administrative, and professional employees. The FLSA does not define what the statute means by an executive, administrative, or professional employee. The Department of Labor (DOL), however, which is responsible for enforcing the FLSA, has issued detailed regulations on the issue. For the most part, these regulations have been accepted by courts and, thus, provide the legal standard for applying the exemption.

The DOL's regulatory definition contains a separate salary and duties test. Under the regulation, the nature of the duties test turns on the amount of an individual's salary. If the individual's salary exceeds the amount specified in the regulation—$250 per week as of January 1, 1999—a short form of the duties test is applied. If, on the other hand, the individual's salary falls below the specified amount, a long form of the test is applied (one that is more difficult to satisfy). The regulation adopts this approach as a way of encouraging employers to provide a certain level of pay to those individuals whom the employer is classifying as exempt. The regulation makes it difficult for an employer to evade the Act's minimum wage requirement by assigning the label of manager or assistant manager to those workers who are more properly viewed as line employees, subject to the reach of the Act.

To meet the definition of an exempt employee, an individual must meet both the salary and duties tests. The salary test is based on the premise that an individual is not properly considered an executive, administrative, or professional employee unless, at a minimum, the individual receives his or her pay in the form of a fixed, predetermined salary. The test does not simply take the employer's method of compensation at face value. Thus, the mere fact that an employee is paid pursuant to a predetermined salary does not satisfy the test. Instead, the test asks whether, for any pay period, the individual is entitled to the full amount of the individual's predetermined amount of pay irrespective of the quality or quantity of the work performed.

One issue of recurring concern under the salary test is whether the test is met where the employee is paid a predetermined salary, but the amount of pay is subject to deductions for disciplinary infractions. Many employers will pay some of their employees on a salary (as opposed to hourly) basis. The employer, however, will retain the discretion to make deductions in pay for specified violations of workplace rules. The position of the DOL is that, in such a case, the salary test is not satisfied (with an exception for penalties imposed in good faith for infractions of safety rules of major significance). The DOL's position has been upheld by the courts, which have extended the rule to both private and public employers.

In some cases, it may be unclear whether an employer has, in practical terms, retained the discretion to make deductions in pay. The DOL takes the position that the salary test denies exempt status to an employee when there is either an actual practice of making deductions or an employment policy that creates a significant likelihood of such deductions. The mere fact that an employee suffers a deduction in pay, on one occasion, might not be sufficient to constitute an actual practice of making deductions if that deduction occurs under unusual circumstances. The mere fact that an employer maintains an employment policy of making deductions in pay might not create a significant likelihood of deductions if there is no clear indication that the policy applies to individuals in the employee's job category. If, however, there is an actual practice of making deductions, as evidenced by more than a one-time deduction in pay in unusual circumstances, or if the employer maintains a policy of making such deductions for individuals in the employee's job category, the employee will fail the salary test.

> **EXAMPLE: A police department compensates its senior officers on a salary basis. As a general matter, a senior officer is entitled to his or her full salary regardless of the number of hours worked during any particular pay period. Under department policy, however, employees in the senior officer job category are subject to suspensions without pay, for periods ranging from a day to six months, for any one of a number of disciplinary infractions. There is evidence that, on several occasions, senior officers have been subjected to deductions in pay pursuant to the department policy. A senior officer sues under the FLSA, claiming that he is entitled to additional overtime pay. The department defends by arguing that the officer falls within the exemption for executive, administrative, and professional employees. The department's defense is likely to fail. Because the officer's pay is subject to deductions for disciplinary infractions, the officer flunks the salary test and, thus, does not fall within the exemption.**

While a policy of making deductions in pay will take an employee out of the exemption, an employer does not fail the salary test in all cases in which the employer makes adjustments of some kind in the amount of an individual's pay. An employer may compensate certain employees on a salary basis. The employer, however, may provide additional compensation for overtime work. The fact that the employer provides such compensation does not, by itself, take the employee out of the exemption. Further, assuming that the exemption otherwise applies, the employer is free to compensate the employee for overtime at a rate less than that required under the FLSA. An employer, in other words, may elect to provide overtime pay to a salaried employee, at an amount determined by the employer, without running the risk that, as a result of that additional pay, the employee will lose his or her exempt status.

Assuming the salary test is met, the duties test must still be satisfied for an employee to meet the exemption. The duties test is intensively fact-specific and, thus, not reducible to a simple formula.

With respect to the exemption for executive employees, the test is met, in its short form (i.e., in those cases in which the employee's salary exceeds the regulatory minimum of $250 per week), when: (1) The primary duty of the employee consists of the management of an enterprise or a department or division of an enterprise; (2) the employee customarily directs the work of two or more employees; (3) the employee regularly exercises discretionary powers and has the authority to order (or influence) the hiring and firing of employees; and (4) the employee devotes no more than 20% of his or her work duties to tasks other than those described in (1) to (3) above.

The exemption for professional employees applies to those employees whose work is predominantly intellectual and varied in character and who exercise significant discretion or judgment in the performance of that work. The exemption has been extended to most professions that normally require licenses to practice (e.g., law, medicine, and teaching). (The law also exempts employees in certain computer-related occupations.)

The duties test may be most difficult to apply with respect to the exemption for administrative employees. According to the DOL's regulations, the duties test is satisfied in this context, in its short form, when: (1) The primary duty of the employee consists of the performance of office or nonmanual work directly related to management policies or general business operations of the employer or the employer's customers; and (2) the primary duty of the employee includes work requiring the exercise of discretion and independent judgment. The DOL has explained that, to meet the test, the employee's activities must relate directly to the administrative operations of a business, not to its production or sales. It is not enough that the employee performs work that has significant financial consequences for the business. It must be work that is substantially important to the administrative operations of the business.

EXAMPLE: A life insurance company employs a number of individuals as marketing representatives. The job of the marketing
representative is to cultivate the independent agent sales force
that the company uses to sell its insurance products. The representative serves as a conduit between the individual agent
and the company's underwriting department, once a customer
decides to purchase an insurance product, but does not
directly initiate a sale or participate in the approval of a sale.
The representative exercises her independent judgment in
determining which agents to contact in a given day and what
information to pass along to those agents. While it is a close
case, a court may well find that the activities of the marketing
representatives are sufficiently related to management policies
or general business operations to qualify for the exemption for
administrative employees (assuming that the representatives
also meet the salary test).

The statutory exemptions aside, one of the more nettlesome
coverage questions raised by the FLSA involves the distinction
between employees and independent contractors. Independent
contractors are not exempt, as such, from the FLSA. However, the
FLSA applies, by its terms, only to employees. By definition, an
independent contractor is not an employee. If an individual is
classified as an independent contractor, that individual falls outside the protections of the FLSA.

It is obvious that the independent contractor label is subject
to manipulation by an employer. An employer, for example,
could require individuals to sign independent contractor agreements while retaining effective control over the individuals'
employment. If such agreements were accepted at face value, an
employer could place large portions of its workforce outside the
reach of the FLSA. To avoid this possibility, courts have taken a
relatively restrictive view of the independent contractor category.
Courts have essentially focused on the economic realities of the
employment situation, ignoring the legal label affixed by the
employer. The factors bearing on the economic reality test

include whether the alleged employer: (1) Has hiring and firing authority with respect to the individual; (2) supervises and controls the individual's work schedules and other conditions of employment; (3) determines the individual's method and rate of pay; and (4) maintains employment records for the individual. At bottom, an individual will be considered an employee of an entity if that entity retains the right of control over the end result of the individual's work and the manner by which that end result is achieved.

> **EXAMPLE: A company requires an individual to sign an agreement stating that the individual is an independent contractor. The company withholds overtime pay from the individual, citing the individual's status as an independent contractor. The individual sues, alleging a violation of the FLSA. The evidence shows that the company retains the authority to discharge the individual. The individual's work is closely supervised by company officials, who require the individual to turn in daily time sheets. The company provides paychecks to the individual, at a fixed rate determined by the company. Notwithstanding the independent contractor agreement, the individual is likely to be viewed as an employee of the company, subject to the protections of the FLSA.**

As the above discussion suggests, there is an important real-world component to compliance with the FLSA. In many cases, it will be difficult to determine in advance whether an employee qualifies for exempt status. The employer will have to make a judgment call on whether to treat the employee as exempt or nonexempt. The law imposes a high price on an employer that improperly classifies an employee as exempt, with the goal of encouraging employers to err on the side of caution and classify the position as nonexempt. Despite this incentive, many employers will take their chances and classify the employee as exempt (if it is at all possible to do so), banking on the fact that their violation of the FLSA will go undetected. In such a workplace, the onus is on the employee to complain about the violation. Unless an employee does so, the employer may well evade the proscriptions of the FLSA.

What Constitutes Compensable Time?

One of the critical areas under the FLSA concerns the computation of compensable time. The FLSA requires an employer to provide a certain amount of pay for work performed. The Act also requires an employee to be compensated at a higher rate of pay when the individual works in excess of forty hours in a workweek. To determine whether an employer has complied with these requirements, one must compute the amount of time (hours worked) for which the individual is entitled to compensation. Based on that computation, one can then determine the amount of pay due the individual.

There are several categories of employee activity for which the employee is not entitled to compensation under the FLSA. First, as a general matter, an employee is not required to be compensated for activities that are preliminary or postliminary to the employee's principal work activity. This could include the time spent commuting between an individual's home and job, as well as other activities that an individual engages in either before or after the individual's normal work shift. There are exceptions to this general rule. Activities performed either before or after the regular work shift are compensable if those activities are an integral and indispensable part of the principal activities for which the individual is employed. Thus, time spent showering and changing clothes, on the premises of the employer, would constitute compensable time if that activity were necessary to maintain safe working conditions. Travel time might also be compensable if integrated in some fashion with work. An employee, for example, who is required to travel away from his or her regular work sites— on company business—is entitled to be compensated for the travel time. Likewise, an employee must be compensated for time traveling to and from job sites, if such travel is necessary to carry out the employee's principal work activity.

In some cases, an employee will be required to adhere to certain company policies while commuting to a job. An employee, for example, may use a company car in commuting to work and may be restricted in the use of that car. In that context, whether the commuting time may be viewed as work time turns on the degree to which the company-imposed restrictions burden the employee. If the burden is *de minimis*, a court may well find that the commuting time is noncompensable, notwithstanding the fact that the commute is regulated, to a degree, by the employer.

> **EXAMPLE: The Immigration and Naturalization Service employs a number of individuals as Border Patrol agent dog handlers. The agents are required to have their dogs reside with them and to transport the dogs to border patrol stations, in agency-owned vehicles, as part of their daily commute. During the commute, agents are required to wear their official uniforms and are prohibited from making any personal stops. The agents have an argument that the commuting time constitutes compensable work time, given the restrictions imposed by the employer. A court might find, nonetheless, that the restrictions are too *de minimis* to require compensation for the commuting time, given the small amount of time involved in the commute and the relatively slight nature of the burdens imposed upon the employees.**

A second category of potentially noncompensable time involves time spent on meals and breaks. The FLSA does not require an employer to allot time for meals and breaks. Many states, however, require that such time be provided, and it is common practice for employers to do so. The DOL takes the position that an individual is required to be compensated for any rest or snack period that does not exceed twenty minutes. This means that, for the typical break period of fifteen minutes, an employee must be compensated. For the half-hour (or more) typically allotted for lunch, the employee is not entitled to compensation.

While an employee is not required to be compensated for the time off for lunch, that assumes that the employee is not performing job-related duties during the lunch period. There are signs that the traditional lunch break is going the way of the dinosaur. More and more employees are working through their lunch periods or are eating at their desks or workstations as they work. This raises the possibility that the time an employer allots for lunch will constitute compensable time. The mere fact that an employee remains at his or her workstation while eating lunch does not convert the lunchtime into compensable work time. If, however, the employee performs his or her assigned job tasks while consuming lunch, the employee is entitled to compensation. Significantly, it is not necessary, in this context, that the employer requires the employee to work. So long as the employer permits the work, the time is compensable.

> **EXAMPLE: A warehouse clerk works a standard eight-hour shift. The clerk is given thirty minutes of his own time to eat lunch. The clerk brings a brown bag lunch to work and consumes his lunch at his workstation. During the thirty-minute lunch period, the clerk continues to carry out his job, directing the unloading of goods and taking orders over the phone. The employer does not require that the clerk perform work during his lunch period. The employer, however, permits the clerk to perform the work and receives a benefit from the work. There is a strong argument that the clerk is entitled to compensation for the work performed during his lunch period.**

Increasingly, employers are requiring or permitting employees to participate in training programs. This raises the question of whether the time spent on training constitutes compensable time. If the individual participating in training is an existing employee, the central question is whether the training serves the interests of the employer. It is likely that the training will be viewed as serving the employer's interests if the training is compelled by the employer or viewed by the employer as important (perhaps necessary) to job advancement. Under the regulations of the DOL, training time is *not* considered compensable if: (1) The training is held outside of working hours; (2) attendance at the training session is strictly voluntary; (3) the training session is not directly related to the employee's job; and (4) the employee does not perform any productive work while attending the training session.

A separate question is whether a job trainee may be considered an employee. Employers frequently require potential hires to go through a period of pre-employment training. If the trainee is not guaranteed a job at the end of the training period, the training is similar in kind to that provided at a vocational school, and the training confers no immediate benefit upon the employer, the trainee will not be treated as an employee. If, on the other hand, the trainee is guaranteed a job at the end of the training period and the training is specifically tailored to the position that the individual will eventually occupy, the trainee may well be considered an employee, thus entitled to compensation under the provisions of the FLSA.

A final category of potentially noncompensable time involves periods in which an individual is on call for work. Most jobs impose obligations on an employee only while the employee is on the job site performing work. Other jobs, however, require that an employee be on call to perform work, even during periods in which the employee is not performing his or her routine duties. The defining principle, in this context, is the degree to which the employer controls the employee during the on-call period. If the employee is required to remain on the work premises or is otherwise significantly restricted in his or her ability to enjoy the time, the on-call time is compensable. If, on the other hand, the employee remains on call but is free to spend the time as he or she wishes (off the work premises), the employee will not be entitled to compensation for the on-call time.

EXAMPLE: An employee works as a troubleshooter for a company that operates a production line. During her regular eight-

hour shift, the employee works on-site, providing assistance in the event mechanical problems develop in the production line. The employee is fully compensated for this work. The employee, however, is also required to be on call during certain evenings and weekends. During the on-call period, the employee is expected to remain close to a telephone. The employee is required to provide on-the-spot advice to employees who need help in resolving a production-line problem. The employee is subject to discipline if she is not immediately available for a telephone consult. Because of the degree to which the employer exercises control over the employee during the on-call period, the on-call time is compensable.

For obvious reasons, compliance with the FLSA turns on an adequate system of recordkeeping. One can state the general rules concerning compensable time, but the legal standards mean nothing, absent evidence that the employee has performed work for which the employee is entitled to compensation. While the Act imposes significant recordkeeping requirements upon employers, there may be cases where an employer defaults on its obligation to maintain records concerning an employee's work history. This, in turn, may impair the ability of the employee to prove a claim for overtime pay. Many courts will be inclined to take the employee at his or her word (as to the number of hours worked), since the lack of any written record is attributable to the employer's nonfeasance. Nonetheless, it is a wise practice for an employee who believes that she is entitled to additional overtime pay to maintain an independent written record of the work performed. If the employee makes a claim for overtime pay and the employer defends by citing the lack of any written record of the work performed, the employee will be able to substantiate her claim with written proof.

Calculating Pay

Ultimately, the focus of the FLSA is on one critical issue—the amount of pay an individual is required to receive for work performed. There are two (related) contexts in which the pay issue arises. The first concerns the employer's compliance with the FLSA's minimum wage requirement. The second concerns the rate of pay that is used to determine the amount of overtime compensation due an employee.

To comply with the FLSA, an employer is required to pay any nonexempt employee no less than the minimum wage. The payment must take the form of cash or something that can be readily converted into cash (e.g., a check). An employer is permitted to deduct the reasonable cost of any food or lodging provided to the employee, meaning, in effect, that the furnishing of such items constitutes a valid form of compensation. Many employers provide their workers with employee discounts. While nothing in the FLSA prohibits an employer from doing so, the value of any such discount is not counted toward the minimum wage requirement. An employer may make deductions in pay for such items as employer-required uniforms and tools of the trade. In no event, however, may those deductions reduce an individual's wage below the minimum.

It is not necessary that an employer pay an employee on an hourly basis. An employer may compensate an employee on a piece rate or commission basis. An employer may also pay the employee on a salary basis, where the amount of the employee's compensation, for any pay period, is fixed in advance. If an employee is paid on a nonhourly basis, an employer's compliance with the minimum wage requirement is determined by dividing the amount the employee is paid during a pay period by the amount of hours actually worked during that period. So long as the resulting average is no less than the hourly minimum wage, the employer is in compliance with the minimum wage requirement.

An employer is excused from paying the full minimum wage with respect to tipped employees (i.e., those employees who customarily and regularly receive more than $30 a month in tips). In the case of these employees, an employer is permitted to consider tips as a part of wages, with the caveat that the employer must pay at least $2.13 an hour in direct wages. So long as the employee's tips are sufficient to cover the difference between the employer's contribution and the minimum wage amount, the minimum wage requirement is satisfied.

If a nonexempt employee works in excess of forty hours in a workweek, the employee is entitled to overtime pay. As a general matter, the overtime rate is one and one-half times the employee's regular rate of pay. The employee's regular rate includes all payments made by the employer to or on behalf of the employee (subject to certain statutory exclusions). The regular rate typically includes such supplemental payments as production bonuses, shift differentials, hazardous duty premiums, and cost-of-living allowances.

The calculation of overtime pay is dictated by the employer's method of payment. If the employee is paid an hourly rate, computing the overtime rate is a relatively easy task. The employee is entitled to one and one-half times his or her regular hourly rate of pay for each hour worked in excess of forty. With respect to those employees paid on a piece rate basis, the regular rate is determined by dividing the employee's total weekly earnings by the total number of hours worked during that week. The employee is entitled to one-half times the regular rate for each hour worked in excess of forty. If agreed to in advance, the employer may choose to pay the employee one and one-half times the piece rate for each piece produced during the overtime hours.

Calculating the amount of overtime pay is more complicated with respect to employees paid on a salary basis. The standard calculation involves dividing the employee's weekly salary by the number of hours that the employer intends the weekly salary to compensate. For each hour worked in excess of forty, the employee is entitled to one and one-half times the regular rate of pay, so determined. The law also permits an employer to adopt an alternative method of overtime compensation for those salaried employees whose hours fluctuate from week to week. Instead of paying the employee a salary for a regular or specified number of hours a week, the employer can reach a mutual under-

standing with the employee that the employee will receive a fixed
amount of compensation per week, regardless of the number of
hours that the employee works in that week. Under this arrangement, the employee's regular rate is determined by dividing the
weekly salary by the number of hours worked each week. The
employee, in turn, receives a rate of 50% of the regular rate for
each hour worked over forty hours. The result of this approach is
that the rate of pay goes down for each additional hour of overtime worked.

For the fluctuating workweek method of pay to apply, certain conditions must be met. First, the employee's hours must
fluctuate from week to week. Second, the employee must receive
a fixed weekly salary that remains the same regardless of the
number of hours that the employee works during the week.
Third, the fixed amount must be sufficient to provide compensation at a regular rate not less than the legal minimum wage.
Finally, the employer and the employee must have a clear, mutual
understanding that the employer will pay the employee the fixed
weekly salary regardless of the hours worked.

The fluctuating workweek method is typically used when
employees work a varying or irregular number of hours in a workweek. The DOL has taken the position, however, that the method
may be used even where the amount of hours for each workweek
is fixed, if the employer alternates between one fixed amount for
one workweek and a different fixed amount for the next workweek. In many cases, the applicability of the fluctuating workweek method will turn on the requirement of a clear, mutual
understanding between the employer and the employee. Courts
have found such an understanding even in the absence of any
written acknowledgment by the employee that the payment
method and the consequences for overtime pay have been
explained to the employee.

> **EXAMPLE: An employee works as a deputy sheriff. The
> employee's hours fluctuate from week to week. The
> employee is paid a fixed weekly salary regardless of the hours**

worked. The employee understands that this is his method of pay, although he is not made aware of how this payment method might affect his overtime rate. The employee works a number of overtime hours for which he is not compensated. The employee files suit under the FLSA, claiming that he is entitled to overtime pay at a rate of one and one-half times his regular rate of pay. The employer acknowledges that it has defaulted on its obligation to pay overtime but rejoins that the rate of pay should be determined under the fluctuating workweek method, which results in less overtime pay. A court may well find that the requirements for using the fluctuating workweek method have been met. While the employee was not apprised of how the use of the fixed method of payment would affect his overtime pay, the employee did have a clear understanding that the fixed salary represented compensation for all straight time hours worked. This might suffice to satisfy the requirements of a clear, mutual understanding.

CHAPTER 8

Employee Benefits

A n increasingly important part of an employee's compensation package consists of the benefits provided under employer-established benefit plans. For most employees, the weekly or monthly paycheck continues to be the principal compensation for work performed. Employees, however, also have concerns about their long-term financial security, not to mention their immediate medical needs. While government programs may address these concerns to a point, the benefits provided by employers can fill the gaps in the government safety net and extend protections far beyond the minimums established under the patchwork of public social welfare programs that exist at the federal, state, and local levels. The financial security of many working Americans is tied not to governmental largesse, but to the benefits provided by the individual employer.

As important as employee benefits may be, the first thing to understand about the legal regulation of such benefits is that, for the most part, the law does not require an employer to provide them. Employee benefits, in other words, are a privilege, not a right. An employer is required to provide a minimum wage for work performed, as discussed in the previous chapter. An employer, however, is not *required* to supplement that wage with employee (or fringe) benefits. Thus, an employer is not required to provide pension or retirement benefits for its employees. An employer is not obligated to provide severance benefits to those employees who are laid off. Nor is the employer required to make health insurance available to its employees. As a general matter, by paying a minimum wage (and appropriate overtime), the employer discharges its legal obligations under the law.

Despite this legal vacuum, employee benefit plans are a commonplace feature of the American workplace. Employers provide such benefits for a variety of reasons. One reason is the free market. If other employers provide employee benefits, an employer may need to do so as well to remain competitive. Employee benefits can also be viewed as a part of the overall compensation provided to an employee. An employer, in other words, can market itself as providing a certain level of compensation while paying less in basic wages or salary. Finally, employers provide employee benefits because the law encourages them to do so. Most notably, there are favorable tax consequences for those employers that establish certain types of employee benefit plans.

Although employers are not obligated to provide employee benefits as an initial matter, the provision of such benefits, pursuant to employer plans, is subject to extensive legal regulation. That is because, once the employer makes the decision to establish a benefit plan, the law intervenes—quite aggressively—to protect the rights of employees. This may seem like an odd approach for the law to take. If an employer is not required to provide a benefit in the first instance, why subject the employer to government regulation (and legal liability) when it chooses voluntarily to go beyond what the law requires? The answer is, in part, political. Business has long opposed attempts to require individual employers to foot the bill for employee benefits. This is particularly true of small business, which is a vigorous critic of virtually any government initiative that imposes financial obligations on an employer. It is largely because of this opposition that legislative attempts to require employers to insure their employees for health care have failed. The idea that individual employers can be required, outright, to provide a comprehensive package of employee benefits is simply not, at this point, politically viable.

More fundamentally, imposing such an affirmative obligation on employers goes against the grain of America's legal and political tradition. The legal culture of this country is rooted largely in negative constraints on behavior. This nation has little difficulty telling a person or entity that it cannot engage in certain conduct. It has more difficulty telling a person or entity that it must take affirmative steps to protect the interests of another. In lieu of imposing a legal requirement that employee benefits be provided, the law has adopted an approach that is uniquely American—encourage employers to adopt benefit plans by using the tax code to enhance free market incentives, and then regulate the benefit plans with vigor once the employer makes the voluntary choice that the law encourages.

There are two general areas of regulation with respect to employee benefits. First, the principle of nondiscrimination, discussed in Chapters 1 to 6, plays an important role in this context. An employer may choose to treat its employees equally by not providing a particular employee benefit. If the employer, however, elects to make the benefit available, the benefit must be doled out in a nondiscriminatory fashion. Thus, an employer may not discriminate on the basis of race, sex, national origin, religion, age, or disability in providing an employee benefit, even if the employer could choose not to provide the benefit at all.

One would be hard-pressed, at this late date, to find a benefit plan that facially discriminates on the basis of race (although it is possible that an otherwise neutral plan could be administered in a racially discriminatory fashion). Historically, many benefit plans did base the level of benefits on certain gender-based assumptions (e.g., that women generally live longer than men), but these plan distinctions were invalidated in a series of Supreme Court decisions. Claims of race or sex discrimination, in the provision of employee benefits, are now less common.

On the other hand, benefit discrimination persists, unabated, with respect to the protected category of age. The reasons for this are discussed in Chapter 5. It is not always clear whether a plan distinction is age-based, since age correlates in some fashion with a number of other factors. Thus, an employer may make a distinction in its benefit plan that is later declared to be age-based, even though it is not explicitly defined by age. Even where a plan distinction is clearly age-based, there are a number of statutory defenses that might save an otherwise discriminatory plan. Because these defenses are not defined in clear terms, employers are encouraged to take an aggressive position, with the hope that a particular age-based distinction can be justified. This, inevitably, leads to a significant amount of litigation under the federal Age Discrimination in Employment Act.

The second area of government regulation more directly focuses on the provision of employee benefits as such. When an employer adopts a benefit plan on behalf of its employees, the employer subjects itself to the reach of the law. There are two basic categories of federal protection (each of which is discussed in this chapter). The first concerns an employer's obligation to maintain health care coverage, under a group plan, for those individuals who become separated from employment. The federal statutes addressing this issue are the Consolidated Omnibus Budget Reconciliation Act of 1985 and the Health Insurance Portability and Accountability Act of 1996. The second category concerns the more general obligations imposed under the Employee Retirement Income Security Act of 1974 (ERISA). ERISA is the principal federal statute that regulates the provision of benefits under employer plans. ERISA is an important and highly complex statute. My goal here is simply to provide a general overview of the statute's basic protections. The adage that you should consult a lawyer (when in doubt) applies more than ever in this context.

The Special Case of Health Insurance Coverage

For many employees, the critical employee benefit—other than salary—is health insurance coverage. As noted previously, employers are not required to provide health insurance benefits for their employees. Many employers, however, do provide such benefits. Typically, these benefits are established as part of a group plan to which both the employer and the employee contribute.

While many employers provide health insurance benefits to their employees, those benefits are tied to the employment relationship. In the absence of a statute providing otherwise, the benefits will cease upon the termination of that relationship. This creates a problem for those employees who lose their jobs. An employee may have been covered by a group health plan. That plan may have extended benefits to the employee and his or her entire family. Suddenly, the employee (and his or her family) is without health insurance coverage. In some cases, public programs (like Medicaid) might be available to cushion the blow. Unless the law intercedes, however, many employees will find themselves without health insurance coverage or with coverage at levels far below that provided by the employer's group plan.

In recognition of this problem, federal law imposes obligations on employers that provide group health insurance coverage to their employees. The principal federal statute is the Consolidated Omnibus Budget Reconciliation Act of 1985 (COBRA), as supplemented by the Health Insurance Portability and Accountability Act of 1996 (HIPAA). The COBRA covers group health plans maintained by employers with twenty or more employees in the prior year. The Act also covers state and local governments that maintain group health plans. The COBRA does not require an employer to maintain a group health plan. It simply imposes a continuation of coverage requirement upon those employers whose plans are covered under the Act.

To be entitled to COBRA protection, an individual must be a qualified beneficiary. A qualified beneficiary is any individual (employee, spouse, or dependent child) covered by the employer's group health plan on the day before a qualifying event. For the employee, a qualifying event is the voluntary or involuntary termination of employment or reduction in the number of hours worked for reasons other than gross misconduct. (This means that an employee terminated for gross misconduct is not entitled to COBRA protection.) For the spouse of an employee, qualifying events include the employee's termination from employment, as well as the employee becoming entitled to Medicare, the death of the employee, or the spouse's divorce or legal separation from the employee. For any dependent child of the employee, qualifying events include all of the above plus loss of dependent child status under the rules of the benefit plan. Notably, while an individual must generally be a qualified beneficiary as of the day before a qualifying event, an exception is made for a dependent child who is not yet born (or legally adopted) at the time of the qualifying event. If the child is born (or adopted) during the period of COBRA continuation coverage, the child is a qualified beneficiary.

With respect to a qualified beneficiary, the COBRA guarantees that, upon a qualifying event, health insurance coverage will be extended for a certain period of time under the employer's group plan. The standard period is eighteen months. Thus, if a covered employee is terminated from his or her job, the employee (and any covered family member) would be entitled to coverage under the group plan for a period of eighteen months following the termination. If the covered employee is disabled or becomes disabled during the first sixty days of COBRA continuation coverage, coverage is extended for a period of twenty-nine months (from the date of the original qualifying event). That period covers the disabled employee as well as any spouse or dependent child covered under the plan. Finally, where a covered employee dies, divorces his or her spouse, or becomes eligible for Medicare (thus ending the covered employee's COBRA coverage), any covered spouse or dependent child may continue coverage for an additional period of thirty-six months from the date on which any of those qualifying events occur, even if the event occurs during a period of COBRA continuation coverage that has already been triggered by some other qualifying event. (If the covered employee becomes eligible for Medicare while employed, the spouse and dependent child are entitled to thirty-six months of extended coverage from the date on which the employee retires.) A dependent child can continue coverage for a period of thirty-six months after the date on which he or she loses his or her status as a dependent child under the plan.

The protection provided under the COBRA is limited by several factors. First, COBRA protection does not kick in by operation of law. The employee must opt for the COBRA benefit within sixty days of the qualifying event. COBRA protection is by no means a free ride. The qualified beneficiary can be required to pay 102% of the premium for coverage under the plan, representing both the employer and employee portions of the premium as augmented by a 2% fee for administrative costs. (While costly, this is still less than what an individual could purchase, on his or her own, in the private market.) Finally, coverage under the COBRA is calibrated to the coverage provided under the group plan at issue. This means, on the one hand, that the employer must provide the same level of coverage to the COBRA beneficiary as it does to any similarly situated beneficiary covered under the plan. It also means, however, that if the employer ends group health insurance coverage for all of its employees (or simply goes out of business), COBRA coverage terminates.

The COBRA was supplemented in 1996 by the HIPAA. The HIPAA expanded on the scope of the COBRA protections. The Act also altered the rules (at least indirectly) for the duration of COBRA continuation coverage. The COBRA provides that an individual's COBRA coverage ceases once the individual becomes covered under another employer's group health plan. The Act contains an exception for cases in which the group plan limits or denies coverage based upon a preexisting condition of the COBRA beneficiary. The HIPAA significantly limits the circumstances under which group health plans may apply exclusions for preexisting conditions. The rules are somewhat complicated, but the bottom line is that many more COBRA beneficiaries, who obtain new employment, will find themselves covered under another employer's group health plan. The net effect of this change is to shift the cost of the health insurance benefit from the old employer to the new one.

To assist individuals in exercising their COBRA rights, the COBRA imposes a significant notice requirement upon employers and plan administrators. When a qualifying event occurs (e.g., an employee is terminated from his or her job), the employer must provide notice to the plan administrator within thirty days of the event. The plan must then notify any qualified beneficiary, within fourteen days, of their right to continued coverage under the plan. Based on this notice, the beneficiary can decide whether to elect COBRA continuation coverage. The HIPAA requires that employers provide a Certificate of Coverage to all individuals whose coverage under a group health plan has expired. That Certificate provides proof of all coverage provided under the plan over a two-year period. The Certificate helps determine an employer's compliance with the provisions in the HIPAA limiting exclusions for pre-existing conditions, which are keyed to the amount of coverage an individual has had under a prior group health plan.

Taken together, the COBRA and the HIPAA provide significant protection for employees. The statutes do not guarantee health insurance coverage for employees. They do, however, ensure that an employee who loses his or her job is not immediately dropped from a group health plan. Studies have shown that of the employees and dependents who become eligible for COBRA coverage, almost one-third opt for the COBRA benefit. An employee who suffers a change in job status, sufficient to trigger the protections of the COBRA, must make an informed choice whether to continue coverage under the employer's group health plan.

Federal Regulation of Employee Benefit Plans— Coverage Issues

Although health insurance coverage is critical to many employees, it is only one of many benefits that an employer may provide to its employees. Many employers establish pension or retirement plans for their employees. Many provide severance benefits to those individuals whose employment is terminated. Some employers even provide such benefits as prepaid legal services or scholarship funds as part of an employee plan. The federal statute that regulates the provision of these and other employee benefits, when provided under a plan established by an employer, is the Employee Retirement Income Security Act, commonly referred to as ERISA.

ERISA is a comprehensive federal statute, passed in 1974, to improve the fairness and financial security of America's private pension system. ERISA was enacted after a lengthy study of the private pension system. The statute was passed because of perceived abuses in the manner in which employers administered benefit plans. ERISA seeks to ensure, among other things, that benefits promised by employers to their employees are in fact paid. ERISA contains two sets of requirements—those that provide protections for employee benefit rights (the labor provisions) and those that provide favored tax treatment to those plans that meet the qualification standards established by the Act (the revenue provisions).

In keeping with the statute's lofty ambitions, ERISA coverage is broad. The Act's labor provisions extend to most private benefit plans established by an employer. A plan can be any regularly conducted employment-based program or practice that has the purpose of affording certain kinds of benefits to employees. Covered plans include such pension plans as defined benefit plans, where an employee is promised a specific level of retirement income, and defined contribution plans (e.g., money purchase plans, profit sharing plans, and employee stock ownership plans), where an employee has an account to which an employer makes specific contributions. The Act also reaches plans that provide benefits for the welfare of the employee, including health coverage, life insurance, or childcare benefits. ERISA makes distinctions in the level of protections provided employees, based on whether a plan is classified as a pension or welfare plan. (Essentially, greater protection exists for pension plans.)

There are some exclusions from the Act. ERISA does not apply to the federal or to any state or local government. ERISA also exempts certain plans maintained by churches and fraternal organizations; plans maintained solely to comply with workers' compensation, unemployment compensation, or disability insurance laws; and plans maintained outside the United States primarily for the benefit of noncitizens residing abroad. Notably, there are distinctions in coverage between the statute's labor and revenue provisions. The labor provisions apply to both pension and welfare plans. The revenue provisions do not generally reach welfare plans but cover certain types of financial arrangements that are not covered under the labor provisions (including individual retirement accounts). An arrangement that is covered only under the revenue provisions is eligible for favored tax treatment but is not subject to the portion of the act that provides specific protections for employees.

In addition to these exclusions, there are at least two other general limitations on the scope of ERISA coverage. ERISA limits its protection to employees. This means that workers acting as independent contractors are not protected against conduct that would otherwise be unlawful if engaged in with respect to an employee. The standards for determining independent contractor status are similar to those applied under other federal statutes. Essentially, courts focus on the hiring party's right to control the manner and means by which the work is accomplished.

A more significant limitation on the reach of ERISA protection is one inherent in ERISA itself. To qualify for tax-favored treatment, a benefit plan must meet detailed requirements designed to ensure that the plan covers a fair cross-section of employees. ERISA further provides that a plan may not impose certain conditions on participation in the plan. Specifically, if a plan requires that an employee complete a period of service with the employer before becoming eligible to participate in the plan, that period may not extend beyond the later of the date on which the employee attains the age of 21 or the date on which the employee completes one year of service. Nor may an employer exclude an individual from a benefit plan because of the age of the individual at the time he or she is hired.

These limitations aside, ERISA does not prohibit an employer from distinguishing between groups or categories of employees. ERISA seeks to provide maximum benefit protection for employees. It does not, however, guarantee the participation of all employees in a benefit plan. An employer may exclude employees from plan participation so long as it does not contravene ERISA's specific nondiscrimination provisions. (Of course, as noted previously, any plan distinction must also comport with the other federal and state laws prohibiting discrimination in the provision of employee benefits.)

> EXAMPLE: Company A retains the services of a number of workers pursuant to leasing contracts entered into with other companies. The leasing contracts provide that the leased workers are the employees of the leasing company, but the workers apply for benefits under the pension and welfare plans maintained by Company A. The plan administrator denies the workers benefits, concluding that the plans cover only regular employees. The workers sue under ERISA, claiming that they meet the definition of a common-law employee and, thus, are entitled to participate in the benefit plans. The workers may be employees within the meaning of ERISA. ERISA, however, does not obligate employers to extend benefit protection to all individuals who meet the definition of an employee. The distinction in this case—between regular and leased employees—is a reasonable one and does not otherwise violate ERISA's nondiscrimination provisions. The plan distinction does not violate ERISA.

Finally, it is important to stress that ERISA is a comprehensive federal statute that supersedes any state or local law that is inconsistent with the federal mandate. This is significant, given the centrality of pension and welfare plans in the national economy and the sheer number of individuals enrolled in benefit plans covered by ERISA (estimated to be over 100 million). Because of its broad reach, ERISA's requirements will often collide with state and local laws that might have an impact on the provision of employee benefits. In such a collision, the federal requirement typically wins out.

> **EXAMPLE: An employee is covered under a company's pension plan. The employee dies. Under the plan, monthly annuities are to be paid to the employee's surviving spouse, in accordance with the requirements of ERISA. The employee, however, was married on a prior occasion. When the employee's first wife died, she bequeathed a portion of her community property interest in the employee's undistributed pension plan benefits to her son. Under the state's community property laws, the son is entitled to a share of the pension benefits. Under ERISA, however, the surviving spouse is entitled to the entire survivor annuity. Because the state's community property law is inconsistent with ERISA's objective of ensuring a stream of income to surviving spouses (under certain pension plan arrangements), the state law is superseded. The surviving spouse receives the full pension benefit.**

Federal Regulation of Employee Benefit Plans— The Basic Protections

Assuming that a benefit plan is covered under ERISA, the question becomes what protection the statute provides to those employees who are covered under the plan. The first point to make here has already been made. ERISA does not require employers to establish employee benefit plans. Nor does it mandate the particular benefits that an employer must provide if it chooses to have such a plan. ERISA regulates the plans (and accompanying benefits) that employers choose to adopt.

In many cases, the level of ERISA protection is dictated by the terms of the plan itself. ERISA provides individuals with a right to bring suit with respect to benefit decisions made by a plan administrator. Thus, if the administrator denies benefits that are potentially available under the plan, the individual can challenge that denial in court. Often, however, the plan will give discretion to the administrator to pay or deny claims. This is particularly true of welfare plans. In such a case, courts will grant substantial deference to the administrator's decision. Unless the administrator acts in an irrational or arbitrary manner, the administrator's decision will be upheld.

> **EXAMPLE: An employer has an employee welfare plan that provides life insurance benefits. An employee covered under the plan dies in an automobile collision. The employee's surviving spouse files a claim for an accidental death benefit. The plan administrator denies the claim, finding that the employee did not die from an accident, within the meaning of the plan, because the employee was legally intoxicated at the time and could have reasonably foreseen that a fatal injury might occur if he drove his car. The surviving spouse brings an action in court, challenging the administrator's denial of the claim. The court is likely to uphold the administrator's decision. While not the only interpretation of the term *accident,* the administrator's view is not unreasonable and, for that reason, is likely to be accepted by the court.**

While plan administrators are given some discretion in carrying out the provisions of a benefit plan, ERISA constrains that discretion in several ways. First, ERISA imposes significant reporting and disclosure obligations upon plan administrators. ERISA requires that participants be provided with comprehensive summaries of employee benefit plans (with updates for major changes) and annual reports on the financing and operation of the plans. If the employer intends to terminate a pension plan, advance notice must be provided to participants. At their request, participants are entitled to a report on the status of their vesting and accrued pension benefits. The report is provided automatically when a participant leaves the employ of the benefit provider. Finally, ERISA mandates that benefit plans report certain financial and actuarial data to government agencies.

The informational issue aside, ERISA achieves the goal of protecting employee benefits in two general ways. First, ERISA imposes substantial fiduciary obligations on those who control and manage employee benefit plans. One of the major goals of ERISA is to ensure that adequate funds are maintained to pay promised benefits. To achieve that goal, ERISA adopts rules designed to ensure that individuals who control plan assets act exclusively in the interest of plan participants and beneficiaries. These rules prohibit certain transactions between plans and parties-in-interest. Parties-in-interest include fiduciaries, plan sponsors, participants and beneficiaries, and persons who provide services to the plan. The rules also require plan administrators to act with prudence in managing plan funds and to diversify the plan's investments to minimize the risk of large losses.

It is not always clear to whom ERISA's fiduciary obligations extend. ERISA requires that every benefit plan covered under the act designate one or more fiduciaries. Obviously, those persons designated as fiduciaries must comport with the statute's fiduciary requirements. So too must the plan administrator, as well as any other person providing investment advice (for a fee) or possessing the power to manage, acquire, or dispose of any plan asset. Sometimes the employer itself will act as plan administrator. In such a case, the employer may engage in conduct that violates one of ERISA's fiduciary rules. The question, however, is whether the employer engaged in the conduct in its status as employer—in which case ERISA's fiduciary obligations would not apply—or as plan administrator—in which case they would. The basic rule is that the *employer cum plan administrator* is treated as a fiduciary for ERISA purposes if, at least in part, it was acting in its fiduciary capacity as plan administrator when it engaged in the improper conduct.

> **EXAMPLE: A company is the administrator of its own welfare benefit plan. The company decides to reorganize its operations by transferring one of its failing divisions to a new, separately incorporated subsidiary. The company's primary goal is to relieve itself of its financial obligations under the benefit**

plan. The company calls a meeting of the division's employees at which it discusses the reorganization, with substantial focus on the reorganization's possible impact on employee benefits. The company knows that the new subsidiary is likely to fail but wants to encourage the workers to transfer voluntarily to the subsidiary. The company informs the employees that their benefits will be more secure if they make the transfer, knowing this to be false. Based on the company's representations, a number of employees accept the voluntary transfer and end up losing their benefits under the welfare plan when the new subsidiary goes under. The employees sue, alleging that the company breached its fiduciary obligation under ERISA to act solely in the interest of the participants and beneficiaries of the plan. The company defends by arguing that it was acting in its capacity as employer when it made the misrepresentations and, thus, is not liable under ERISA. The company's argument lacks merit. The meeting at which the company made the misrepresentations focused largely on the issue of employee benefits. The company, in providing information (or misinformation) about employee benefits, was acting, in part, as plan administrator.

In addition to regulating the activities of fiduciaries, ERISA adopts specific vesting requirements for pension plans. Under ERISA, a pension plan must follow one of two vesting schedules. The first schedule requires that an employee be 100% vested after no more than five years of service. The second requires that an employee be partially vested after no more than three years of service and 100% vested after no more than seven years of service. (These are the statutory minimums. If it chooses, a plan can adopt a more generous vesting schedule.) Once 100% vested, an employee cannot lose his or her pension benefits. This is true even if the employee leaves his or her job before the normal retirement age.

ERISA's vesting rules apply only to pension plans. There is no vesting requirement for welfare plans, meaning that employees do not have a nonforfeitable right in the benefits provided under such plans. While ERISA does not require the vesting of welfare benefits, ERISA does not leave employees without protection. As noted earlier, ERISA adopts rules that regulate the conduct of plan fiduciaries. These rules apply to both pension and welfare plans. ERISA, moreover, requires plans to adopt specific procedures for amending or modifying a plan. An employer is generally free under ERISA to adopt, modify, or terminate its welfare plan. In doing so, however, it must act in accordance with the formal procedures set forth in the plan. If the employer fails to follow those procedures and takes action calculated to strip individuals of their benefits under a welfare plan, the employer may well violate the statutory rights of those employees covered under the welfare plan.

> **EXAMPLE: An employer maintains a welfare benefit plan for its workers. The employer shuts down one of its subsidiaries and opens the work to competitive bidding. The employer engages in the reorganization with the purpose of reducing its financial obligations under the welfare plan. As a result of the reorganization, employees are relegated to the inferior benefits provided by the company that prevails in the competitive bidding. The employees sue, alleging that the employer unlawfully interfered with the employees' rights under the welfare plan. The employer had the authority to modify or terminate its welfare plan in accordance with the formal procedures established in the plan. The employer, however, did not invoke those procedures, choosing instead to achieve its goal of reducing its employee benefit costs by outsourcing work. Even though the benefits under the welfare plan are not vested, the employer's conduct may well violate ERISA.**

As the above example suggests, proving an ERISA violation can be a difficult task. Because of the statute's vesting requirement, few employers are going to openly strip an individual of his or her vested pension benefits. Even with welfare plans, an employer may be reluctant to declare openly that benefits are being reduced or terminated. In many cases, employers will act clandestinely, hoping to achieve a reduction in their benefit costs without openly acknowledging that they have in fact cut back on benefits.

To address this problem, ERISA adopts a framework for resolving benefit disputes not unlike that adopted in the antidiscrimination statutes. ERISA makes it unlawful for an employer to discriminate against a plan participant (or beneficiary) for the purpose of interfering with the attainment of any right to which the participant may become entitled under the plan. This means that an employer may not discharge, fine, suspend, or discipline an employee as a way of interfering with an employee's benefit rights. The key in cases of this nature is the motivation for the employer's action. If the employer acts out of legitimate purpose (e.g., the employee is a poor performer), the employer's conduct is not unlawful under ERISA even if, as it turns out, the employee loses benefits as a result of the adverse employment action. If the employer acts with the intent of interfering with an individual's rights under an employee benefit plan, the employer violates ERISA.

> EXAMPLE: An employee is one month away from vesting in her pension plan. The plan is a "cliff" plan, meaning that the employee is 0% vested in the plan until the date on which the employee becomes vested (at which point the employee becomes fully vested). The employer fires the employee, claiming that the employee's job performance is unsatisfactory. There is substantial evidence that the employee is a superb worker, who had received glowing evaluations from her supervisors just before the termination. There is also evidence that, during the same time frame, company officials made statements about the need for reducing the company's financial obligations under its pension plan. The evidence supports a finding that the employer unlawfully terminated the employee to prevent the employee from vesting in the pension plan.

In some cases, ERISA claims overlap with claims of discrimination under the Age Discrimination in Employment Act, the federal age discrimination statute. As discussed in Chapter 5, the age statute makes it unlawful for an employer to discriminate on the basis of age in the provision of employee benefits. ERISA also prohibits conduct that, in some circumstances, might constitute unlawful age discrimination. ERISA, for example, prohibits a pension plan from ceasing or reducing benefit accrual based on an employee's attainment of a particular age. That same prohibition is contained in the federal age discrimination statute. In many cases, an employer's adverse action with respect to an employee benefit will subject the employer to potential liability under both ERISA and the Age Discrimination in Employment Act.

Finally, it should be stressed that ERISA establishes the minimal statutory requirements for employee benefit plans. An employer can always bind itself to additional obligations either in the plan itself or through contractual understandings with employees or their bargaining representative. ERISA exists because it assumes that, without the impetus of the law, many employers will provide little protection for employee benefits. While this assumption may hold true in many cases, some employers may contract to provide for an even greater level of protection than that demanded under ERISA. If an employer does so, the employer can be held to its word.

CHAPTER 9

Family and Medical Leave

A s the preceding chapters suggest, the primary responsibilities of an employer are to treat applicants and employees in a nondiscriminatory fashion, to provide a fair wage for work performed, and to live up to any obligations that the employer has assumed in the provision of an employee benefit. An employer's legal duties, however, do not end there. An employee is paid to work, but there are times when an employee may need (or want) to take time off work. An employee, for example, may contract a disease or illness that requires hospitalization. An employee may have a child who is in need of medical care. Or, an employee may give birth to a child and wish to stay home with the child in the initial months following birth. In such a case, an employer could take the position that if the employee is not able to work, the employee should be fired. The employer's position can be defended as the embodiment of the principle of at-will employment, but it can also be seen as unfair and short-sighted. Should the employer have the unfettered right to terminate the employment of an individual who has a family or medical need that requires the employee's absence from work?

Congress answered this question in 1993 when it enacted into law the Family and Medical Leave Act (FMLA). The FMLA provides that, in certain circumstances, an employer is required to provide leave to an employee with an assurance that the employee can return to the same (or equivalent) job at the end of the leave. The Act provides for up to twelve workweeks of leave during a twelve-month period. The Act applies to leave taken for one or more of the following reasons: (1) the birth and care of an employee's newborn child; (2) the placement with the employee of a son or daughter for adoption or foster care; (3) the care of an immediate family member (spouse, child, or parent) with a serious health condition; or (4) the inability of an employee to work because of a serious health condition.

The FMLA reflects fundamental societal changes in family and work relations. In years past, the law assumed that only one family member (usually a man) worked. If there were newborn children or dependent family members who were sick, there was another family member (usually a woman) who could attend to those needs. That patriarchal model has eroded as women have flooded the job market. More generally, the FMLA reflects a change in the approach to work itself. Work has long occupied a central role in the American experience, but so too have family and leisure. As employees have found themselves working longer hours for the same (or less) pay, family has increasingly taken a backseat to work. The FMLA seeks to encourage a more balanced approach to family and work life.

While the FMLA represents an important symbolic change in this nation's approach to family and work issues, there are significant limits to the protection provided under the Act. First, the Act guarantees *unpaid* leave only. The Act provides that if an employee is in need of leave, that employee can take the leave and return to his or her job at the expiration of the leave period. The employer can choose to pay the employee for the leave if it so chooses, but it is not legally obligated to do so (assuming that it treats all employees the same with respect to the leave).

A second limit on the reach of the FMLA is that a significant number of small employers are exempt from the Act. Many federal statutes establish coverage thresholds for employers. Typically, an employer is exempt if it has less than fifteen (or twenty) employees. The FMLA, which was vigorously opposed by small business, contains such a coverage limitation but with a much higher threshold. With respect to private employers, the Act reaches only those companies that employ fifty or more employees for at least twenty workweeks in the current or preceding calendar year. (The Act reaches all public agencies, including state, local, and federal employers.) Although many states (just over half) have their own leave statutes, coverage under the federal and state statutes is far from comprehensive.

Finally, even concerning those employers that meet the coverage threshold, the protection of the FMLA is not universal. To receive the protection of the FMLA, an employee must have worked for a covered employer for a total of twelve months. While that twelve months need not be consecutive, the employee must have worked 1,250 hours during the twelve months prior to the start of the FMLA leave. (This means actual work time.) An employee is covered under the act only if the employee works at a location in the United States and only if at least fifty employees are employed at the location or within a seventy-five-mile radius of the location.

Despite these limitations, the FMLA provides significant statutory protection for many employees who are need in of leave and who would lose their jobs in the absence of the federal statute. In this chapter, I deal briefly with three general issues that arise under the federal Act: (1) the employee's obligation to provide notice and medical certification; (2) the employer's duties with respect to leave, health care protection, and job restoration; and (3) the relationship between the FMLA and the other laws that may provide for leave protection.

Employee Notice and Medical Certification

The FMLA is a statute that imposes obligations on the employer. Those obligations, however, do not exist in the abstract. They arise only if the employee takes the steps necessary to trigger the protections of the Act. Since the employee is seeking what might be viewed as an extraordinary measure of protection—the right to miss work and retain his or her job—the employee carries the initial burden of putting the leave issue on the table and shifting to the employer the burden of complying with the specific requirements of the Act.

The most important precondition to FMLA protection is that the employer be given reasonable notice of the need for the leave. An employer is not expected to be clairvoyant. An employee cannot simply disappear from work, expecting that the employer will treat the leave as covered under the FMLA. Nor is the employer expected to guess at the reason for the leave, where the employee provides notice of a work absence but does not specify the grounds for the absence. The employee must provide the employer with notice sufficient to make the employer aware of the employee's need for the type of leave that qualifies for protection under the FMLA.

Where practicable, the employee is required to provide at least thirty days' advance notice of the need to take FMLA leave. Thus, if an employee is pregnant and wishes to take leave for a certain period following the birth of the child, the employee should provide notice to the employer no later than thirty days before the expected date of the birth. In some cases, of course, it will not be possible to provide thirty days' notice, either because the need for the leave is unforeseeable (e.g., a medical emergency) or because the leave, while foreseeable, must be taken within thirty days of the point at which the reason for the leave first arises. In such a case, the employee must provide notice as soon as practicable. Typically, notice should be provided within one or two days of the event precipitating the need for the leave.

Not surprisingly, the notice issue has generated some controversy. The controversy stems less from when the notice must be provided than from what form the notice must take. On the one hand, it is clear that an employee is not required to expressly mention the FMLA in making the request for leave. The employee is not expected to be a lawyer. If the employee provides a clear explanation for why the leave is needed (e.g., "My son is seriously ill;" "I need to undergo surgery;" "I want to stay home with my baby following childbirth"), the employee discharges his or her notice obligation. On the other hand, it is not enough for an employee to make vague references to a sick child or a need for time off. Many employers have policies requiring the discharge of those individuals who have unexcused absences from work. The FMLA trumps those policies to the extent they would lead to the discharge of an individual who qualifies for FMLA leave for one of the four reasons set forth in the Act. For that legal trump to occur, however, the employee must fairly apprise the employer of the reason for the requested leave. If the employee fails to show up for work and does not furnish the employer with notice sufficient to place the employee within the reasonable ambit of the FMLA, the employer may invoke its normal work rules and terminate the employee.

> EXAMPLE: An employee learns that his child has a serious medical condition that will require a protracted period of bed rest. The employee notifies the employer of his need for leave, based upon the child's condition. The employee does not specifically assert his rights under the FMLA and, in fact, does not mention the statute at all. The employer, upon receiving the request for leave, discharges the employee. The employee has a claim under the FMLA. The employee has provided notice sufficient to apprise the employer of the possibility that the leave requested is FMLA-qualifying leave. The employer, without further investigation, has terminated the employee because of his request for leave.

> EXAMPLE: Same example as above except the employee calls into work and vaguely mentions that he will be staying home that day because his child is sick. The employee does not provide any details of his child's condition and does not ask for an extended period of leave. Over the next three workdays, the employee stays at home without calling in to report his absence. This is in direct violation of the employer's atten-

dance policy. The employer discharges the employee, invoking the attendance policy. The employer's action may be justified. The notice provided by the employee may not have been sufficient to trigger the protections of the FMLA. The employee, moreover, violated the employer's attendance policy by failing to call in to report his absence.

Significantly, the FMLA does not require that the request for leave be in writing. Verbal notice is sufficient if it makes the employer aware that the employee needs FMLA-qualifying leave. The result may be different if the employer has a policy of requiring that all leave requests be put in writing. An employer is entitled to adopt its own procedural requirements for the handling of leave requests. While an employee's failure to follow those requirements might not disentitle the employee from the protections of the FMLA, an employer can insist that the employee, at some point, provide the necessary paperwork for approval of the leave request. At bottom, an employee is well advised to follow the employer's customary procedures when making a request for FMLA-qualifying leave.

Assuming that the employee has provided the requisite notice of the need for leave, the ball is then placed in the employer's court. The employer can take the employee at his or her word and provide the leave. The employer, however, may not be satisfied with the employee's initial explanation. The employer may want further information concerning the circumstances surrounding the need for leave. If the employee's notice does not, by itself, bring the employee within the protection of the FMLA, the employer may press the employee for additional evidence that the leave is FMLA-qualifying.

In cases in which the leave is for medical purposes, the employer is entitled to seek medical certification of the employee's (or family member's) condition. The FMLA guarantees leave to any covered employee who needs to care for an immediate family member with a serious health condition. The Act also applies when the employee himself or herself is unable to work because of such a condition. A serious health condition means an illness, injury, impairment, or physical or mental condition that involves: (1) any period of incapacity or treatment connected with inpatient care; (2) a period of incapacity that involves continuing treatment by a health care provider, and which requires absence of more than three calendar days from work, school, or other regular daily activities; (3) any period of incapacity due to pregnancy, or for prenatal care; (4) any period of incapacity due to a chronic serious health condition (e.g., asthma); (5) a period of incapacity that is permanent or long term due to a condition for which treatment may not be effective (e.g., a terminal disease); or (6) any absences to receive multiple treatments by, or on referral by, a health care provider for a condition that likely would result in incapacity of more than three consecutive days if left untreated (e.g., chemotherapy). In some cases, it may be obvious that a medical condition qualifies for leave protection. In other cases, however, the question may be in doubt. The requirement of providing a medical certification serves to ensure that the medical condition is serious enough to meet the statutory standard for protected leave.

An employer must allow an employee at least fifteen days to obtain the medical certification. The certification is to come from a health care provider, typically the employee's physician. (The Department of Labor has issued a standard form that can be completed by the physician.) If the employer doubts the opinion of the employee's health care provider, the employer (at its own expense) may require the employee to provide a second medical certification to be obtained from a health care provider of the employer's choosing. If the second certification differs from the certification provided by the first health care provider, the employer can press for a third opinion (again at the employer's expense), which is binding on the parties. An employer may require an employee on leave to provide subsequent recertifications, although, as a general matter, where an employee suffers from a chronic condition, the employer may not request recertification more than once every thirty days.

While the employer may ask for additional certifications or recertifications of medical need, the employer is not obligated to inquire any further when the initial certification does not support the leave request. An employee may wish to have leave designated as FMLA-qualifying leave. The employee visits a health care provider, who confirms that the employee is suffering from a chronic health condition. The provider, however, does not certify that the employee's condition is the kind of incapacitating condition that would qualify for leave protection under the FMLA. An employer, in such a case, is entitled to rely upon the physician's certification until it receives some additional word from the employee. If no such word is forthcoming and the employee misses work in violation of an employer's attendance policy, the employer may invoke its normal work rules and discharge the employee.

> **EXAMPLE: An employee suffers from a chronic illness. The employee takes paid sick leave, as provided under the employer's leave policy. During her period of paid leave, the employee sees a physician, hoping to obtain medical certification of a serious health condition so that the employee can qualify for FMLA leave once her paid leave is exhausted. The physician confirms that the employee has a serious chronic condition but certifies that the employee is not presently incapacitated and, thus, is able to work. The employee eventually returns to work and is informed that, in light of the physician's certification, any future absences will be counted against her under the employer's attendance policy. Two weeks later, the employee again becomes ill and calls into work sick. The employer, invoking its attendance policy, fires the employee for excessive absenteeism. The employee sues under the FMLA, claiming that the employer was required to investigate further and require an additional medical certification, once it learned that the employee was again sick. The employee is unlikely to prevail on her claim. The employee suffered from a chronic condition. Only a few months before,**

the employee's own physician had refused to certify that the employee was eligible for FMLA-qualifying leave. While it is possible that the employee's condition worsened during the intervening period, the employer can make a fair argument that it was entitled to rely upon the previous medical certification until provided with a different certification by the employee.

Lastly, it must be stressed that the FMLA seeks to provide leave protection to employees with as little disruption to the employer's operations as possible. Where an employee seeks leave on an intermittent basis or requests reduced schedule leave, the employee is expected to cooperate with the employer in scheduling the leave. In some cases, there may be an alternative job that would accommodate recurring periods of leave better than the employee's regular job. In such a case, the employer may transfer the employee to the alternative job so long as the job provides equivalent pay and benefits. For the FMLA to work, there must be a substantial level of cooperation between the employee and employer.

The Employer's Obligations

Once the employee provides notice of his or her need for leave and satisfies the employer that the leave is FMLA-qualifying leave, the guarantees of the FMLA come into play. The employer's principal obligation under the FMLA is (not surprisingly) to provide leave. As noted previously, an employee is entitled to twelve weeks of leave in a twelve-month period. The employer is permitted to choose from among four methods for determining the twelve-month period (e.g., the calendar year; any fixed twelve-month leave year) but, of course, may not manipulate the period in a way that would deprive the employee of the twelve weeks' leave to which he or she is entitled. The leave need not be consecutive. Thus, an employee can take four weeks' leave at one point, due to an FMLA-qualifying event, and eight weeks' leave at a later point, due to another such event, so long as the leave falls within the twelve-month period designated by the employer. In some circumstances, an employee is permitted to take a leave on an intermittent or reduced schedule basis, thus allowing the employee to take leave in blocks of time or to reduce his or her normal work schedule.

There are some limits on the use of leave with respect to leave taken for the care of a newborn child or for a newly placed (adopted) child. First, the leave must conclude within twelve months of the birth or placement of the child. Second, where spouses are employed by the same employer, the spouses are limited to a combined total of twelve weeks' leave. Finally, intermittent or reduced schedule leave may be taken for the care of a newly born or adopted child only with the employer's approval. (Intermittent/reduced schedule leave may be taken to care for a seriously ill family member only where there is a medical need for leave that can best be accommodated through an intermittent or reduced leave schedule.)

The leave issue is complicated by the fact that the Act requires the employer to designate the leave (where appropriate) as FMLA leave. Where the employee notifies the employer of the need for leave and the employer acquires sufficient information to verify that the leave is being taken for an FMLA-required reason, the employer must promptly notify the employee (typically within two business days) that the leave is being designated as FMLA leave. Notably, the employer is permitted to designate paid leave taken under an existing leave plan as FMLA leave. In other words, if the employer has a policy of providing paid vacation or sick leave to its employees and an employee is in need of leave that is FMLA-qualifying leave, the employer can require the employee to substitute the accrued paid leave for FMLA leave. (The employee has the option of substituting paid leave for FMLA leave in the event the employer does not require the employee to do so.) If the employer requires that paid leave taken under an existing plan be counted as FMLA leave, it must designate the leave as FMLA-qualifying leave prior to the start of the leave period unless the employer does not have sufficient information, at that point, to determine whether the leave is FMLA-qualifying leave.

That an employer can count accrued paid leave as FMLA leave suggests that the protection of the FMLA may be less than what it first appears. The FMLA purports to guarantee to each eligible employee a total of twelve weeks' leave for a twelve-month period. Many companies, however, already have leave plans that provide for several weeks of paid leave per year. For employees of these companies, the FMLA may add little in the way of additional leave protection, since the employer can simply designate the leave as FMLA leave (assuming it qualifies for such treatment). This reduces the amount of any additional leave available under the FMLA to the difference (if any) between the twelve weeks guaranteed under the FMLA and the leave already provided under the company's policy. The FMLA can provide important leave protection in some cases. It is far from a panacea, however, for those employees struggling to balance family responsibilities and work needs.

> **EXAMPLE: An employee works for a company that allows two weeks of annual vacation leave (paid) and up to eight weeks of annual sick or personal leave (paid). An employee adopts a child and elects to take leave to care for the child. The leave is FMLA-qualifying leave. The employer requires the accrued paid leave (ten weeks total) to be substituted for the FMLA leave. This leaves the employee with two weeks of additional unpaid leave that can be claimed under the FMLA. The employee receives twelve weeks of leave to care for the child, but the employee would have been entitled to ten weeks' leave under the company's leave policy. The FMLA results in only two weeks of additional leave.**

In addition to its guarantee of leave, the FMLA requires that the employer maintain an employee's group health insurance coverage during the period of any FMLA leave. This is not unlike the COBRA provision discussed in Chapter 8. Like the COBRA, the FMLA does not require an employer to provide health insurance coverage to its employees. Instead, the Act requires that if the employer provides group health coverage to its employees, that same coverage must be extended to an employee who is on FMLA leave. There is one critical distinction between the COBRA and the FMLA. Under the COBRA, the employee (or former employee) may be required to pay the full amount of the insurance premium. Under the FMLA, the employer is required to pay its share of the premium, as is the employee. The employer may discontinue coverage if the employee fails to pay his or her share of the premium. The employer may also discontinue coverage if the employee informs the employer that he or she will not be returning to work or if, in fact, the employee does not return to work at the end of the leave period.

Finally, and most critically, the FMLA contains a requirement of job restoration. Guaranteed leave would mean little if the employer were not required to bring the employee back to work after the leave period has expired. The Act requires that upon the expiration of FMLA leave, an employee must be restored to his or her original job or to an equivalent job. An equivalent job is one that is virtually identical to the original job with respect to pay, benefits, and other terms and conditions of employment. The FMLA also prohibits an employer from stripping the employee of any employment benefit to which the employee was entitled before taking the FMLA leave.

There are some limits to the job restoration requirement. First, the FMLA requires the employer to treat the employee the same way the employee would have been treated had the employee continued working. This means that the employer must return the employee to the same or equivalent job even if, during the employee's absence, the employee has been replaced or the job restructured to accommodate the employee's absence. On the other hand, there may be cases in which the employee would have lost his or her job even if the employee had not taken leave. An employer, for example, may engage in a mass layoff of workers during the period of an employee's leave. If the employee would have been laid off even if the employee had not taken leave, there is no obligation on the employer's part to reinstate the employee.

There is also an exception to the job restoration requirement. The Act permits an employer to designate an employee as a "key" employee. A key employee is defined as a salaried employee who is among the highest paid 10% of employees within seventy-five miles of the work site. An employer is permitted to deny job restoration to a key employee if it can show that reinstating the employee will cause substantial and grievous economic injury to its operations. To invoke the key employee exception, the employer must notify the employee—*at the time the employee provides notice of intent to take leave*—of his or her status as a key employee. The employer must also notify the employee as soon as the employer decides it will deny job restoration, explain to the employee the reasons for the denial, and provide to the employee a reasonable opportunity to return to work once the period of leave ends.

Bound up with the requirement of job restoration is the principle that an employer may not take adverse action against an employee because the employee has exercised his or her rights under the FMLA. The FMLA contemplates that the employee will engage in an interactive process with the employer to determine eligibility for FMLA leave. The effectiveness of this process turns on an employee feeling free to approach his or her employer with a leave request. An employer is entitled to question the request for leave and, if there is an absence of evidence to substantiate the leave as FMLA-qualifying leave, deny the request. The employer, however, may not engage in reprisals against the employee because the employee has invoked the protections of the FMLA.

> **EXAMPLE: An employee has a chronic condition that is caus-
> ing the employee some discomfort. The employee wishes to
> take a leave of absence from work and approaches the**

employer with the leave request. It is doubtful whether the employee has the type of serious health condition that would qualify the employee for FMLA leave. The employer, therefore, would be justified in denying the leave request. Instead, the employer grants the leave. One day after the employee goes out on leave, the employer terminates his employment under circumstances that are suggestive of an intent to sanction the employee for having requested FMLA leave. The employee has a claim that his discharge violates the FMLA.

Relationship to Other Laws

The observant reader will have realized that the leave protections of the FMLA overlap to some degree with the protections provided under other federal laws. Specifically, the leave issue arises under the Americans With Disabilities Act (ADA), where a medical leave of absence can be a reasonable accommodation. The issue also arises with respect to the prohibition against sex discrimination, which, as discussed in Chapter 2, includes protections against pregnancy discrimination. More generally, an employer may violate the antidiscrimination laws by refusing to provide leave to an employee if it provides such leave to individuals of a different race, gender, or national origin.

It is important to distinguish among the various statutory protections that are implicated when an employee requests leave. The FMLA guarantees a certain period of leave to any covered employee. In other words, the Act requires that a covered employer provide leave to an employee if the leave is FMLA-qualifying leave. No such per se requirement exists under the other federal statutes. The ADA, for example, merely provides that, in some circumstances, an employer is required to provide leave to an employee who meets the Act's definition of disability. Similarly, the prohibition against pregnancy discrimination is implicated only when the employer treats a pregnant worker different from a similarly situated nonpregnant employee. If an employer provides paid leave to employees with temporary disabilities, it must provide the same leave to a pregnant employee. The employer, however, does not engage in unlawful sex discrimination by denying leave to a pregnant worker if it denies leave to other workers under similar circumstances.

By the same token, the FMLA has limits that are not found in the other federal laws that touch upon the leave issue. The leave provided under the FMLA is capped at twelve weeks in a twelve-month period. No such limit exists under the ADA. While the ADA does not support a claim for indefinite leave, leave can extend beyond the FMLA's fixed period of twelve weeks if it satisfies the ADA's requirements for a reasonable accommodation and does not impose an undue hardship on the employer. Under the ADA, moreover, the leave can be paid leave if the employer otherwise provides such leave to similarly situated employees. The same is true with respect to a pregnant employee, who can claim sex discrimination if the employer provides paid leave to other workers who suffer from temporary disabilities and denies such leave to the pregnant employee. An employer may well comply with the FMLA but nonetheless violate federal law in denying leave to an employee.

> **EXAMPLE: An employee has a chronic health condition that is incapacitating during periods when it is symptomatic. The employee has an outbreak of the condition and is given twelve weeks' leave in accordance with the FMLA. The employee returns to his job and works successfully for three months. The condition again flares up, and the employee seeks additional leave. This time the employee wants to be placed in a two-month treatment program. The employee provides the employer with a physician's opinion that the treatment program carries with it a reasonable prospect for a full recovery and a return to work, with little risk of a reoccurrence. The employer, citing the FMLA, denies the leave request, stating that it has provided all the leave that is required under federal law. The employee sues, claiming that the employer violated the ADA by not allowing the employee**

to participate in the treatment program (on leave) as a reasonable accommodation. The employer is correct that it was not required to provide additional FMLA leave. The FMLA, however, does not dictate the level of protection under the ADA. If the employee is a disabled individual within the meaning of the ADA, the employee might well have a claim that the employer violated the ADA by failing to provide the employee with two months' leave to participate in the treatment program.

EXAMPLE: An employee is pregnant. The employer provides four weeks of annual paid leave to those employees with temporary disabilities. Following childbirth, the employee is given four weeks of paid leave. The employee desires to stay home with the child for a longer period and asks for an additional period of eight weeks' leave (unpaid). The employer denies the request, explaining that it has provided the employee with the full amount of leave available under its leave policy. The employee sues, claiming a violation of the FMLA. The employer did not engage in unlawful sex discrimination by denying the request for additional leave, since it treated the employee no differently than it did other similarly situated employees. In this case, however, the FMLA provides the employee with additional protection. Assuming the employer is a covered employer and the employee has properly notified the employer of her request for additional leave, the employer has violated the FMLA.

As the above examples suggest, the leave question can be legally complex. Because of the complexity of the issues and the increasing importance of leave protection in the workplace, employees must educate themselves on their legal rights (and duties) in this area.

CHAPTER 10

Wrongful Discharge

The first principle of the American workplace is employment-at-will. Employment-at-will means that the employee serves at the complete will of the employer. In the absence of an employment contract providing otherwise, the employer retains the absolute right to discharge the employee for any reason that the employer deems appropriate.

This book should make clear that at-will employment is a doctrine under siege. A number of federal statutes regulate various aspects of the employment relationship. These statutes encroach upon employer discretion by prohibiting certain forms of discrimination and mandating compliance with minimal standards of fairness. For every federal statute that speaks to the employment relationship, there are scores more at the state and local levels, all providing protections for individual employees and, thus, further tying the hands of the employer.

While statutes provide the principal source of employment protection, there are other ways that the law can impact the workplace. In the American legal system, law emanates from a number of sources. Principally, law is the product of Congress and state and local legislative bodies. But courts also play a role in making law by fashioning what are known as "common law" doctrines. These doctrines cannot be inconsistent with statutory law but can fill the gaps in the governing statutes or take the law into areas not expressly covered by such statutes.

In the employment context, courts have played a significant, albeit secondary, role in adopting doctrines that constrain the conduct of employers. The most prominent of the judge-made doctrines is the theory of wrongful discharge. Wrongful discharge means precisely what its name implies—that an employer has discharged an individual under circumstances that are viewed as improper, thus triggering the protection of the law. The theory is typically invoked in one of two circumstances. First, an employee can assert a claim of wrongful discharge if the employer has made an implied promise not to terminate the employee or to do so only for cause. Second, a wrongful discharge claim can be asserted where the termination contravenes some well-established public policy.

The critical thing to understand about the wrongful discharge theory is that it is a doctrine created largely by state courts. As such, the protection provided by the theory is not uniform. An employee working in California may have substantial protection against wrongful discharge. An employee working in some other state may have little or no protection. This chapter does not provide a comprehensive state-by-state examination of wrongful discharge law. It provides a brief overview of the wrongful discharge theory, as generally applied.

The Implied Contract

As noted above, the principle of at-will employment assumes that the employer retains the right to discharge an employee for any reason. An employer, however, can choose to cede away its absolute discretion to terminate an employee as part of an employment contract. An employment contract can take many forms. A common form of employment contract is the collective bargaining agreement. Where an employer negotiates an agreement with a union, the employer obligates itself to the specific promises contained in the agreement, including, in the typical collective bargaining agreement, a promise not to terminate a member of a bargaining unit in the absence of just cause. An employer can also enter into an individual employment contract. This type of contract is commonplace for professional athletes and high-ranking executives. It is a rarity, however, for the average worker. Most American workers do not work under a formal employment contract and, thus, cannot cite such a contract as a limitation upon the employer's authority.

In some cases, it is possible that an employer will obligate itself to a specific protection for an employee without formalizing the obligation in a written contract. Not every contract is reduced to a formal agreement. Not every contract reflects an express promise. At times, an employer will engage in conduct or make statements from which a binding commitment can be inferred. In such a case, a court may recognize an implied contract that trumps, to some degree, the principle of at-will employment. If the employer fires the employee in violation of the contract, it engages in an act of wrongful discharge for which the employee has a legal remedy.

An implied contract can arise in a variety of circumstances. It is not uncommon for an employer (or one of its agents) to make statements to an employee concerning the employee's job status. An employer, for example, may provide assurances of job security to an employee, implying that the employee will retain the job so long as he or she performs satisfactorily. An employer can communicate the same level of protection through its conduct. An employer may have an established practice of not terminating employees except for good cause. Or, an employer might have a practice of providing job security to those employees who have worked for the employer for a number of years and who have received promotions and salary increases. At some point, the statements and/or conduct of the employer are sufficient to give rise to a binding implied contract.

A fertile ground for the implied contract theory is the employer's own personnel documents. Employers often issue written personnel documents and policies. The most common of

these is the employee handbook or manual. Employee handbooks often speak to the issue of job security. Some state, quite
specifically, that employees will be terminated only for good
cause. Employers make these representations to entice individuals
to work for the employer and to buttress morale among existing
employees. In doing so, however, employers might well bind
themselves to an agreement not to terminate an employee
except for good cause.

> **EXAMPLE: An employee is fired from his job, following
> twenty-five years of service with the company. He was told at
> the time that he was hired that if he performed his job well,
> his job was secure. The employee had been promoted on
> numerous occasions, had consistently received favorable per-
> formance reviews, and had not engaged in any serious mis-
> conduct in the workplace. The company also has an
> employee handbook, suggesting that an employee's job will
> be secure if the employee performs satisfactorily. The
> employee sues, claiming wrongful discharge. The employee
> invokes the implied contract theory, citing the statements
> made at the time of his hiring, the representations in the
> employee handbook, the length of his service, and his con-
> sistently solid job performance. The employee has a strong
> wrongful discharge claim.**

The implied contract theory does not provide absolute protection from discharge. An employer could enter into an employment contract that expressly guarantees lifetime employment to
an individual, regardless of the individual's job performance.
While an employer might be held to an explicit agreement of that
nature, such a momentous commitment is rarely implied. Instead,
the law binds the employer to a promise not to discharge the
employee except for good or just cause. This means essentially
that the employer must have a business justification for the discharge, related to such factors as performance deficiencies, misconduct, or economic need. If the employer has good cause for

terminating the employee, the employee cannot successfully invoke the wrongful discharge theory, even if an implied contract can be established.

> **EXAMPLE: An employee is fired after striking a supervisor in the face. The attack is unprovoked. The employer has an employee handbook that specifically states that an employee can be fired only for good cause. The employee sues, alleging wrongful discharge based on an implied contract theory. The employee may have a strong argument that an implied contract exists by virtue of the provision in the employee handbook. It is likely, however, that the employee's violent act provides good cause for termination. If so, the wrongful discharge claim fails.**

In some cases, an employer might in good faith believe that an employee has engaged in misconduct that would justify the employee's discharge under a good cause standard. Based on that good faith belief, the employer discharges the offender. As it turns out, the employee can demonstrate that the misconduct did not in fact take place. A court may hold, nonetheless, that because the employer had a good faith belief that the misconduct occurred, the requirement of a "for cause" discharge is met.

> **EXAMPLE: An employee claims that she was sexually harassed by a supervisor. The employer thoroughly investigates the harassment, taking detailed statements from both the complainant and the alleged perpetrator and interviewing other employees. Based on its investigation, the employer concludes that the harassment took place. Because the harassment was serious in nature (involving the alleged grabbing of the complainant's breasts), the employer decides to discharge the supervisor. The supervisor sues, claiming wrongful discharge. There is evidence that the employee has an implied contract to be discharged only for good cause. There is also evidence that, as it turns out, the harassment may not**

have taken place. Nonetheless, the evidence also shows that the employer conducted a conscientious investigation of the alleged harassment and believed in good faith that the harassment took place. A court may conclude that the employer was justified in terminating the supervisor, thus defeating the wrongful discharge claim, even though the supervisor may be able to demonstrate, after the fact, that the misconduct did not occur.

It should be apparent that, the just cause limitation notwithstanding, the implied contract theory has broad implications. It is not uncommon for an employer (or its agents) to make general statements about an employee's job security. Even where no such representations are made, employers can engage in conduct that could arguably convey the impression that an employee is guaranteed a job if the employee performs the job in a satisfactory fashion. Taken to its logical endpoint, the implied contract theory could serve as a complete trump of the employment-at-will doctrine, providing employees with what amounts to a "for cause" employment relationship.

There are two factors that work against this broad level of employee protection. First, employers have become increasingly sophisticated in their understanding of the implied contract theory. Most notably, employers have carefully vetted their employee handbooks to avoid making representations that could give rise to an implied contract. One way to accomplish this is to remove any reference to job security issues (e.g., statements that imply that an employee will be fired only for cause). Another is to place a disclaimer in the handbook, stating that the handbook is not intended to be a contract of employment and that the employer retains the unilateral right to modify any of the provisions contained in the handbook. It is not clear that all courts will give effect to such a disclaimer to the extent there is other evidence supportive of an implied contract. Nonetheless, by massaging its employee handbook (and other personnel documents) and counseling its managers to guard against making oral assurances of job security, the employer can undercut the effectiveness of the implied contract theory.

More generally, there has been a tendency on the part of most courts to cabin the implied contract theory to discrete circumstances supportive of an actual promise of job security. The case for recognizing an implied contract is easy where the employer has made specific statements that an employee's job is secure if the employee performs the job satisfactorily. This is an implied form of the type of formal employment contract that can always override the at-will doctrine. The case is more difficult where the implied contract is purportedly based on such amorphous factors as the longevity of the individual's employment or the general practices of the employer. The mere fact that an employee has worked for an employer for a substantial period of time, while receiving pay raises, stellar performance evaluations, and promotions, may not be enough (at least in some courts) to sustain a wrongful discharge claim under an implied contract theory.

Public Policy

The implied contract theory focuses on the conduct of the employer in creating a binding promise to provide a certain level of job protection to the employee. The second ground for asserting a wrongful discharge theory shifts the focus to broader public policy concerns. Under the public policy prong of the wrongful discharge theory, an employee is entitled to assert a claim for wrongful discharge if the employer has terminated the employee in contravention of a well-defined public policy.

The critical question with respect to the public policy exception to at-will employment is definitional—what constitutes a well-defined public policy? The question is not easily resolved. The public policy theory has been invoked most frequently in cases in which an employee has been discharged for engaging in statutorily protected activity. A typical example involves state workers' compensation statutes. Most states have laws that allow employees to be compensated for on-the-job injuries. These laws require that the employee file a claim for compensation. In many cases, however, the statutes do not contain a specific provision making it unlawful for an employer to discharge the employee for having filed such a claim. Nonetheless, it is obvious that if the employer is allowed to discharge an employee who asserts a claim for compensation, employees will not feel free to exercise their rights under the statute, thus undermining the protections of the statute. The fact that the employer's conduct (if unchecked) would undermine enforcement of a statute enacted for the employee's benefit supports the existence of a well-defined public policy.

> **EXAMPLE: An employee is injured on the job. The injury is severe enough to qualify the employee for compensation under the state's workers' compensation law. The employee files a claim for benefits. Two days later, the employer discharges the employee. The evidence supports a finding that the employer fired the employee in retaliation for the employee having filed a claim under the workers' compensation law. The employee sues, alleging wrongful discharge. The employee specifically claims that the employer's action contravenes the well-defined public policy embodied in the workers' compensation statute. A court is likely to uphold the employee's claim (assuming the court recognizes the public policy basis for a wrongful discharge claim).**

A well-defined public policy has also been found where an employee is discharged for having refused to engage in an illegal act. If an employer instructs an employee to do something illegal (e.g., falsify information on a government form), the employee refuses, and the employer fires the employee because of that refusal, the employee has a viable claim of wrongful discharge. In a similar vein, the public policy theory typically extends to an employee who has disclosed illegal or improper conduct on the part of his or her employer. This amounts to a form of whistleblower protection for those employees who promote the public interest by making such conduct known.

Sometimes, the public policy claim is based upon the state's own laws against unlawful discrimination. As discussed in previous chapters, most states have statutes that make it unlawful to discriminate on the basis of race, gender, or age. These statutes typically provide an aggrieved individual with a cause of action. Often, however, the statute is not comprehensive. It may not apply to certain categories of employers. Or, it may limit relief to back pay. (A wrongful discharge claim might support an award of compensatory and punitive damages.) In these circumstances, a wrongful discharge claim can be used as a way of supplementing the state's existing statutes on workplace discrimination.

> **EXAMPLE: An employee is terminated from her job. The evidence shows that the employer fired her because of her gender. The employee has a claim of sex discrimination under the state's antidiscrimination law. The state law, however, only provides for back pay relief. The employee asserts a claim for wrongful discharge, in addition to her claim of sex discrimination under the state law, because she hopes to recover compensatory and punitive damages. A court may recognize a separate claim for wrongful discharge (with the resulting compensatory and punitive damages), based on the well-defined public policy embodied in the state antidiscrimination statute.**

The more controversial applications of the public policy theory occur where the public policy is not rooted in any specific statutory or constitutional provision. Some courts have determined that a well-defined public policy cannot be derived from anything other than the positive law (i.e., a statute or constitutional provision). Thus, if an employee were fired for refusing to perform a certain act, there would be no wrongful discharge claim if that act, while undesirable, was not itself illegal. Other courts, however, have recognized that a well-defined public policy can be one that is identified by the court itself. In such a case, the court plays a dual role—it identifies the public policy at issue and provides the cause of action for its vindication.

> **EXAMPLE: An employee works as a respiratory therapist. The employee is fired after he refuses to work the evening shift at a hospital. The employee refuses to work the shift because he would have been the only respiratory therapist working at the time. The employee claims that permitting only one respiratory therapist to be on duty poses a threat to the health and safety of the patients. There is no state law concerning the scheduling of respiratory therapists. Thus, the employer would not have violated a state statute in requiring the employee to work alone. Some courts would hold that the employee is not entitled to assert a claim of wrongful discharge, based on public policy, because the policy being vindicated is not reflected in any state statute. Other courts, however, might embrace a wrongful discharge claim, based on a general societal concern for qualified patient care.**

As with the implied contract theory, the public policy theory has potentially broad implications. One could argue that public policy is implicated anytime an employer has fired an employee for what is viewed as a bad or nonlegitimate reason. Permitting the employer to discharge a good employee for no legitimate reason affects the public interest by depriving the workforce of an effective employee and possibly forcing the employee into unemployment, with consequences for the employee and his or her family as well as the public fisc. Most courts have been reluctant to take the doctrine that far, suggesting that it would essentially impose a "for cause" regime upon all employment relationships. The principle of public policy can be broadly defined. The principle, however, must be anchored in something more than the mere fact that an employee has been unfairly terminated from his or her job.

EXAMPLE: An employee works at a state school for the men-
tally retarded. The employee is fired following an internal dispute with the school administrator. The employee sues, alleging a wrongful discharge. The employee claims that her termination is against public policy because her job is socially important and because she was discharged for having disagreed
with the administrator on a matter that was significant to the
operation of the school. A court is unlikely to sustain the
wrongful discharge claim. The mere fact that the employee's
job is socially important is not enough. While there may be a
public interest in permitting disagreement and debate on an
issue of societal importance, that interest is generally super-
seded by the employer's right to control the workplace.

Recent Trends

The wrongful discharge theory is constantly evolving. Twenty-five
years ago, the theory was in its developing stages. During the intervening period, the theory has grown at a rapid rate. Even now,
however, the theory is not universally accepted. The legal status of
the wrongful discharge theory continues to be in a state of flux.

There are some signs of a continued expansion of the theory. First, some courts have identified additional legal grounds for
a wrongful discharge claim (other than implied contract and public policy). Courts, for example, have invoked the implied
covenant of good faith and fair dealing. The narrow version of
this doctrine merely constrains the employer in the manner in
which it carries out an existing employment contract. Broadly
applied, however, the doctrine amounts to an implied-in-law
obligation not to terminate an employee without good cause.

Some courts, moreover, have extended the rationale of the
wrongful discharge theory to adverse employment actions other
than a discharge. Courts, for example, have permitted employees to challenge a demotion under the same standards that apply
to a wrongful discharge claim. Conceivably, this approach could
extend to a wide variety of other employment actions, thus bring-

ing the wrongful discharge theory into all aspects of the employment relationship.

Despite these developments, there is also a countervailing movement against the wrongful discharge theory. Having let the genie out of the bottle, some courts have started to pull the reins in. With respect to the implied contract theory, this means limiting the theory to cases in which there are concrete representations of job security. With respect to the public policy theory, it means limiting the theory to cases in which the public policy is derived from a specific statute or constitutional provision.

In some cases, the movement against the wrongful discharge theory has come from the legislative branch. To cite one example, the Arizona legislature recently passed a statute that severely restricts the wrongful discharge theory. The statute specifically provides that the employment relationship is contractual in nature. The statute states that the employment relationship is severable at any time unless there is a written contract stating otherwise. The statute limits the wrongful discharge theory to three discrete circumstances: (1) where the employer breaches a written contract by discharging the employee; (2) where the employee is discharged after being asked to violate an Arizona statute (and refusing to do so); and (3) where the employee is discharged in retaliation for performing a protected act.

Ultimately, it is the legislative branch that holds the cards. Courts can fashion common law doctrines, but when the legislature speaks to a specific issue, its word is final (assuming its action is not unconstitutional). The crazy quilt of legal standards in this area suggests that it may be time for a more uniform approach to the issue. The era of at-will employment is over. In typically American fashion, the denouement has come, not from any frontal assault upon the doctrine, but from a series of individual acts billed as exceptions to the rule. It is perhaps time for the law to catch up with itself and adopt, as the rule, a standard that provides basic protection against unjustified terminations in accordance with the modern realities of the employment relationship.

Part II

Workplace Rights in Practice

Part I of this book sets forth the basic legal rights of employees in the American workplace. Part II takes these rights and applies them in the real world. The employee's position is a difficult one. The employee does not make the rules. The employee does not initiate the action. The employee reacts to the employer's moves, often with little information to go on and little time to make decisions that may be crucial to the employee's ability to protect and vindicate his or her legal rights. It is one thing to say that a legal right exists in theory. It is another to say that it can be meaningfully exercised in practice.

While Part I addresses a broad range of issues involving employee rights in the workplace, Part II focuses essentially on a case of workplace discrimination. This is done for two reasons. First, discrimination is an increasingly important part of employment law. Certainly, discrimination claims comprise a substantial percentage of those employment claims litigated in court. Second, the pre-suit procedures established under the antidiscrimination laws are, relatively speaking, complex. For the average worker, these procedures can be confusing and daunting in their own right. This part is designed to assist the worker in navigating this complex process.

As it turns out, many of the points addressed in Part II are apropos to other areas of employment law. This part, for example, focuses on the kind of evidence that might call into question the credibility of the employer's explanation for an adverse employment decision, thus supporting a claim of discrimination. This discussion is relevant to any legal claim that turns on the validity of the employer's explanation for an adverse employment decision. This part also focuses on the principle of unlawful retaliation. The federal antidiscrimination statutes all contain protections against retaliation, but so do a number of other federal and state laws not addressing discrimination. Much of the discussion of this issue would apply equally to those laws. Finally, this part addresses the litigation of discrimination claims. Again, a number of the points explored in this discussion would apply more generally to litigation of any employment claim.

The goal of Part II is not simply to counsel the employee who has made a decision to pursue a claim of unlawful discrimination. It is to assist the employee in *making the decision* whether to pursue such a claim. A right may exist. That right may have been violated. The employee, however, must still decide whether, all things considered, embarking on a course of potentially divisive and protracted litigation is in the employee's best interest.

CHAPTER 11

Do I Have a Claim?

The story begins this way. Al is a forty-nine-year-old African American. For twenty-five years, he has worked for a company that distributes machine parts. The company is based in the Northeast, with its headquarters in Philadelphia. Al has worked in the Pittsburgh office. He began as a low-level salesman and received a number of promotions and pay raises over the course of his employment. He now works as a district sales manager.

Two years ago, the company initiated a corporate reorganization. As part of that reorganization, a new management team was installed. In particular, a new individual took over the position of regional sales manager, the position directly above Al's in the corporate hierarchy. The new sales manager is a white male, ten years Al's junior. At the time of the reorganization, the company president made public comments about the future of the company. The president stated that it was time for the company to "tighten its belt" and rid itself of the "deadwood." The president stated that the company wanted more aggressive managers, who were "lean and mean" and not "set in their ways." The president stated that those from the "old way" of doing things needed to adapt to the "new methods" or get out.

Since the reorganization, Al has received criticism for his work, for the first time in his career. The regional sales manager has been particularly critical of certain aspects of Al's job performance. He has focused on Al's hands-off management style and his inattention to detail, as evidenced by Al's failure (on occasion) to complete the necessary paperwork on time. The regional sales manager has documented these criticisms, at some length, in Al's semiannual performance evaluations. Nevertheless, he has rated Al as a satisfactory employee (two steps below the highest rating possible). In addition, the sales figures for Al's district have remained high. Indeed, in the last two years, Al has received a substantial bonus for having generated the highest sales figures for any district in his region. He has also received annual increases in pay.

The company is relatively diverse. Al is not the only African American in the Pittsburgh office. Nor is Al the only African American at the company in a management position. On occasion, Al has overheard co-workers making racial comments. In one case, one of the salesmen in Al's office stated that "blacks are lazy" and should "stop complaining." In another case, a fellow district manager used a racial epithet in referring to one of his subordinate employees.

One day Al arrives for work. There is a message on Al's voice mail that the regional manager will be visiting the office and wishes to speak with him. The manager arrives at the office and calls Al into the conference room. After some awkward small talk, the manager informs Al that the company has made a decision to let him go. Stunned, Al asks why. The manager offers two explanations. First, he explains that Al's work has not been up to par, citing the criticisms in the recent performance evaluations. Second, he informs Al that the company, as part of its ongoing reorganization effort, needs to cut back on the number of managers. The manager implies that Al's position is being eliminated as part of a corporate downsizing.

For several days, Al is left reeling. Eventually, Al gathers his wits and begins to think through his situation. Al is aware that he is not the only district manager that the company has let go. In fact, two other district managers have been fired in the past two years. Both managers were in Al's age range, and both were replaced by (or had their job responsibilities assigned to) individuals who appeared, to Al, to be much younger. Both of the other district managers who were let go were white. One of the replacements was African American.

Several weeks later, Al receives a phone call from a friend, who still works for the company. He informs Al that an individual recently arrived in the workplace and began occupying Al's old office. It is not clear that the individual has the title of district manager. He appears, however, to have assumed all of Al's responsibilities. He has told other workers that he has been brought in to supervise sales in the district. This individual is in his 30s and white.

Armed with this information, Al begins to consider the possibility of pursuing a claim against the company. Al strongly believes that he was an effective district manager who performed his job well. He doesn't deny that he had a hands-off management style, but that style had been very effective. After all, his district continued to set the pace for sales. As for his supposed paperwork deficiency, it is true that he did not always complete the necessary paperwork on time. This, however, had been the case for years, and nobody complained (until the new regional sales manager took over). Al knows for a fact that other district managers were no better at this task. In fact, the managers frequently joked among themselves about the amount of pointless paperwork involved in the job. And how about the fact that an individual appears to have assumed Al's job duties, despite the regional manager's claim that he was being let go because the company needed to cut back on the number of managers? Surely this is all suspicious. But is it enough to sustain a legal claim? And if Al has a claim, what exactly is it?

The Employer's Explanation

The starting point for answering these questions is the explanation offered by the employer. As discussed in Chapter 1, there is a well-established framework for resolving claims of employment discrimination. The centerpiece of that framework is the principle of pretext. In litigation, pretext is a part of the three-step standard of proof known as the *McDonnell Douglas* standard. The plaintiff (employee) must establish a prima facie case. The defendant (employer) is required to articulate a legitimate, nondiscriminatory explanation for its decision. The plaintiff can seek to prove discrimination by proving that the explanation proffered by the employer is a pretext (i.e., is not the true reason for the decision). From evidence of pretext, a court (or jury) can infer a discriminatory motive.

Although geared to litigation, the pretext model has relevance in the real world. An employer is not required to provide a contemporaneous explanation for an adverse employment action (although its failure to do so once a case gets to court can prove costly). Most employers, however, do explain to the employee at the time of an adverse action why the action is being taken. This explanation provides the employee with a vital tool for assessing the possible merits of a discrimination claim. The employee, at that point, will not be privy to all of the evidence that might support a claim of discrimination. He or she will, however, be aware of a considerable amount of relevant information, as the above hypothetical example suggests. Based on that information, he or she can put the employer's explanation to the test. Does the explanation seem valid? Or does it suggest that the employer is covering up the real reason for its action, perhaps discrimination?

There are two basic questions that an employee should ask. First, the employee should ask whether the reason provided by the employer is a true one. In other words, is the purported basis for the employment decision accurate, as a factual matter, or is it false? The law does not require an employer to be honest. The mere fact, moreover, that the employer provides a false reason does not mean that the employer has discriminated or even that the employer is lying about its motivation. The employer, for example, may have believed in good faith that the factual underpinning for its decision is true even if, as it turns out, it is not.

Nonetheless, the fact that the explanation provided by the employer is untrue is significant. It suggests that the employer is making up a reason for its decision to cover up something. That something could be discrimination.

The most obvious case of a false explanation occurs when the employer purports to base its decision on some misconduct on the part of the employee. The employer, for example, may state that it discharged the employee because the employee was absent from work. If it turns out that the employee was not absent, there is strong evidence of pretext. A false explanation can also be detected from a general criticism of the employee's performance. An employer, for example, may state that an employee was fired for poor performance. Yet, the contemporaneous evidence may demonstrate that the employee was consistently rated as a superior employee. Such evidence suggests that the employer is concocting the performance rationale to cover up its true reason for the discharge.

The second question that an employee should ask is whether the proffered explanation, even if arguably true, actually motivated the employer. There are several factors to consider. First, the employee should assess whether the explanation for the employment action—say a discharge—is the type of thing that would lead a reasonable employer to discharge an employee. No employee is perfect. An employer can always seize upon some minor performance deficiency to attempt to justify a decision. The question is whether this deficiency in fact prompted the decision. A key factor to consider is the bottom line. The employee may have been deficient in some peripheral aspect of the job, but if the employee was, at bottom, an effective employee, there are reasons to question whether a rational employer, whose chief concern typically is the bottom line, would rid itself of such an employee.

Another factor to consider is whether the employer has been consistent in its explanations for its action. Once a discrimination case ends up in court, this factor can be critical to the employee's case. An employer may have provided one explanation at the time of decision only to shift to some other explanation by the time the employee files suit, thus supporting an argument that the employer is fishing for an explanation in order to cover up the true reason for its action. Obviously, the shifting explanation approach to pretext is not as helpful to the employee at the time of the adverse employment action, at which point there is less time for the employer to have contradicted itself. It is possible, however, that an employer might shift explanations, or contradict itself, even in the context of providing the initial justification for its decision. Indeed, it might be a wise strategy for the employee to ask for an explanation from more than one official or to simply ask the decision maker himself or herself to repeat the explanation. By doing so, the employee may flesh out inconsistencies in the employer's explanation that could support a claim of discrimination.

Finally, the employee should ask whether other individuals in the workplace, similarly situated, have engaged in the same conduct cited by the employer as the basis for the adverse action without the same consequences. Discrimination is all about relative treatment. An employer has no right to fire even the worst performer if it would not have treated an individual of a different race, gender, or age in the same manner. When an employer states that an employee was fired because of some transgression—say absenteeism—and there is evidence that other similarly situated employees have committed the same infraction without suffering the same adverse action, there is reason to question the veracity of the employer's explanation for the action.

As suggested in Chapter 1, comparative evidence of this nature is dicey. Courts (and juries) feel comfortable in imposing liability on an employer when the employer's explanation is shown to be factually false. When, however, it is essentially conceded that the employee has engaged in some questionable conduct, there is a tendency to side with the employer, even if there is evidence that the employer has not consistently sanctioned employees for what might appear to be similar conduct. If there is any factual variation between the circumstances surrounding the incidents being compared (e.g., the decision makers are different, the time frame is not the same, the conduct of the comparator is different in some fashion), the comparative evidence may well fail.

With this as a background, let us return to our friend Al. As you recall, Al was given two reasons for the discharge. First, Al was told that he was being let go because of the performance deficiencies that had been noted in his recent evaluations. Second, Al was told that the company was cutting back on managers and that his position was being eliminated.

Al should first ask whether either of the explanations advanced by the company is true (as a factual matter). In this case, there are certainly reasons to question the probity of the second reason—that Al's job was being eliminated—given the information that Al has received from his friend in the office. It is not clear that an individual has filled Al's position in a formal sense. It appears, however, that an individual has assumed Al's job responsibilities. That would seem to contradict the assertion that Al is being fired as part of an effort to reduce the number of managers. If, in fact, Al's position has not been eliminated, there may be reason to believe that the regional sales manager has concocted an explanation for the discharge, perhaps in an attempt to cover up some discriminatory reason for the discharge.

Al also has reason to question the performance-based explanation tendered by the company. Al was a twenty-five-year employee of the company. Al had been a superior performer for years. While it is true that his recent performance evaluations contained criticisms of his work, Al was still rated as a satisfactory employee, even by his most vigorous critic (the regional sales manager). Al, moreover, continued to be a successful manager, running a productive district and receiving substantial bonuses for his district's high sales. Any blanket claim that Al's performance was inadequate seems hard to square with the contemporaneous record.

On the other hand, there may be some truth to the specific criticisms of Al's work. Al concedes that he had a relaxed management style and that his attention to paperwork could have been better. Because these performance-based deficiencies may be true (and were documented by the company at the time), Al should ask whether there are reasons for questioning if, in fact, these deficiencies were the motivating factor behind the discharge.

There are two things for Al to consider. First, Al worked in sales. The bottom line in sales is, well, the bottom line. Al may have done things that irritated the regional sales manager. But he had the highest sales of any district in the region. Al, moreover, had worked at the company for years. He had always been a hands-off manager and had never been known for his proficiency with paperwork. It seems odd that, at this late date, these concerns would now prompt the company to terminate Al's employment. Even if the performance criticisms are true, there are reasons to question whether these factors would have led the company to terminate a veteran manager who had a proven track record in generating sales.

A second point for Al to assess is whether the company's reliance on these performance-based factors is consistent with its treatment of these factors, as a general matter, in the workplace. Al is not in a position to know precisely how the company has treated other employees who may have had similar performance problems. Al is aware of the fact, however, that he was hardly unique in his inability to keep up with the paperwork. Indeed, the managers joked among themselves about the silliness of the paperwork requirements. A company can fire an employee for any reason, even a trivial one, so long as it is not a discriminatory (or illegal) one. Nonetheless, it seems suspicious that the company would have axed Al for his failure to process paperwork in a timely fashion, a seemingly minor point to begin with, given the evidence that this failure was widespread among the managers and had been tolerated for years by the company.

In sum, Al has a substantial basis for questioning the veracity of the company's explanation for the discharge. At the very least, this should prompt Al to further examine the circumstances surrounding the discharge.

Specific Evidence of Discriminatory Bias

The next question an employee should ask is whether there is more specific evidence of a discriminatory bias on the part of the company or the relevant decision makers. There is rarely smoking gun evidence of discrimination. Employers do not typically say to employees that they're being fired because they're black, or because they're women, or because they're old. Nor do most employers memorialize a discriminatory motivation for an employment action in some written document. Even if such documentary evidence exists, it is unlikely to be available to the aggrieved employee at the time of the employment decision. In making an initial assessment of the possible basis for a discrimination claim, the employee must rely on what he or she has overheard or seen in the workplace.

Smoking gun evidence aside, company managers and decision makers often make statements that are reflective of a discriminatory attitude. These statements may have been uttered in the context of the employment decision at issue. Or, they may have been made in the context of some other employment decision or as part of the general conversation in the workplace. It is not at all unusual for an employee to have been witness to discriminatory statements or remarks by company officials or co-workers. When an employee suffers an adverse employment action, the employee should consider whether there is evidence of the kinds of discriminatory statements that might support a claim of unlawful discrimination.

There are three factors that bear on the probative value of discriminatory statements made by other individuals in the workplace. The first is the identity of the individual making the statement. Obviously, a discriminatory statement is most probative when it is uttered by the individual making the employment decision at issue. If a decision maker has expressed a discriminatory attitude about a particular race or gender, it is reasonable to infer that this attitude may have influenced the decision maker's judgment in the case at hand. The evidence is less probative if the individual making the statement had no role in the decision. This is particularly true if the statement is made by a co-worker, who has no management authority or who is in no position to influence company policy or decision making.

While statements made by non–decision makers are less probative, there are circumstances where a non–decision maker's attitudes can prove significant. Employment decisions are not made in a vacuum. A particular employment decision is often the product of an overall corporate attitude. That attitude, in turn, is set by high-ranking corporate officials, such as company presidents or CEOs. A high-ranking official may not have directly participated in a particular employment decision. If, however, that official has made discriminatory statements—and publicized those statements in a way likely to filter down through the corporate ranks—there is reason to believe that the statements could have an influence on company decision making. To paraphrase a commercial jingle, when the company president speaks, people (managers, in particular) listen.

The second factor to consider is the context and timing of the statement. Statements are most probative when made in the context of the employment decision at issue. Statements are least probative when they have no connection to company decision making and are remote in time from the decision at issue. Often, statements will fall somewhere in between these two extremes. A statement may have been made in the context of an employment decision of some kind, thus suggesting the possibility that the same discriminatory bias affected other employment decisions (such as the decision at issue). Or, the statement may have been made in the context of an overall corporate reorganization or restructuring to which the decision at issue can be fairly linked. The more connected a statement is to employment decision making and to the time frame of the employment decision at issue, the more supportive the statement is of the employee's claim.

Finally, the probative value of a discriminatory statement is affected by how closely related the statement is to a prohibited factor. In the ideal case (for the employee), the connection between the statement and the prohibited factor will be direct (e.g., "I don't like blacks," "We shouldn't hire women"). In some cases, the discriminatory nature of the statement may not be immediately apparent. We live in an increasingly sophisticated world. Many individuals, even those with discriminatory attitudes, are careful not to express those attitudes in clear terms. Instead, these individuals use carefully chosen code words designed to disguise, albeit imperfectly, the underlying discriminatory attitude. If these code words can be fairly identified with an improper bias (against individuals of a particular race, gender, or age), they can be cited in support of a claim of discrimination.

So how does all of this affect our hypothetical case? Al was not told that he was fired for a discriminatory reason. Thus, as in the typical case, there is no smoking gun evidence of discrimination. Al, however, recalls a number of statements or comments in the workplace that might be suggestive of a discriminatory bias.

The first thing Al remembers is statements made by the company president himself. Specifically, the president made comments in the context of a corporate reorganization that began two years before Al's discharge. There is no evidence that the president was directly involved in the decision to discharge Al. On the other hand, the president is in a position to influence the overall direction of the company. His comments in this case were very public and, thus, likely to have fallen on the ears of the company's decision makers. The statements, moreover, were made in the context of a corporate reorganization, with the implication that the company was going to make changes in its personnel to achieve the president's goal of a more "lean and mean" workforce. There is reason to believe that Al's discharge may have been tied to this reorganization, since his chief antagonist, the regional sales manager, was installed as part of the reorganization initiative. While the president's statements were made two years prior to Al's discharge, the statements strongly hint at an ongoing effort to achieve a significant change in the makeup of the workforce. Finally, the president's remarks are suggestive of an age bias. The president did not state explicitly that the company wanted to rid itself of its older workers. The president, however, used the kinds of code words that can be reasonably linked to an age bias (e.g., that the company needed to get rid of the workers who were "set in their ways" and unable to adapt to the new methods). From all of this, Al could reasonably infer that his discharge may have been the product of a reorganization initiative, which was motivated by a desire to purge the workforce of older managers such as Al.

The second category of statements that Al recalls has to do with race. Al is an African American. Al recalls overhearing racist statements made by co-workers. The statements are obviously offensive and clearly tied to race. The statements, however, were not made in the context of employment decision making. The statements, in fact, were not made by any individual involved in the decision to discharge Al or by any individual who was in a position to influence corporate policy. If the racist remarks were pervasive, the remarks could be cited as evidence of a corporate culture of racism, which, in turn, could support a claim that Al fell victim to that culture when he was terminated. Al, however, can recall but a few isolated instances of inappropriate racial verbiage in a career that spanned twenty-five years. Standing alone, the comments of the co-workers do not provide strong evidence of any racial bias in the company's decision to discharge Al.

The Relevant Context

Al has now considered the specific explanations for the discharge. He believes that these explanations do not ring true. He has also considered the specific evidence of discriminatory bias in the workplace, some of which is at least suggestive of an age bias. The final task is to place this evidence (or information) in the relevant context.

Context should be examined from two perspectives. First, an employee should take a careful look at the context of the particular employment decision at issue. Several questions come to mind. Who is the individual who made the adverse decision?

What is the race or gender of that individual? How old is the individual? If the case involves a discharge, how long had the employee worked at the company? If the employee is a recent hire, it may be harder to draw an inference of discrimination, at least where the company official who makes the decision to terminate the employee is the same official who hired the employee just a short time ago. On the other hand, the mere fact that the company once hired an employee (who is a racial minority or a woman) hardly immunizes the company from a claim of unlawful discrimination in the discharge of that employee. Things can often change at a company in the intervening period between the initial decision to hire and a discharge. The individual making the decision to hire may be free of any discriminatory bias. A different individual, one who harbors discriminatory attitudes, may be responsible for the discharge decision. In the case of a veteran employee, one change is obvious—the employee himself or herself has grown older. The company may have been thrilled to hire the employee when he or she was young. Now that the employee has aged, the employer may be looking for another younger employee to take the older worker's place. By simply growing older, the employee may have gone from the favored status of a younger applicant to the disfavored status of an older employee for whom the company is seeking a replacement.

A critical piece of context to consider is the identity of the individual who ends up with the job at issue. In a refusal-to-hire case, this is the individual who is actually hired for the job. In a discharge case, this is the individual who replaces the employee who has been terminated. Obviously, the case for discrimination is stronger when the individual getting the job is of a different race or gender or is much younger, as the case may be. Indeed, as discussed in Chapter 1, once a case ends up in court, the law adopts an analytical framework that requires the employee to make out a prima facie case of discrimination. For discharge cases, some courts require a showing that the replacement be of a different race or gender than the claimant to make out a standard prima facie case, although there are other ways to prove the claim. For age cases, the individual would have to be substantially younger. Even if there is no such legal requirement, the persuasiveness of the claim is buttressed by evidence that the employer has favored the hiring of an individual who is of a different race or gender or who is much younger than the claimant.

Having considered the context of the specific decision at issue, the employee should next consider the broader context of the workplace as a whole. It is possible for an employment decision to be an entirely isolated event. More often, there is some connection between employment decisions made in the same workplace. In the strongest case, an employer will have a single apparatus for employment decision making. Decisions made during the same general time frame as part of that decisional structure are likely to be affected by the same discriminatory taint. Even where there is no single decisional structure, the same decision maker may be involved in one or more employment decisions. Or, there may be evidence of an overall corporate policy of decision making, as reflected in a number of individual employment decisions. In any event, so long as there is some plausible connection between the decision at hand and other employment decisions, those decisions can be a highly relevant source of contextual evidence. If the decisions suggest a discriminatory bias against members of a protected group, they can provide strong support for a claim of discrimination.

To be sure, an employee may not be aware of other decisions made in the workplace, at least to the degree necessary to draw any significant conclusions of possible discriminatory bias in those decisions. Typically, however, the employee will have a general sense of the company's bottom line. Some employers are known for their efforts to diversify their workforce. Others may have the opposite reputation. When an employee suffers an adverse employment action, the employee should look around. How many minorities or women work for the company? How many are in positions of authority? Is this the kind of place where minorities or women are welcome? Or is the kind of place largely dominated by a decision-making hierarchy of white males?

It should be stressed that context is nothing more than that—context. The fact that a company is stocked with minority managers does not rule out the possibility that, in a particular case, the company has discriminated against a member of a minority group. The fact that a female worker is fired and replaced by another woman does not preclude the possibility that a sexual bias of some kind, perhaps involving a sexual stereotype, has infected the discharge decision. By the same token, the fact that a company has a low number of minority or female employees or managers does not mean, by necessity, that the company has engaged in unlawful discrimination. There is no bottom-line defense to a claim of employment discrimination (e.g., "You can't sue me because I've hired a lot of minorities"), but nor is there any per se rule of liability based on a low number of minority or female employees. Context can be vital in informing the other evidence bearing upon a possible claim of discrimination. It does not, however, standing alone, dictate the existence or nonexistence of discrimination in a particular case.

In this case, there is a good deal of context for Al to chew on. Al is a veteran employee, age 49. It is obvious that the regional sales manager played a critical role in Al's discharge. The regional sales manager is much younger than Al. This is significant because a younger manager sometimes has difficulty supervising an older worker, who may be more experienced and more knowledgeable than his or her superior. It is also noteworthy that the regional sales manager was installed as part of a reorganization effort that may well have been tainted by an age bias. The younger sales manager is also white, which may be relevant to a claim of race discrimination.

A more critical piece of context for Al is the identity of the individual who appears to have assumed Al's job responsibilities. Al does not know the precise age of this individual. According to Al's friend, however, the individual appears to be in his 30s. If true, this could be critical to Al's ability to prove a claim of age discrimination. If nothing else, it would help Al establish a prima facie case of discrimination. The individual assuming Al's job responsibilities is also white, which could lend support to a claim of race discrimination.

The broader context sheds further light on Al's potential claims. Al does not have knowledge of every employment decision that has been made by the company in recent years. Al, however, does know that two other district managers have been let go by the company in the past two years. In each case, the manager (who was roughly Al's age) was replaced by a much younger individual. These employment decisions do not necessarily relate to Al's discharge. The decisions, however, could be seen as part of the company's reorganization initiative. In announcing that initiative, the company president made public comments that are highly suggestive of an intention to purge the company of its older workers. The fact that the company has since cashiered three veteran managers (including Al) and replaced them with younger individuals would seem to confirm that the president's message has gotten through to other managers (such as the regional sales manager, who was installed as part of the reorganization). Taking all of the evidence together, there are solid reasons to believe that Al may have fallen victim to an age-based employment decision.

The broader context is not so helpful to a claim of race discrimination (the other claim that could be on Al's mind). The individual who assumed Al's job responsibilities is white. However, the two other district managers who were let go were white. One was replaced by an African American. This does not rule out the possibility that Al's discharge was racially motivated, but it does suggest that Al was not terminated as part of some overall effort to reduce the number of black managers working at the company. Al also knows that the company is relatively diverse. There are other black managers working at the company, and Al himself has consistently received promotions and pay increases over a twenty-five–year career. Again, this does not preclude the possibility of racial bias in the discharge, since the regional sales manager, who is relatively new to his position, may hold his own discriminatory biases. It does suggest, however, that if Al has been the victim of race discrimination, the discrimination does not stem from some general corporate bias against minority employees.

Putting It All Together

We can now answer the question posed in the title to this chapter. In Al's case, we start with the fact that Al was a veteran employee of the company. Al had a successful track record at the company and was continuing to generate high sales within his district. The reasons provided for Al's discharge are questionable. One—that Al's job was being eliminated—does not appear to be true. The other—that Al suffered from performance-based deficiencies—also has a false ring. Certainly, there are reasons to question whether the relatively trivial criticisms identified by the regional sales manager would have prompted a rational employer to fire a twenty-five-year employee who had just received performance bonuses for his outstanding work in producing a high volume of sales. Al has reason to believe that the explanations offered by the company are a pretext.

If there are reasons to doubt the veracity of the explanations provided for Al's discharge, the question is why the false explanations? The other information gathered by Al—largely contextual—points to one possible answer. Al was terminated two years after the company initiated a corporate reorganization. At the time, the company president made comments that were highly suggestive of a corporate campaign to rid the company of its older workers. Al's nemesis, the much younger regional sales manager, was installed as part of the reorganization. The criticisms of Al's performance began at that point. Al is aware that two other similarly situated district managers were fired in recent months. Al knows that each of these individuals was replaced by a much younger individual. More critically, Al himself appears to have had his job responsibilities assigned to a much younger individual. All of this suggests that Al may have been the victim of an age-based decision.

Does this mean that Al has a lock solid case? Not at all. Al's case is entirely circumstantial. Al has solid evidence of age bias, but there is nothing that directly ties that bias to Al's discharge. Al has a good pretext case, but it is far from perfect. Indeed, it will undoubtedly hurt Al's case that the regional sales manager documented criticisms of Al's performance in written evaluations. This means that one of the classic forms of pretext evidence—that the performance criticisms cited as the basis for an employment action are undocumented—will not be available. Still, at this point, Al is looking only at possibilities. He is not asking whether he can necessarily prove a claim of age discrimination. He is asking whether there is a basis for a claim. The answer is yes.

What about Al's possible claim of race discrimination? Al is an African American. Given the history of race discrimination in this country, a minority employee has at least some reason to suspect that race may be involved in a discharge when the explanation offered by the employer appears dubious. Here, Al has grounds for questioning the company's explanations for the discharge. There are some contextual factors, moreover, that might support a race claim. The individual who assumed Al's job responsibilities is white. The key decision maker, and Al's principal antagonist (the regional sales manager), is also white.

Still, there are factors that should give Al pause. Al worked at the company for twenty-five years. During that period, he witnessed only a handful of isolated racial incidents. Al himself was a prized employee, and the company, in general, was relatively diverse, even at the management level. Indeed, an African American replaced one of the white district managers who was terminated in the aftermath of the reorganization initiative. If Al was the victim of race discrimination, it does not appear that the discrimination stemmed from any general bias against minority employees.

Ultimately, the case might turn on the mind-set of the regional sales manager, the pivotal figure in Al's termination. Did this individual harbor his own racially discriminatory attitudes? Did he express those attitudes to other officials? Did he participate in other decisions that might be suggestive, in one way or another, of his racial attitudes? (For example, was the regional sales manager involved in the decision to hire the African American replacement? Or did some other official participate in that decision?) At this point, Al does not know the answers to these questions. Al, however, might uncover additional evidence of this nature if he were to pursue a legal claim. The race claim is plausible, if not as compelling as the age claim.

Are there other claims that Al might assert? In theory, yes. Al is protected from discrimination on the basis of sex. There is nothing to suggest, however, that this factor or any other (besides age or race) was behind the decision to discharge Al. As we shall see, the first step of the legal process, in this area, is to file a charge of discrimination with a federal or state agency. At that point, the employee is not legally required to produce any evidence in support of his or her claim. It is the agency's job to investigate the charge. Nonetheless, there are risks involved with even the simple act of filing a charge. Before an employee takes such a step, the employee should have at least some basis for believing that discrimination may have occurred. If Al is going to pursue a a formal claim, he should do so on the basis of age (his strongest claim) or race.

CHAPTER 12

Should I Pursue a Claim?

W hen an employee suffers an adverse employment action, it makes sense for the employee to first ask whether there is a possible claim of discrimination. If the employee concludes that there is no credible claim, the inquiry ends and the employee moves on. If, however, an employee has reason to believe that discrimination may have occurred, the employee should inquire further. O.K., I have a possible claim. But do I want to pursue that claim? What are the possible downsides? What are the risks (if any) to my future employment prospects? Is it better for me, in the long run, to maintain an amicable relationship with the employer?

To a degree, these questions have a legal component. The law recognizes the dilemma faced by the employee. If the employee decides to pursue a legal claim, the employee risks retaliation by his or her employer (or former employer). If the employee chooses to forgo a claim, due to the threat of retaliation, the employee forfeits his or her statutory right to be free from unlawful discrimination. To ensure that the employee is not coerced to relinquish statutory rights, the law contains significant protection against retaliation. It is important for an employee, contemplating the filing of a legal claim, to know precisely what that protection is.

Knowing the legal protection against retaliation, while important, is not enough. It may be unlawful for an employer to take action against an individual who has engaged in some protected activity (e.g., filing a charge of discrimination). Many employers, nonetheless, will take such action. An employee cannot be naïve. Whatever the legal protection, asserting a claim of discrimination carries with it some risk. There are also real-world consequences to pursuing a claim of discrimination. When an employee asserts a claim against an employer (or former employer), word tends to get around. This is particularly true if the employee works in a specialized industry, where individuals move from job to job on the strength of reputation. A prospective employer may be unwilling to hire an individual who is viewed as a troublemaker (i.e., an individual who is likely to complain of discrimination when subjected to an adverse employment action). That unwillingness is unlikely to support any legal claim of retaliation (or discrimination), meaning that the employee could lose out on an employment opportunity without any legal recourse.

More generally, an employee must consider the ramifications of embarking upon a legal challenge to an employment action. To assert a legal claim is to invite acrimony. When an employee cries discrimination, an employer is likely to bite back. Typically, the employer will attack the employee's performance on the job; it might even point to supposed misconduct by the employee or raise questions about the employee's integrity or ethics. The result of this battle can be both distasteful and harmful to the employee. There is an alternative that an employee must at least consider. An employer will often discharge an employee with a wink of an eye. The employer will signal that it might be willing to give the employee a favorable reference if the employee is willing to go along. In other words, the employer will be willing to say to prospective employers that the employee was fired for reasons unrelated to any performance-based deficiencies. An employee must consider whether, in the long run, his or her employment (and life) prospects are better served by playing the employer's game.

In this chapter, I address these legal and real-world considerations. Where appropriate, I return to our hypothetical employee, Al. Al has some potentially viable claims of discrimination. But should Al pursue those claims? What are Al's legal protections? What are the real-world risks to Al if he does pursue the claims? What does Al gain, if anything, by backing away from the claims? Will Al be better off, in the long run, by asserting his claims or by letting the claims go and moving on with his life?

Retaliation: The Legal Protection

Federal statutes make it unlawful for an employer to discriminate on the basis of certain prohibited factors. These statutes also provide for a system of enforcement, based largely on the complaints of individual employees. Specifically, employees are permitted to file administrative charges with the U.S. Equal Employment Opportunity Commission (or the relevant state agency). Based on those charges, the Commission investigates the claim of discrimination. If discrimination is uncovered, the Commission seeks to resolve the matter voluntarily, through a conciliation agreement. If attempts at conciliation fail, the Commission either brings suit in its own right or authorizes the individual filing the charge to bring his or her own suit. Ultimately, the issue of the lawfulness of the employer's conduct is resolved in court. If the employer is found to have violated the statute, the employer can be required to pay damages to the aggrieved employee. The court, moreover, may issue an injunction against the employer, thus deterring the employer from engaging in discrimination of the same kind in the future.

It is self-evident that for the antidiscrimination statutes to be effective, individual employees must feel free to come forward and lodge complaints of discrimination. Most employers do not savor the prospect of being called to answer for their employment decisions. Employers would love nothing more than to eliminate the filing of charges or claims of discrimination. One way for an employer to achieve this goal is to retaliate with impunity against those employees who complain of discrimination. If an employer could fire any employee who filed a charge of discrimination, the impact on the enforcement of the antidiscrimination statutes could be devastating. Few employees (if any) would be willing to complain of discrimination, leaving the employer free to discriminate against its employees with little risk of legal liability.

To protect against rampant retaliation of this kind, most employment statutes contain antiretaliation provisions. Essentially, these provisions make it unlawful for an employer to discriminate against an individual because that individual has engaged in some protected activity under the statute. Protected activity falls into two categories. First, protected activity can involve participation in legal proceedings initiated under the statute. This could include the filing of an administrative charge or a lawsuit alleging unlawful discrimination or testifying as a witness in an administrative or judicial proceeding. Second, protected activity can involve opposition to an unlawful employment practice. Some employees are reluctant to initiate formal proceedings against an employer. They may, however, want to oppose an employment practice that they believe to be unlawful. Even if they do not initiate legal proceedings, their opposition to that practice, in the workplace, is a protected activity.

Opposition activity can take many forms. Typically, it involves complaining to the employer (or one of its agents) about what the employee perceives as discriminatory conduct. For the complaint to constitute protected opposition activity, it must typically be framed in terms of discrimination (i.e., be a complaint about discrimination, not about some general mistreatment that is not rooted in discrimination). Opposition activity can also involve a threat to file a charge of discrimination or a refusal to obey an order that is itself discriminatory (e.g., fire an employee because he is black). There are limits on the manner in which opposition activity may be carried out. An employee is permitted within reason to agitate against unlawful discrimination. An employee, however, cannot engage in activity that is unduly disruptive of an employer's operations. Certainly, an employee cannot engage in conduct that is illegal even if the conduct might further the employee's opposition to the employer's unlawful discrimination.

Significantly, an employee is protected against unlawful retaliation even if, as it turns out, there is no underlying discrimination. With respect to participation in legal proceedings, the protection is absolute. If an employee files a charge of discrimination, the employee is protected from retaliation even if there is no basis at all to the claim of discrimination set forth in the charge. With respect to opposition activity, the law is not quite so generous. The employee, in such a case, need not prove that the practice being opposed was in fact unlawful. The employee, however, must have had a reasonable and good faith belief that the practice was unlawful. For the most part, courts have tended to side with the employee in assessing whether the employee had such a belief. Only where it is clear that the practice being opposed could not be an act of unlawful discrimination have courts declined to extend the protection of the antiretaliation provisions to the individual expressing opposition to the practice.

The scope of protection under the antiretaliation provisions is broad. Obviously, these provisions extend to any employee or applicant for employment who engages in a protected activity. The provisions also extend to a former employee, including an individual who has been discharged by an employer and who files a charge challenging the discharge as discriminatory. A former employee is in a unique position. On the one hand, the employee has suffered the ultimate employment action. There is nothing more that the employer can do, in the workplace setting, to injure the employee. The employee, however, may still need the assistance of the employer. The employee, for example, is likely to be applying for a new job. The employee may want to procure a positive job reference from his or her former employer. If the employee files a charge of discrimination challenging the discharge, the employee runs the risk that the former employer will retaliate by providing a negative job reference, thus costing the employee a possible employment opportunity.

From the employee's perspective, the problem with the anti-retaliation provisions is that the provisions may not reach all adverse or hostile actions taken by an employer. Historically, courts took an expansive view of the types of employment actions that could give rise to a claim of unlawful retaliation. In keeping with the purposes of the antiretaliation provisions, courts recognized that an employer should be prohibited from engaging in any action that might deter protected activity. This could include threats, reprimands, harassment, or any other adverse treatment.

More recently, courts have begun to ratchet down on the protections of the antiretaliation provisions. Some courts, for example, have taken the view that these provisions apply only to ultimate employment actions. Under this view, an employer would be prohibited from discharging or demoting an employee. It would not be prohibited, however, from engaging in conduct that, while threatening to an employee, does not result in some final employment decision. Thus, an employer could provide a negative employment evaluation to an employee, in retaliation for the employee's activity, without running afoul of the law. Or, an employer could threaten to discharge the employee if the employee files a charge of discrimination. A shrewd employer could engage in conduct that falls just short of an ultimate employment action but which, nonetheless, is sufficiently threatening to deter employees from exercising protected rights.

Some courts have also suggested that retaliatory actions, to be unlawful, must be employment-related. In other words, the action taken must have some nexus to the employment relationship itself. The implications of this approach are severe. Over the years, employers have engaged in a wide variety of retaliatory actions. These have included: filing criminal charges against the employee; filing a lawsuit against the employee; canceling a symposium honoring the employee; withdrawing a workers' compensation settlement offer; securing a subpoena for the employee's telephone records; referring to allegations of criminal conduct concerning the employee; and engaging in acts of violence against the employee. If the antiretaliation provisions are strictly limited to employment-related actions (e.g., demotions, discharges, or suspensions), actions of this nature could be carried out lawfully. The result could be a serious chill in the willingness of individuals to come forward and complain about discrimination.

It is not clear how far the retrenchment in retaliation protection will go. Some courts have continued to adhere to the liberal view of the antiretaliation provisions. Even those courts that have taken a more restrictive approach—limiting the provisions to actions that are employment-related—tend to apply that standard with some flexibility. Almost all courts, for example, have recognized that it is unlawful for an employer to provide a negative job reference to a former employee's prospective employer in retaliation for that employee's protected activity. This is true because the negative reference, while not affecting the individual's present terms or conditions of employment, does pose a threat to the individual's prospective employment. One could apply this same logic to other retaliatory actions, (e.g., the filing of criminal charges), since those actions could easily tarnish an individual's reputation, thus impairing his or her ability to obtain employment. It should also be remembered that the federal antiretaliation provisions are just one source of legal protection for an employee. If an employer engages in particularly egregious conduct by, for example, threatening physical violence against an employee, that conduct might give rise to legal liability, even if it falls outside the scope of the antiretaliation provisions.

All of these factors should weigh heavily on Al. Al has yet to engage in any protected activity. Al, however, might be inclined to file a charge of discrimination. If he were to file such a charge, Al would be legally protected against retaliation. Al might also be inclined to engage in opposition activity of some kind. Al, for example, could complain to company officials about his discharge. It is possible, in fact, that the company maintains a grievance procedure that Al could invoke. Al might even want to make his case public by contacting a media outlet and telling his story. Al is entitled to engage in such conduct, within reason, but he must be careful. It is tempting for an employee, embittered by an unfair employment decision, to cross the line from legitimate opposition activity to unprotected and potentially illegal conduct. One recurring scenario has been an employee who removes confidential documents or surreptitiously tapes phone conversations in an attempt to buttress his or her case of discrimination. These actions are not likely to be protected and may well lead to criminal charges or a civil lawsuit by the employer.

As a former employee, Al is covered under the antiretaliation provisions. The problem for Al is to determine precisely what conduct by his former employer would be considered unlawful. The most obvious way that the company can injure Al, at this point, is by harming his future job prospects. As noted previously, providing a negative job reference, if done in retaliation for an employee having engaged in protected activity, is unlawful. (The refusal to provide a job reference can also be an act of unlawful retaliation if there is evidence that the employer would have provided a reference if not for the protected activity.) There are other ways, however, that Al's former employer could retaliate, particularly if Al has any skeletons in his closet. The company, for example, could file a suit against Al, claiming that he has done something in the course of his employment that is improper. The company could "dig up the dirt" on Al and threaten to take some action against him. Since it is not clear that these actions fall within the scope of the antiretaliation provisions, Al is at some legal risk of suffering the brunt of the employer's wrath.

It is also fair to say, however, that most employers are not inclined to resort to such extreme tactics unless the employee has done something, beyond the filing of a charge, to provoke the employer's anger. For a current employee, the threat of retaliation is immediate—the employee is still in the workplace and could well feel the heat from company managers. For the former employee, the threat is more oblique, although still real. The former employee's main concern is that the employer not do anything that will jeopardize the employee's ability to secure another job. For the most part, Al knows that if he engages in protected activity, he will be legally protected against the most common form of retaliatory conduct visited upon a former employee.

Retaliation in the Real World

It is important for an employee to understand the legal protections of the antiretaliation provisions. But that is only half of the story. It is one thing to say that a legal right exists. It is another to say that the right, in fact, provides meaningful protection to the employee. An employee must look beyond the law as written to assess the application of the antiretaliation provisions in the real world.

The first thing to understand about retaliation is that it occurs quite often. The law prohibits employers from taking reprisals against individuals who exercise their protected rights. Employers, however, sometimes ignore the law. Retaliation is commonplace in American workplaces and goes on despite the clear prohibitions against it. An employee who is considering the possibility of lodging a complaint of discrimination must not be naïve. The law may make it illegal for an employer to retaliate, but the law cannot prevent the employer, if it so desires, from getting its pound of flesh.

It is true, of course, that if the employer engages in unlawful retaliation, the employee has a right of action against the employer. The employee, in other words, can sue for damages caused by the retaliation. As noted above, this is true even if, as it turns out, there is no merit to the underlying claim of discrimination. Often, an employer will take an adverse action against an employee that is not discriminatory. The employer, however, steamed by an employee's complaint, will retaliate. Although innocent of the underlying charge of discrimination, the employer exposes itself to legal liability by engaging in an act of reprisal.

The problem for the employee is that a claim of unlawful retaliation must be proved. The employee, in other words, must be able to establish a causal link between the protected activity and the adverse action. This is not always easy to do. In most retaliation cases, a critical evidentiary factor is the proximity in time between the protected activity and the allegedly retaliatory act. If an employee has worked for a company for years and is discharged one day after she files a charge of discrimination (alleging discrimination in a denial of promotion), there are substantial grounds to believe that the discharge was retaliatory (i.e., was caused by the employee's protected activity). Many employers, however, are savvy enough to avoid such a snap decision. These employers will bide their time, slowly building a case against the complaining employee. Eventually, perhaps months after the filing of the charge, the employer will take action, discharging or demoting the employee.

Unfortunately, some courts have unwittingly provided employers with the legal cover to engage in such a retaliatory campaign. These courts have suggested that there is a point at which the gap in time between the protected activity and the retaliatory act is too great to sustain a claim of unlawful retaliation. The temporal gap has been set at as little as four months, meaning that no inference of retaliation can be drawn if the adverse action takes place more than four months after the protected activity. Absent smoking gun evidence of retaliation, the employee, in such a case, would not be able to prevail on any claim of unlawful retaliation.

For the former employee, the issue is complicated by the fact that the employee's claim turns, in many cases, on the transmission of information from one employer to another. As noted above, it is unlawful for an employer to provide a negative job reference for a retaliatory reason. It might also be unlawful for an employer to inform a prospective employer about a former employee's protected activity, since this may brand the employee a troublemaker. The problem is that there are hidden ways in which information about a former employee's protected activities can be passed among prospective employers and their decision-making agents. In many cases, it will be impossible for the employee to prove that the former employer has disclosed the employee's protected activity to a prospective employer. In some cases, in fact, the information will have been acquired by the prospective employer without any specific input from the former employer, meaning that the employee will have no claim against the former employer. While it is unlawful for a prospective employer to reject a job applicant because of the applicant's prior protected activity, proving that such an employer has done so is a very difficult task. The employee must prove that the prospective employer knew about the protected activity and that it was in fact the protected activity that led to the employer not hiring the employee.

The situation for the former employee is most perilous where the employee works in an insular or specialized business or industry. In that context, employees are often hired by word of mouth, largely on the strength of reputation. It is likely that the managers of one company in a specialized field are going to be aware of the protected activity of a former employee of another company in the same field, particularly if that activity mushrooms into a lawsuit. What's worse, the employee may have experience and skills that are uniquely tied to his or her specialized field or industry, such that the employee's job prospects, outside of that narrow field, are limited. An employee in this situation faces the very real prospect of being effectively blackballed from meaningful employment if the employers in that field have an aversion to hiring an individual who complains about discriminatory treatment.

This connects quite directly to the situation confronting Al. Al knows that if he engages in protected activity of some kind, he is covered by the antiretaliation provisions. Al also knows that he is legally protected if his former employer sabotages his efforts at obtaining another job by providing a negative job reference (for a retaliatory reason) or trash-talking about Al's protected activity. Al, however, cannot ignore the realities of his situation. Al works as a salesman. This is the type of business where word spreads quickly among those in the field. No matter how discreet Al tries to be, it is very possible that word of Al's protected activity will spread to other companies and their decision makers. Even if Al's former employer provides a negative job reference to a prospective employer, Al still must prove that the employer did so for a retaliatory reason. Al may have difficulty doing so, since the employer will undoubtedly claim that it merely told the truth—that Al's performance was deficient and that he was discharged for his poor performance. Al can prevail on a retaliation claim only if he can show that the employer would not have provided the negative reference in the absence of the protected activity. Would Al be able to make such a showing? Would Al be effectively foreclosed from employment in his chosen field if word spread that Al is charging his former employer with unlawful discrimination?

There is no way to answer these questions with any certainty. The important thing is that Al be aware of the risks. For a number of reasons, Al may want to throw caution to the wind and pursue his claims. Al may feel strongly that he has been treated unfairly. He may feel an obligation to other employees (and to the law) to carry the banner against his former employer, which may be on a campaign to purge the workforce of older employees. Certainly, Al has reason to believe that he could prevail on at least one of his possible claims. These are valid, perhaps compelling, reasons for Al to proceed. Al must realize, however, that he exposes himself to some risk of reprisal. This is true despite the legal protections that exist against unlawful retaliation.

Other Considerations

In deciding whether to pursue a claim of discrimination, an employee has much to consider. An employee should assess the merits of any claim that he or she might assert. The employee should also bear in mind the legal and real-world risks of retaliation by the employer. The employee's calculus, however, should not end there. The decision to pursue a claim of discrimination is a momentous one. The employee's initial reaction to an adverse employment action may be anger. The employee may feel strongly that an injustice has been done and may want to punish the employer for its wrongful conduct. This emotional urge, understandable as it may be, needs to be tempered by a reasoned assessment of all of the factors that bear upon the decision to pursue a claim. If the employee is going to go to the mat with the employer, the employee should do so with his or her eyes open.

A critical feature of the federal antidiscrimination statutes is the unique pre-suit procedures that govern the assertion of discrimination claims. In most areas of the law, the first step taken by a claimant is the filing of a lawsuit. To file a suit, a claimant must have at least some factual basis for asserting a claim or else the claimant can be sanctioned for initiating a frivolous suit. Once a lawsuit is filed, the claimant is subject to the normal rules of discovery, meaning that the individual can be deposed (under oath) and required to produce documents relevant to the case. In short, the claimant must hit the ground running, knowing that he or she will have to produce evidence to support the claim and that the other side is likely to hit hard in its attempt to discredit the claimant's case.

The federal antidiscrimination statutes take a different tack. As discussed more thoroughly in Chapter 13, these statutes establish an elaborate pre-suit mechanism. Under these pre-suit procedures, an individual is required to file a charge of discrimination as a precondition to bringing suit in court. That charge must be filed with the U.S. Equal Employment Opportunity Commission, assuming the individual wants to pursue a federal claim. (The federal charge must be cross-filed with the relevant state agency, a point discussed in Chapter 13.) It is the Commission's responsibility to investigate the charge and decide whether there is reasonable cause to believe that discrimination has occurred. If the Commission finds cause, it tries to conciliate the dispute. If that fails, the Commission brings suit in its own right or issues a right-to-sue letter to the individual, which entitles the individual to bring a lawsuit in court.

In theory, the pre-suit procedures are user-friendly. They provide an employee with an opportunity to allege employment discrimination without the substantial costs and risks of a full-fledged suit. The Commission, not the employee, develops a factual record. The Commission, not the employee, seeks to resolve the dispute. Only after these pre-suit procedures are exhausted is the employee confronted with the decision to pursue a claim in court. In short, the employee is given an opportunity to test the waters before stepping into the adversarial system.

There are two problems with this rosy scenario. The Commission is an overburdened agency. The Commission has a huge inventory of charges with limited resources to resolve those charges. The likelihood that the Commission will promptly investigate a charge and resolve the matter to the satisfaction of the employee is not great. For many claimants, the Commission is nothing but a necessary stopping point on the way to court.

Second, even where the Commission plays its assigned role and thoroughly investigates a charge, there is a risk to the individual filing a charge. Once a charge is filed with the Commission, the Commission takes over. The Commission investigates the charge. The Commission attempts to conciliate the charge. If conciliation fails, the Commission, if it so chooses, brings suit in court. The Commission can do all of this without the formal consent of the employee because federal law provides the Commission with independent enforcement theory. An employee who has second thoughts about pursuing a claim might refuse to cooperate with the Commission or even seek to withdraw his or her charge. If, however, the Commission is determined to pursue a claim, it can do so without the assistance of the employee. By the simple act of filing a charge, the employee may end up the pawn in a hotly contested dispute between the Commission and the employer, one that could lead to protracted litigation.

The antidiscrimination statutes are designed to make it easy for an employee to raise questions about the validity of an employment decision. It is easy, however, to be seduced into thinking that the filing of a charge is an act without consequences. By filing a charge, the employee starts the ball rolling. Once the process is under way, it may be difficult to stop. An employee should not approach the filing of a charge with the same trepidation that he or she might approach the filing of a lawsuit. The employee, however, should not treat the step of filing a charge lightly.

The employee should also consider the likely reaction of the employer once it is formally charged with discrimination. As noted earlier, there is always some risk that an employer will retaliate against an individual who asserts a claim of unlawful discrimination. Even if no retaliation occurs, one thing is almost certain—the employer will attempt, quite vigorously, to justify its employment action. To do that, it must, by necessity, attack the employee. Discrimination claims are resolved under a framework that forces the employer's hand, once the employee makes the minimal showing necessary to establish a prima facie case. Specifically, the employer must articulate a legitimate nondiscriminatory explanation for its decision. If the employer offers no explanation for the decision, it loses. If the employer offers a flimsy one, it risks having the explanation declared a pretext for discrimination. This legal framework creates an incentive for an employer to offer some explanation for its adverse action, one that can be defended against claims of pretext and fabrication.

In keeping with this framework, an employer will begin building a case against the employee from the moment a charge is filed (if not before). Theoretically, the employer does not have to be overly critical of the employee's job performance. The employer, for example, could say that the employee did his job well but, ultimately, was not as productive as he could be. In the real world, this rarely occurs. For whatever reason, employers feel compelled to trash the employee's work record. Many employers will adopt a "scorched earth" approach, attempting to dig up the dirt (if any) on the employee. Others, at the very least, will hone in on the employee's weaknesses. Even the best employee has had his or her bad moments. The employer will uncover those moments, if possible, and exploit them in an attempt to discredit the employee's case. The employee must be prepared to have his or her work record sullied and, in some cases, his or her reputation tarnished.

The employee must also be prepared for what may be an emotionally wrenching experience. In the ideal case, the employee will file a charge of discrimination and the matter will be resolved consensually. If, however, the case proceeds to court, the employee may be headed for a bumpy ride. The employer is likely to bring all guns to bear. If unwilling to settle, the employer will do everything it can to discredit the employee. It may take years for the case to go to trial and years more for any appeals to be resolved. Many individuals, drawn into such a milieu, become obsessed with the case. Many individuals leave the process with nothing to show for it but the emotional scars of a hostile confrontation. Before embarking upon such a journey, an individual should take stock of himself or herself and the situation. How important is this to me? Am I prepared to go to the mat to vindicate my rights? Is it better for me to let it go and get on with my life?

Finally, the employee must consider the lost opportunity costs of pursuing a claim of discrimination. This is particularly an issue for an employee who has been discharged. As discussed earlier, when an employee is fired, there is often a carefully choreographed minuet between the employer and the employee. The employer will want the decision to appear justified. The employer, however, may want to extend an olive branch to the employee as a way to head off a possible lawsuit. Thus, the employer will offer muted criticisms of the employee's performance, while hinting that it would be willing to put in a good word for the employee with a prospective employer. The implication is obvious: If you play along, we'll help you out; if you don't, we won't. The employee must carefully assess such a quid pro quo before choosing to charge the employer with an unlawful act.

An example from my own experience illustrates the point. I knew a man who worked as a director of human resources for a medium-sized company. The individual had worked for the company for years. At age 49, he was abruptly fired. The explanation seemed fishy, and a younger man, whom the 49-year-old had trained, moved into his position. The situation had the makings of a strong claim of age discrimination. The dilemma for the older individual was this. He knew that if he pursued a claim, word would get around. He knew that in his field, human resources, complaining of discrimination would tarnish his reputation, making it difficult for him to obtain another job in that field. He also sensed, given the nature of the company, that if he charged discrimination, the company would contest the matter vigorously.

In this case, the individual chose not to pursue a claim. He sought, instead, to focus on securing another job. While he had a tough go initially, he eventually ended up with a far better job than what he had, retiring a wealthy man. Meanwhile, the company that fired him went under. Even if the individual had prevailed on his claim—after what might have been a lengthy struggle—he would have ended up with nothing. For this individual, the decision not to pursue a claim was clearly the correct one.

Does this mean that an employee should never pursue a claim of discrimination? Of course not. Thousands of employees file charges of discrimination each year. Many of these individuals have their complaints resolved to their satisfaction. Indeed, the perception among employers is that they are held hostage to individuals who charge discrimination, forced to either settle baseless claims or end up in protracted and costly litigation. One does not have to agree with this tired complaint to recognize that the employee does have a certain leverage, stemming from the relative ease with which the employee can charge discrimination and a built-in advantage in litigation—the employee, if he or she prevails, can recover his or her attorney's fees; the employer (typically) cannot. An employee should know that there is much in the law that favors the employee's interest. The employee, however, should also know that if push comes to shove, as it often does in cases of this nature, there are costs (and risks) to the employee.

At bottom, the decision to bring a claim is personal and individual. Obviously, the decision is heavily influenced by the merits of the claim. If there is nothing to suggest that discrimination has occurred, even the simple act of filing a charge could be ill-advised. If, on the other hand, there is a possible basis for a claim, the employee must carefully assess the possible costs and benefits of pursuing a claim.

In some respects, it is surprising and heartening that so many individual employees are willing to take up the banner against their allegedly wrongdoing employers. Many assume that most employees claim discrimination to make money—to force the employer into a lucrative cash settlement or to recover substantial damages in a court action. That has not been my experience. No doubt, financial conditions come into play. For many employees, however, the primary motivation is far more ennobling. They want to punish the employer for its wrongdoing and, in so doing, deter the employer from taking similar action in the future against other employees.

All of which leads us back to Al. Al knows that he has possible claims of discrimination. At least one appears strong even without the benefit of the kind of discovery that Al could get in a formal legal proceeding. Al also knows, however, that, at age 49, his employment situation is precarious. If he pursues a claim, he could be jeopardizing his job prospects. If there is not a quick resolution of the claim and Al feels compelled to push forward, Al could be embroiled for years in costly litigation, with no guarantee of a favorable resolution. Ultimately, Al must decide what is best for him. Al may feel that he has nothing to lose in pursuing a claim. Al may believe that the company is engaging in a campaign to rid the workforce of older managers. Al may feel obliged to take action, notwithstanding the possible implications for his future job prospects.

For our purposes, we will assume that Al decides to pursue his claim. The next question is what Al must do, as a legal matter, to assert those claims.

CHAPTER 13

The Pre-Suit Procedures

When Congress enacted the Civil Rights Act of 1964, it was aware that many states had their own laws against discrimination in the workplace. Congress was concerned that the new federal protections not trump the existing antidiscrimination laws in place in many states. Congress was also concerned that the new federal statutes not open the floodgates to costly and contentious litigation. Congress wanted to empower employees who were victims of discrimination. Congress, however, also wanted to encourage the voluntary resolution of employment disputes. To achieve these goals, Congress set up a relatively elaborate pre-suit mechanism for resolving claims of unlawful discrimination. That mechanism requires an employee to file a charge of discrimination as a prerequisite to bringing suit in court. It also requires that the employee first attempt to resolve his or her claim before the state agency responsible for resolving claims of discrimination in the state where the discrimination occurs.

In theory, the pre-suit procedures established in the federal statutes make it easier for the employee to claim discrimination. The critical first step for the employee is the filing of a charge of discrimination, typically with an office of the U.S. Equal Employment Opportunity Commission (EEOC). The charge does not have to be supported by any evidence. It is simply a sworn statement that contains the employee's own allegations of discrimination.

Based upon the charge, the EEOC investigates the employee's claim to determine whether there is reasonable cause to believe that discrimination has occurred. The idea is that the EEOC will carry the ball and work out an agreement with the employer to resolve the matter where there is cause to believe that the employer has discriminated. This roots out the unlawful discrimination and provides the employee with a prompt remedy for the adverse action while avoiding costly and divisive litigation.

As is so often the case, what looks good on paper doesn't work as well in practice. Congress contemplated that the EEOC would serve as a major buffer to court litigation. Congress made it a *requirement* that an employee first file a charge with the EEOC before proceeding to court. The problem is that Congress never provided the EEOC with the resources necessary to carry out its assigned role. Thousands of charges are filed with the EEOC each year. There is simply no way that the Commission can fully investigate and meaningfully resolve each charge. In many cases, the EEOC is nothing more than a way station for those who intend to pursue a claim in court.

Another problem is that the pre-suit procedures are not at all simple. To initiate the pre-suit procedures, an employee need only take the minimal step of filing a charge on a form provided by the EEOC. The employee, however, must act promptly or risk losing his or her right to bring a claim in court. The employee, moreover, must also satisfy the requirement of first presenting his or her claim to the appropriate state agency, a procedure known as the *deferral requirement*. Fortunately, the EEOC has entered into work-sharing agreements with most such agencies, permitting the employee to satisfy the deferral requirement by the simple act of filing a charge with the EEOC. Finally, the employee must take care to include within his or her charge all of the possible grounds of discrimination. If the employee fails to reference a specific claim of discrimination, the employee may be precluded from asserting that claim in a subsequent court action.

Once a charge is properly filed, the EEOC takes over the case. In practice, many charges pend with the EEOC for some time. After a charge has been with the EEOC for 180 days, the employee has a right to obtain a right-to-sue letter from the EEOC. The employee has an important tactical decision to make at this point. If the employee asks for a right-to-sue letter, the employee must be prepared to file suit and to go it alone. If the employee allows the EEOC to investigate the charge, he or she risks having the EEOC assume control over the case. The EEOC might find there is no cause to believe that discrimination has occurred, leaving the employee free to bring his or her own suit, but with the black mark of a no-cause finding. The EEOC might find cause and then bring suit in its own right, where its primary allegiance is to the broader public interest, rather than to the individual employee. More generally, the employee must decide whether to accept any offer of settlement that the employer may make or whether to submit the claim to arbitration (or mediation), a method of alternative dispute resolution sometimes favored by employers.

On occasion, the pre-suit procedures work precisely as intended, leading to a relatively prompt and nonacrimonious resolution of the dispute. More often than not, however, these procedures serve as a trap for the unwary. An employee who wishes to go forward on a claim of discrimination must be aware of the pre-suit procedures and the potential pitfalls of not adhering to the letter of those procedures.

Filing a Charge

The centerpiece of the pre-suit procedures is the charge-filing requirement. On paper, this requirement is simple enough. The EEOC enforces the federal statutes that address discrimination in the workplace. These include the statutes prohibiting discrimination on the basis of race, sex, religion, national origin, age, and disability. The EEOC has offices located throughout the country. Many of these offices exist exclusively for the purpose of receiving and investigating charges. When an individual wishes to file a charge of discrimination, he or she should contact the closest EEOC office. The EEOC will draw up a charge based on the information provided by the charging party. The charging party needs only to sign the charge to initiate the pre-suit procedures.

What complicates this seemingly simple process is that the employee must act promptly in filing a charge and, in doing so, satisfy the statutory deferral requirement (i.e., the requirement that the claim first be presented to a state administrative agency). The federal antidiscrimination laws adopt a two-tiered approach to the charge-filing procedure. In cases where the discrimination occurs in a state that does not have an agency with the authority to grant or seek relief for unlawful discrimination of the kind alleged, an employee is required to file a charge within 180 days of the adverse employment decision at issue. This is a relatively simple requirement, although, as we shall see, there may be questions as to when the limitations period begins to run. If the employee files the charge within the 180-day period, the employee is protected. If the employee does not file a charge within that period, the employee loses the right to bring suit on the claim, absent some special doctrine that would extend the charge-filing period.

In cases where the discrimination occurs in a state that does have an agency with the authority to grant or seek relief for unlawful discrimination of the kind alleged, the procedures are more complex. The employee is given 300 days in which to file a charge with the EEOC. The employee, however, must first commence proceedings with the state agency. A charge is not considered filed with the EEOC until 60 days after state proceedings are commenced (unless the state terminates the proceedings before the 60-day period has expired). In essence, the employee must comply with two administrative requirements. The employee must commence proceedings with the appropriate state agency while filing a charge with the EEOC within the 300 days allotted by federal law.

As it turns out, most states have state agencies with the authority to grant or seek relief for the kinds of discrimination prohibited under federal law. Thus, in most cases, the employee will be subject to the 300-day period for filing a charge. This favors the interest of the employee in one sense, since it provides the employee with more time in which to file a charge. The problem is that the employee must also comply with the deferral requirement. If the employee does not take the steps necessary to commence and terminate state proceedings before the 300-day period elapses for the filing of a charge with the EEOC, the employee could lose the right to pursue his or her claim in court.

Fortunately, the EEOC has entered into work-sharing agreements with most state agencies responsible for resolving claims of discrimination. Under these agreements, the state agency agrees in advance to waive the deferral requirement for certain categories of charges. Typically, the agreement provides that if a charge is first filed with the EEOC, the EEOC assumes responsibility for the charge. State proceedings are deemed to be commenced and terminated either upon the filing of the charge with the EEOC or upon the EEOC's transmittal of the charge to the state agency, which should occur within a few days of the filing of the charge with the EEOC. For the most part, these agreements have been upheld by the courts.

The bottom line is that in most (although not all) cases, an employee will have 300 days from the discriminatory action to file a charge with the EEOC. Assuming that the EEOC has entered into a work-sharing agreement with the relevant state agency, the employee will not be obligated to file a separate complaint with the state. The agreement might be read as achieving a waiver of the deferral requirement based merely on the filing of the charge with the EEOC. This means that the employee could file a charge with the EEOC on the 300th day and comply with all of the statutory requirements. The agreement might be construed as achieving compliance with the deferral requirement only upon the transmittal of the charge to the state agency. Since that transmittal may take 2 or 3 days to occur, the employee would have to file a charge a few days before the 300th day. To be absolutely safe, the employee would need to file with both the EEOC and the state agency within 240 days of the adverse employment decision. This would ensure that the federal charge is timely, since the state would have at least 60 days to pass upon the complaint before the 300-day period expires.

It should be kept in mind that the deferral requirement is simply a component of the pre-suit procedures established under federal law. In other words, satisfying the requirement is a precondition to the assertion of a federal claim. An employee may wish to pursue a claim under state law. If the employee chooses to do so, he or she must comply with the state's own filing requirements. The employee must be careful how far he or she takes the state claim. An adverse determination by a state administrative agency is not binding in an employee's federal case. That determination becomes binding, however, once it is reviewed by a state court. An employee who loses before a state agency and then appeals his or her claim to a state court would be precluded from pursuing a parallel claim of discrimination under federal law should the state court affirm the agency's ruling.

It is also important to stress that the procedures discussed in this chapter do not apply to employees of the federal government, who are subject to a different set of pre-suit procedures. These procedures are, in some respects, more onerous, requiring the employee to act even more expeditiously and to work through a more elaborate system of administrative procedures before filing an action in court.

Another factor that complicates the charge-filing process is the difficulty, in some cases, of determining what event triggers the running of the charge-filing period—whether it be 180 days or 300 days. Take, for example, the case of an employee who is terminated from a job. Does the period for filing a charge begin to run when the employment decision is made? Or does it begin running when the employee receives notice of the decision? And what if the employer maintains an internal grievance procedure for its employees? Is the charge-filing period tolled while the employee grieves the termination?

The U.S. Supreme Court has resolved these questions. The Supreme Court has taken the view that the period for filing a charge begins to run when the employee receives notice of a final decision to terminate his or her employment. A decision is considered final even though the employee might be entitled to challenge the termination decision under an internal grievance procedure. Thus, the time for filing a charge is not tolled or abated merely because the employee is grieving the adverse decision. On the other hand, the mere suggestion that an employee might lose his or her job or that a workforce reduction is on the horizon is typically not enough to require the employee to come forward. There must be an element of finality (and specificity) to the decision, fairly putting the employee on notice that a decision has been made to discharge the employee. From that point, the employee has 180 or 300 days, as the case may be, to file a charge with the EEOC.

In other cases, the triggering event for the charge-filing period may be more difficult to pinpoint. An employer, for example, could adopt a policy that discriminates against members of a protected group in the provision of an employee benefit. The problem is that the discriminatory distinction may not yet have been applied to the individual employee (in a way that causes any tangible injury). Does the charge-filing period begin to run at the time the employer adopts the allegedly discriminatory policy, or can the employee wait until the policy is specifically applied to the employee? There is no clear answer to this question. If the policy is facially discriminatory—that is, on its face, makes a distinction between or among protected groups—the employee can wait until the policy is applied to the employee. That is because each application of a facially discriminatory policy gives rise to a separate violation of the law. (For that reason, discrimination in the level of pay provided to members of different protected groups can be challenged each time an employee receives a discriminatory paycheck.) If, on the other hand, the policy is not facially discriminatory—that is, it adopted for a discriminatory reason but not one that is apparent on the face of the policy—it is conceivable that a court would require the employee to challenge the policy at the time of adoption (assuming that the employee has fair notice of the policy). To be safe, an employee who is aware of a potentially discriminatory policy and who knows that the policy is likely to be applied to the employee's detriment at some point may want to take action promptly to ensure that the complaint is timely and to prevent the policy from being applied in a way that would cause the employee injury.

In a narrow range of cases, an employee might be given additional time in which to file a charge. This occurs when the employer misleads the employee concerning the basis for an employment decision. An employer, for example, may inform an employee that he is being terminated as part of a reduction-in-force, meaning that the employee's job is being eliminated. At that point, the employee has no reason to question the validity of the employer's explanation for the discharge. Several months later, however, the employee learns that his job has not in fact been eliminated. Only at that point does the employee have reason to question the basis for the employment decision. Since the employee was lulled into inaction by the employer's misrepresentation, the time for filing a charge would not begin to run until the employee learned the truth about the elimination of his job (unless the employee, in the exercise of due diligence, could have discovered that fact at some earlier point).

For the employee, the charge-filing requirement can be demanding. Relatively speaking, the period of time for filing a charge is short. At most, the employee has 300 days in which to file the charge. The theory is that filing a charge is a simple step, one that can be taken without a great deal of thought or investigation. As discussed in prior chapters, this is not altogether true. There are risks to filing a charge. An employee, moreover, may want to hold back on filing a charge until some internal grievance plays out or until the employee is secure in some other employment position. The law forces the employee into what may be a hasty decision to initiate legal proceedings.

The charge-filing procedure is complicated by one additional factor. The purpose of the charge-filing requirement is to provide the EEOC (and state agencies) with the opportunity to obtain a voluntary resolution of a claim before the employee embarks upon a course of contentious litigation. For the EEOC to play this role, the employee must include the claim within the EEOC charge. If the employee fails to do so, the EEOC has no opportunity to seek a voluntary resolution of the claim. To avoid this result, the law requires that, as a precondition to asserting claims in court, the employee include those claims (each of them) in his or her EEOC charge. If the employee omits a claim from the charge, the employee may well be barred from pursuing that claim in court.

This latter point has particular relevance to our hypothetical employee, Al. Al has potential claims of age and race discrimination. The age claim would appear to be the stronger claim. It is possible, however, that through additional discovery, Al could uncover information that is supportive of his race claim. For this reason, Al may want to include the race claim in his charge, even though he has more confidence in the age claim. If Al fails to include the race claim in his charge and information emerges in support of that claim, it is possible that Al will be precluded from asserting that claim in court.

In other respects, Al's task is relatively simple. Al was terminated from his job. Assuming that the discrimination occurred in a deferral state—one with a state agency empowered to remedy discrimination of the kind alleged—Al would have 300 days from the date he was notified of the discharge to file a charge with the EEOC. As noted previously, the law may provide an employee with additional time to file a charge in those cases in which the employee has been misled with respect to the circumstances surrounding an employment decision. This might be such a case, since the company suggested to Al that his job was being eliminated, a fact that Al now has reason to question in light of information that he came across after the employment decision. Al, however, should not go to the bank on the possibility that he will be given additional time to file a charge. If Al wants to pursue a claim, he should file his charge within the time allotted by statute.

The one thing that complicates this picture is that Al must also satisfy the deferral requirement (assuming that he is subject to the 300-day charge-filing period). The procedures for meeting this requirement will vary (to a degree) from state to state, depending on the nature of the work-sharing agreement, if any, between the EEOC and the particular state agency. To be safe, Al should approach the EEOC well before the 300-day period has elapsed. The EEOC should be aware of the provisions of the work-sharing agreement and should take the steps necessary to ensure that the deferral requirement is satisfied. It is likely that if Al files his EEOC charge some time before the 300-day period has expired (with his age and race claims included), he will have taken all of the steps necessary to protect his legal rights under federal law.

On occasion, the EEOC provides an employee with false information concerning the employee's pre-suit obligations. The EEOC, for example, may tell a charging party that she need not file a separate claim with the state, due to the provisions of a work-sharing agreement, when, in fact, the work-sharing agreement does not relieve the employee of her burden to commence state proceedings. For the most part, courts have been sympathetic to employees who lose out on statutory rights because of misstatements of law by the EEOC. If it was reasonable for the employee to rely upon the representations of the EEOC, the employee will not be held accountable for the EEOC's blunder.

Processing a Charge

Once a charge is filed with the EEOC, the pre-suit procedures begin in earnest. There are two ways in which this process can play out. First, the employee can permit the EEOC to conduct a full investigation of the charge (assuming the EEOC is inclined to do so). Under this scenario, the EEOC would investigate the charge of discrimination. The EEOC would determine whether there is reasonable cause to believe that discrimination has occurred. If the EEOC found that no such cause exists, the EEOC would notify the employee of its no-cause finding. (The EEOC now calls this a dismissal "without particularized findings.") The employee would then have 90 days to file a suit in court. If the Commission found cause, it would attempt to conciliate the charge with the employer. If a conciliation agreement were worked out, the matter would be resolved. If no agreement was reached, the EEOC could bring suit in its own right. Or, the EEOC could provide the employee with a right-to-sue letter. Again, the employee would have 90 days in which to file a lawsuit.

The second course of action is for the employee to pull the claim out of the administrative process as quickly as possible. Federal law requires that an employee file a charge with the EEOC as a precondition to suit. It does not require that the employee leave the charge in the administrative process indefinitely. In the case of a charge alleging discrimination on the basis of race, sex, national origin, religion, or disability, the EEOC has exclusive jurisdiction over the charge for a period of 180 days. The employee can request a right-to-sue letter at any time, but the EEOC is not required to provide the letter during that 180-day period. If, at the end of that period, the EEOC has not yet resolved the charge, the employee can demand a right-to-sue letter from the EEOC. The EEOC is obligated to provide the letter promptly, leaving the employee with 90 days in which to file a lawsuit. In the case of a charge alleging discrimination on the basis of age, the employee is required to let the charge pend with the EEOC for a period of 60 days. After 60 days, the employee can file a lawsuit on the charge. (The employee does not have to obtain a right-to-sue letter from the EEOC to file a suit alleging age discrimination.)

As the above discussion suggests, the pre-suit procedures present the employee with an important tactical decision. The employee can allow the EEOC to carry the ball and (if it is willing to do so) fully investigate the charge. The advantage of this course is obvious. The EEOC has full investigative authority. The EEOC can demand information from the employer and, where necessary, subpoena documents. The EEOC might build a persuasive case against the employer, thus forcing the employer to settle on terms favorable to the employee. Even if the EEOC does not find reasonable cause (or is unable to reach a conciliation agreement with the employer), the EEOC may have created a substantial factual record concerning the employment decision at issue. The employee can use the information gathered by the EEOC in building his or her own case against the employer.

There are some potential downsides in permitting the EEOC to have free rein. The EEOC finds reasonable cause in a relatively small percentage of cases. The EEOC does not always conduct the type of thorough investigation that the antidiscrimination statutes contemplate. Even if it does, it may well find that there is no cause to believe that discrimination occurred. While the EEOC's cause determinations are not controlling in a subsequent action brought by the employee, they can be introduced as evidence (at least in some courts). That the EEOC did not make a finding in the employee's favor might work against the employee's ability to prove his or her claim in court. (This concern is ameliorated by the fact that the EEOC no longer issues a no-cause finding, as such, when it dismisses a charge without finding cause. Instead, the EEOC dismisses the charge without particularized findings.)

More fundamentally, there is a tension between the interests of the EEOC and the individual employee. The EEOC represents the broader public interest. That interest overlaps, to a large degree, with the interest of the individual employee, but the two interests can diverge. The EEOC, for example, may believe that a settlement offer is adequate to serve the deterrent purposes of the statute. An employee may believe that he or she is entitled to additional relief. The EEOC, at the pre-suit stage, cannot compromise the rights of the employee. The EEOC, however, can make it difficult for the employee to say no, should the EEOC work out a conciliation agreement with the employer that provides some relief to the employee. The deeper into the process the EEOC goes, the less control the employee retains over the claim.

The other scenario—quickly moving out of the administrative process and into court—also has its pros and cons. On the plus side, the employee increases the chances of being able to pursue his or her claim unhindered by the efforts of the EEOC. If the employee pulls the claim out of the administrative process, it is unlikely that the EEOC will continue to pursue an investigation. The downside is that the employee loses the benefit of the EEOC's investigative efforts. Some employees file a charge simply to test the waters. These employees want to see what the EEOC will turn up in an investigation. If an employee does an end run around the investigative process, the employee forfeits the possible benefits of having an EEOC investigation. The employee, moreover, will have to act quickly to protect his or her rights, since the employee has a mere 90 days to file a lawsuit once the EEOC issues a right-to-sue letter. An employee should adopt a strategy of giving short shrift to the administrative process only if the employee is confident that he or she has the goods on the employer and is not in need of the EEOC's investigative assistance.

With respect to claims of age discrimination, there is an additional consideration. The antidiscrimination statutes adopt a dual system of public and private enforcement. The EEOC has the authority to bring a public enforcement action stemming from a charge of discrimination filed by an individual employee. That employee may also bring suit in his or her own right. For the most part, these statutory rights are complementary—that is, both the EEOC and the employee can assert claims, often with either the EEOC or the employee intervening in the lawsuit of the other. The federal age discrimination statute takes a different approach. That statute gives the upper hand to the EEOC. Specifically, it provides that the filing of a lawsuit by the EEOC cuts off the suit rights of the employee (assuming that the employee has not yet filed suit). Since the age statute permits an employee to file suit once a charge has sat with the EEOC for at least 60 days, an employee can take the steps necessary to ensure that he or she (rather than the EEOC) wins the race to the courthouse. The employee should be prepared to file suit once it becomes clear that the EEOC itself is preparing to initiate a lawsuit.

On occasion, an employee will have second thoughts about the decision to file a charge. The EEOC's regulations permit an employee to withdraw a charge. The problem is that the act of withdrawing a charge does not necessarily end the process. Under the age statute, the EEOC has the authority to act without the benefit of a charge. Thus, even where the employee withdraws the charge, the EEOC retains the authority go forward with an investigation and, eventually, to file suit. The EEOC's enforcement authority under Title VII of the Civil Rights Act is charge-driven. The EEOC, however, has the authority to file its own charges (known as "Commissioner's charges") where the EEOC has a reason to believe that a company is engaging in practices that violate the statute. The EEOC could act on a Commissioner's charge even where the charging party is no longer willing to cooperate in the investigation and, in fact, has withdrawn the charge.

The fact that the EEOC can go forward on a possible claim—without the voluntary participation of the employee—underscores an important point about the EEOC's enforcement role. The EEOC has the full authority to act on information provided by an employee. The EEOC can file a lawsuit, based on a charge, even if the employee filing the charge no longer has an interest in pursuing the claim. An employee must understand that once a charge is filed with the EEOC, there is no way to maintain total control over the process. The genie, so to speak, is out of the bottle. Typically, the EEOC acts only with the cooperation of a charging party and in close contact with the charging party. As a legal matter, however, the EEOC is not circumscribed by the interests or desires of the employee filing a charge.

Assuming that the EEOC fully investigates a charge and finds reasonable cause to believe that discrimination has occurred, the next step is for the EEOC to seek a conciliation agreement with the employer. The EEOC cannot bring a lawsuit in its own right without first seeking to achieve a voluntary resolution of the dispute. The EEOC is obligated by statute to engage in reasonable efforts to conciliate (or settle) a charge. No such requirement exists for the employee filing the charge. Nor is the employee required to accept a conciliation agreement reached between the EEOC and the employer. The EEOC attempts to work out an agreement with the employer. If an agreement is reached and the employee accepts the agreement, the matter is resolved. Both the employer and the employee—as well as the EEOC—can be held to the agreement. If the employee refuses to accept the agreement, the employee will be issued a right-to-sue letter, authorizing the employee to bring suit in court.

While the charging party is under no legal obligation to accept a conciliation agreement, the employee's freedom is not unlimited. First, an employee may not refuse to accept a conciliation agreement only to sue for precisely the same relief offered by the employer as part of the conciliation package. In other words, the employee can reject a conciliation agreement and still bring an action in court only if the employee is seeking relief in addition to that offered by the employer in conciliation. If the employee rebuffs a conciliation agreement and then sues for nothing more than the relief that would have been provided under that agreement, the employee can be precluded from maintaining the suit.

There is also a financial risk to the employee should the employee go forward on a lawsuit in the face of the rejection of a proffered conciliation agreement. An individual cannot be forced into settling a claim. The law, however, wants to encourage parties to settle. To create an incentive to settle, the law requires a plaintiff to pay the costs of the defendant if the plaintiff obtains a judgment that is less than an offer or judgment (or settlement) made by the defendant. The law also prohibits the plaintiff from recovering any attorney's fees as the prevailing party past the point at which the offer of judgment is made. If an employee rejects a conciliation agreement, sues the employer, and ends up recovering less from the employer than that offered as part of the conciliation agreement, the employee can be required to pay the employer's costs. The employee would also lose out on any attorney's fees for work done after rejection of the conciliation agreement, which would include all of the work done in litigation. (The risk that a plaintiff will be denied attorney's fees, even if the plaintiff is the prevailing party, may well dissuade an attorney from taking the plaintiff's case.)

Given the legal implications of rejecting a conciliation agreement, an employee must give careful consideration to any offer of settlement advanced during the conciliation process. An employee must also assess whether there is a realistic chance of recovering more in litigation than what the employer has put on the table in conciliation. Just as two birds in the hand are better than one in the bush, what the employee is guaranteed under a conciliation agreement (the employer willing) may well prove better than what the employee *might* be able to recover after years of contentious litigation.

Settlement and the ADR Option

The possibility of settlement does not arise just in the context of a conciliation agreement. At any point in the process, an employer may offer a sum of money to resolve a claim (or threatened claim) of discrimination. The employee must give careful consideration to such an offer. If the employee accepts the offer and settles the claim, the dispute is resolved—permanently. The employee is bound by the agreement to settle so long as the agreement is knowing and voluntary. An agreement is knowing and voluntary if the agreement is reached in the context of an existing dispute, the terms of the agreement are reasonably clear, and there is no evidence of coercion or fraud by the employer. While the decision to settle a claim is pregnant with meaning (and consequence), so too is the decision not to settle a claim. The employee does not want to reject a generous settlement offer only to litigate the claim and end up with nothing.

To fully assess the merits of a settlement offer, an employee must understand two things: the nature of the relief provided under the antidiscrimination laws and the chance of prevailing on the claim and recovering that relief (if it is in addition to the amount offered in settlement). As always, the employee must also consider the personal and financial costs of litigating a claim, since any victory in litigation is likely to be hard fought.

Historically, the federal antidiscrimination laws provided relief of a relatively limited nature. Title VII of the Civil Rights Act authorized the award of back wages for an individual who was fired from a job, demoted, not hired, or denied a promotion. The Act did not provide for compensatory damages (e.g., damages for emotional pain and suffering). Nor did the Act permit the award of punitive damages—that is, damages designed to punish a wrongdoer for its illegal conduct. In many cases, particularly those involving claims of sexual harassment, an employee was left with very little in the way of monetary relief for an employer's unlawful discrimination.

The other civil rights statutes were a bit more generous. The age discrimination statute has always permitted the award of liquidated damages in those cases where the plaintiff proves a willful violation of the statute. Liquidated damages allow the plaintiff to recover twice the amount of back wages otherwise owed to the plaintiff. In cases of race discrimination, employees could also bring suit under a Civil War–era statute, 42 U.S.C. 1981. That statute was construed to permit the award of compensatory and punitive damages, although it was not clear that the statute applied to the bread-and-butter claim of employment discrimination. An employee could also bring suit under the applicable state law. The problem is that the protection varied from state to state. Some states have authorized the award of compensatory and punitive damages on generous terms, while others have provided for only limited relief.

In 1991, Congress substantially upped the ante for unlawful discrimination. In a civil rights statute, Congress provided for the award of compensatory and punitive damages in cases of intentional discrimination under Title VII of the Civil Rights Act and the Americans With Disabilities Act (ADA). Congress defined compensatory damages to include damages for emotional pain, suffering, inconvenience, mental anguish, and loss of enjoyment of life. Congress authorized the award of punitive damages in those cases in which the employer engages in discrimination with malice or with reckless indifference to the federally protected rights of an aggrieved individual. Congress also amended Section 1981 (the Civil War–era statute) to make clear that the statute applies to most race-based claims of employment discrimination.

The new damage provisions contain a number of statutory caps geared to the size of the employer. The lowest cap is $50,000 (for an employer with fewer than 101 employees). The highest cap is $300,000 (for an employer with more than 500 employees). No cap applies to the award of compensatory and punitive damages under Section 1981. The net effect of these provisions is to establish two different tracks for the award of compensatory and punitive damages. In cases involving claims of discrimination based on sex, national origin, religion, or disability, the employee can recover compensatory and punitive damages but be subject to the caps imposed by statute, meaning that the combined total of compensatory and punitive damages may not exceed the cap applicable to the employer in question (based on the number of employees working for the employer). In cases involving a claim of race discrimination, the employee can recover compensatory and punitive damages without any statutory limitation on the amount of the recovery. (Courts themselves can reduce the amount of damages awarded by a jury when the award appears to be excessive.)

While the 1991 Civil Rights Act created new damages for discrimination claimants, it would be a mistake to assume that these damages are easily obtainable in a case of employment discrimination. To date, the track record for the award of damages under the 1991 Act has been mixed. Juries have awarded substantial compensatory damages to employees who have proved unlawful discrimination. In many cases, however, courts have reduced the amount of damages, leaving the employee with little to show after hard-fought litigation. There is a downside, moreover, to asserting a claim for compensatory damages. By seeking damages for emotional pain and suffering, the employee opens the door to inquiries about the employee's personal life. In a sexual harassment case, for example, the employee may claim that the harassment caused her severe emotional pain. The employer may want to test this claim by probing whether there are other things that occurred in the employee's personal life, more so than the harassment, that caused the emotional distress. The employer may want to obtain discovery of the employee's medical records, including records of any psychiatric counseling, to verify the employee's claim of an emotional injury. An employer may also want to probe whether, given her sexual proclivities, the employee is the type of person who is likely to be offended (in a serious way) by sexual overtures or advances. It is questionable whether the employer may pursue this latter course of inquiry, since there are rules that limit questions about a claimant's sexual history. A court, however, might be willing to permit some questioning in that area, within limits. Certainly, many courts will be willing to permit the employer to ferret out other information of a personal nature, some of which could prove embarrassing to the employee.

Punitive damages have also proven to be somewhat elusive. There is an argument that a jury should be allowed to consider an award of punitive damages in most cases in which there is evidence that an employer has intentionally discriminated against an employee. Many courts have taken a different view, permitting a jury to consider an award of punitive damages only where there is evidence of egregious discrimination. (This issue was before the Supreme Court as of the writing of this book.) Even where juries are allowed to consider an award of punitive damages, courts have been willing to reduce the amount of punitive damages awarded by the jury. This is true even where the jury's award falls below the applicable statutory cap.

Knowing all of this is important because few employers will be willing to pay a significant amount of compensatory damages in settlement, at least for such intangible harms as emotional pain, suffering, inconvenience, mental anguish, and loss of enjoyment. Nor will they readily agree to pay out in settlement any significant amount of punitive damages. What an employer might be willing to do is settle a claim for a healthy amount of "make whole relief" (i.e., back wages) and, perhaps, certain types of pecuniary compensatory damages (e.g., medical costs, out-of-pocket expenses). There are exceptions to this, of course. In cases where there is compelling evidence of discrimination and the employer's exposure (for substantial compensatory and punitive damages) is great, the employer may be willing to cut a deal that includes an amount for compensatory and punitive damages. By and large, however, employers will settle (if at all) for such tangible damages as lost wages and out-of-pocket expenses and, perhaps, a relatively small amount of nonpecuniary compensatory and punitive damages.

This creates a dilemma for the employee. The employee knows that he or she can assert a claim for compensatory and punitive damages. The employee may have reason to believe that a jury would award such damages if the case goes to trial. An employee should also know, however, that there is no guarantee that at the end of the process the employee will end up with any damages of that kind. Of course, as always, the employee must consider the strength of his or her claim. If the claim is weak (as a relative matter), the employee may want to take whatever reasonable offer is put on the table. If the claim is strong, the employee may want to go forward (unless the employer tenders a very substantial settlement offer), particularly if the employee is passionate about the merits of the claim and the need for sanctioning the employer for its allegedly unlawful conduct. Nonetheless, even with a strong claim, the employee may want to accept a settlement offer that provides for meaningful monetary relief, albeit less than what the employee could theoretically recover in litigation, given the chances that a jury will decline to award any significant compensatory or punitive damages or, if it does, that a court will reduce or rescind the jury's award.

In some respects, the employee's course of action will be dictated by the nature of the claim that the employee is asserting. In a case involving a discriminatory discharge, the employee is likely to have a substantial claim for back wages, since the employer has removed the employee from a job that the employee would have continued performing if not for the alleged discrimination. In such a case, the employee may be able to extract a favorable settlement from the employer on the basis of back wages alone. On the other hand, in a case involving workplace harassment, there is often no tangible injury to an employee, in the sense that the employee has been fired, demoted, or transferred to a less desirable job. The employee's claim for relief will focus on punitive damages and such compensatory relief as emotional pain and suffering. In such a case, the employer may be unwilling to forward any significant monetary relief as part of a settlement. Unless the employer does so, there will be little chance for settlement.

Settlement is one way that a case can be resolved without the need for litigation. It is also possible to do an end run around litigation by submitting a claim to some form of alternative dispute resolution (ADR). A common form of ADR is arbitration. Under an arbitration procedure, a claim is submitted to an arbitrator in a nonjudicial forum. Typically, the normal rules of evidence and discovery, applicable in court, do not apply (in a strict sense). The arbitrator takes evidence and renders a decision. The process is relatively quick, with less opportunity for the types of delays and backlogs that plague the court system.

In recent years, some employers have attempted to integrate arbitration into the employment relationship. Specifically, they require, as a condition of employment, that an applicant or employee agree to submit any future claim of discrimination to arbitration. This is a highly controversial and questionable practice (known as mandatory arbitration). The EEOC opposes mandatory arbitration. The practice has been challenged in court, with some success, and is currently being debated in the political arena. As of the writing of this book, the legality of mandatory arbitration is up in the air. In some parts of the country, courts have invalidated mandatory arbitration agreements. In others, the practice has been upheld.

For the employee, there is very little choice involved (assuming that the practice of mandatory arbitration is upheld). If the employee wants the job, the employee must agree to arbitrate any future claim. If the employee enters into such an agreement and later suffers some adverse action in the workplace, the employee will be held to the agreement and forced to arbitrate any claim of discrimination arising from the adverse action, with no chance (typically) to bring a claim in court. If the employee refuses to sign the agreement and, as a result, loses a job, it is unlikely that the employee will have any legal recourse.

For obvious reasons, mandatory arbitration is a problem for employees. There is, however, a less controversial form of arbitration that may actually prove beneficial to employees. This is the type of arbitration that an employee agrees to after a dispute has arisen. Some employers do not insist that, as a condition of working for the employer, the employee agree to submit any future claim to arbitration. They do, however, offer the option of submitting a claim to arbitration once a dispute arises and there is a possibility of litigation. When confronted with such an option, the employee must decide whether to seek resolution of the claim through arbitration.

There are several factors that an employee should consider before embarking upon arbitration (or some other form of ADR). The first (and most critical) factor is whether the arbitration system at issue results in a binding decision—that is, whether a decision by the arbitrator, if adverse to the employee, would preclude the employee from bringing a claim in court. In some cases, arbitration is nonbinding. The hope is that the chance of resolving the claim without the necessity of going to court will be increased if the parties first seek resolution in an arbitral forum. The only downside to this type of arbitration is that without the hammer of a binding award, the whole exercise may be a waste of the employee's time (and money). More typically, an arbitration decision will be binding on both the employee and the employer. This means, in effect, that by submitting a claim to arbitration, the employee is agreeing to arbitrate the claim *in lieu of* bringing the claim in court.

The second factor to consider is the cost of the arbitration procedure. Court costs are relatively slight. The individual bringing suit need only pay the standard filing fee. Arbitration can work differently. First, the filing fee for arbitration is sometimes higher (much higher, in fact) than the filing fees imposed by courts. In addition, arbitrators are not judges, who receive compensation from the government. They are private citizens who are performing a service for a fee. As such, they need to be paid. Some arbitration systems require that the parties split the arbitrator's fees, which can sometimes be in the thousands of dollars. The employee may be required to pay these fees even if the employee prevails on his or her claim in arbitration.

Next, the employee needs to assess the overall fairness of the arbitration procedure at issue. Arbitration procedures can vary greatly. Rarely will an arbitration procedure provide an individual with the full array of procedural protections that exist in federal courts. The very purpose of arbitration is to provide a relatively cheap and quick alternative to litigation. Some arbitration arrangements, however, will do a better job than others in ensuring that the employee has a fair shot at proving his or her case. A critical factor is the degree to which the arbitration procedure permits reasonable discovery. Does the arbitration arrangement permit an employee to take depositions? Does it limit the number of depositions that may be taken? (Some arbitration arrangements limit each side to one deposition, a ridiculously low figure.) Can the employee force the employer to turn over documents that have relevance to the employee's case? The employee must also check carefully to determine what relief is available under the arbitration arrangement. It is likely that the arbitrator will have the power to award back wages and other out-of-pocket losses. But is the arbitrator authorized to award broad compensatory or punitive damages? Some arbitration arrangements do not permit the award of such damages. Others severely limit the amount of the award (with caps that are far below the amounts permitted under the Civil Rights Act of 1991). By agreeing to arbitrate, an employee might, in effect, be agreeing to forgo any meaningful compensatory or punitive damages.

Finally, the employee should carefully examine the method by which the arbitrator is to be chosen. The employer may have its own arbitration arrangement. The employer may have gamed the system to ensure that the arbitrator is sympathetic to the employer's position. If nothing else, the fact that the employer is a repeat player in the process increases the likelihood that the arbitrator will rule in the employer's favor, since the arbitrator knows that the employer is more likely to seek the arbitrator's services in the future if the arbitrator has ruled in the employer's favor. The fairest arbitration arrangements are those that use a reputable organization like the American Arbitration Association, which has protocols in place that are designed to ensure fairness and impartiality. If the arbitration arrangement makes reference to the procedures of the American Arbitration Association, there is a good chance that the arrangement will be minimally fair in its selection of arbitrators. If, instead, it appears that the procedure is a fly-by-night operation, set up entirely by the individual employer, there are reasons to be skeptical of the basic fairness of the system.

There is much to be said in favor of arbitration and other forms of ADR. Federal courts are increasingly overburdened. It may take years for an employee to navigate through the judicial process. Even then, there is no guarantee that the employee will prevail. In some cases, arbitration can provide the best result for the employee—either a quick victory or a (mercifully) quick defeat. Still, there is much that an employee gives up by agreeing to arbitration, at least where the arbitration is binding. The employee loses the full range of discovery options provided in federal court. The employee substitutes a private citizen (the arbitrator) for a federal judge, a figure of constitutional stature who is armed with the full authority to enforce federal law. Most notably, the employee cedes away the right to have the case heard by a jury, a right of such importance that it is contained in the Constitution. Opting for arbitration in lieu of an action in court is an important step, one that should not be taken lightly.

Returning to our friend Al, we can only speculate how Al's situation would play out. Al's strongest claim is his age claim. Al is not entitled to recover compensatory and punitive damages on that claim, unless such damages are available under state law (which is possible). Al would, however, be able to seek back wages and liquidated damages for his termination. Perhaps the employer would be willing to cut a favorable deal. Or, the EEOC would work out a conciliation agreement that is amenable to both parties.

One thing that may work against settlement of Al's claim is that Al's discharge appears to have occurred in the context of a reorganization initiative that has claimed the jobs of a number of employees. Where a claim appears to stem from an isolated event, an employer may be willing to settle to make the case go away, if nothing else. Where, however, the claim appears to arise from a more general pattern of employment decision making, settlement is a touchier issue for the employer, since word will invariably get around that a deal has been struck, thus encouraging other employees in their efforts to pursue claims against the employer. In cases of this nature, the company might be inclined to take a hard-line stance against any settlement.

Given this scenario, it is entirely possible that Al will emerge from the pre-suit stage without a deal. Al will then be faced with the choice of taking his claim to the next level. Arbitration might be an option, but Al may be reluctant to opt for that approach, for the reasons discussed above. If Al does not go the arbitration route (or otherwise pursue some method of ADR), he is left with one option—litigating his claim.

CHAPTER 14

Litigation

We now come to the last stage of the process. Most of us know something about litigation. If nothing else, we have watched Court TV, the O.J. Simpson trial, or *Perry Mason* reruns. We know that there is judge, a jury, witnesses, and lawyers who ask questions of the witnesses and make arguments to the judge and the jury.

The problem with this superficial understanding, as gleaned from the real and dramatic depictions of television, is that it reveals only the end point of litigation—the trial itself. This is the proverbial tip of the iceberg. Most of what we refer to as litigation occurs well before the trial itself begins (assuming that one takes place at all). First, a suit must be filed in court. The suit must be filed on a timely basis. In the case of the federal antidiscrimination laws, there are important issues that arise at the initial stage of the suit, particularly when both the U.S. Equal Employment Opportunity Commission (EEOC) and the charging party desire to bring suit or to participate in the same proceeding. Next, the case must proceed through what may be a lengthy period of pre-trial discovery. This could last months, even years, and could well result in the dismissal of the suit under a procedural device known as summary judgment, where a single judge (not a jury) decides that the employee has not produced sufficient evidence to take his or her case to a jury. Only after the case has made it through the arduous pretrial process and cleared the summary judgment hurdle does it finally go to trial. Even if the case is tried and the employee prevails, there are likely to be post-trial motions filed by the employer and appeals made to the court of appeals and, perhaps, the Supreme Court. Typically, any judgment in favor of the employee is stayed during the appeals process, meaning that the employee will be unable to collect on any judgment in the employee's favor until the process is completed in its entirety.

For the employee, the litigation process can be taxing. The employee will have to sit for one or more depositions. Those depositions will be given under oath. Without a doubt, the employer will be aggressive in asking questions about the employee's performance on the job. The employer may try to dig up the dirt on the employee, if any exists. This scenario will be reprised, in front of a jury, should the case make it to trial. If the employee prevails before a jury and rides out the almost inevitable appeals process, the employee will have earned the victory.

Filing the Suit

Almost all court actions are subject to a statute of limitations. Typically, the statute of limitations requires that a suit be brought within a certain period of time after the occurrence of the event giving rise to the suit. For the most part, the federal antidiscrimination laws take a somewhat different tack. As discussed in Chapter 13, the federal statutes establish an elaborate pre-suit procedure for the assertion of discrimination claims. Because of that procedure, the limitations period for filing suit in court is geared to what occurs in the pre-suit phase. Specifically, the employee is given a certain period of time, after receiving notice of a right-to-sue, to file suit. That period is 90 days. The 90 days is measured from the date on which the employee receives notice of the right-to-sue (by letter).

The limitations period operates somewhat differently under the respective statutes. With respect to Title VII of the Civil Rights

Act and the Americans With Disabilities Act, the employee cannot bring suit until a right-to-sue letter has been issued. The employee can request a right-to-sue letter at any time but is not entitled to receive one until a charge has pended with the EEOC for 180 days. Under the age statute, by contrast, the employee can proceed without a right-to-sue letter. The employee need only let the charge sit for 60 days before the EEOC. The employee can, if he or she chooses, wait for the EEOC to investigate and resolve the charge. When the EEOC disposes of the charge, it provides notice to the employee. That notice triggers the 90-day period for filing an action in court. (Historically, age suits were subject to a 2-year limitations period, as measured from the date of the discrimination, except in cases of a willful violation, where a 3-year limitations period applied. This limitations scheme was borrowed from the Fair Labor Standards Act. Congress changed the law, with respect to the age statute, in 1991.)

There is at least one exception to these filing rules. Claims of race discrimination may be brought under Title VII. Such claims, however, may also be brought under the Civil War–era statute, 42 U.S.C. 1981. That statute does not have a pre-suit procedure. There is no requirement, in other words, that the employee file a charge as a precondition to bringing suit. Because Section 1981 does not contain its own statute of limitations provision, courts have borrowed a limitations period from the law of the state in which the discrimination occurred, usually appropriating the limitations period applicable to personal injury actions in that state. Thus, to file a timely lawsuit alleging race discrimination under Section 1981, an employee must file suit within the limitations period borrowed from state law, as measured from the date of the discriminatory event. Of course, an employee can also bring a discrimination claim under state law (assuming the state in question has a law prohibiting the type of discrimination involved). Each state will have its own timeliness requirement for the assertion of a state law claim.

This procedure is complicated somewhat by the fact that the EEOC has the independent authority to bring suit in its own name. Thus, in certain cases, both the EEOC and the employee (the charging party) may desire to bring suit. Under Title VII and the Americans With Disabilities Act, both the EEOC and the employee retain their legal rights, although the rights of one are usually asserted by intervening in the action of the other. If the EEOC files suit first, the employee is limited to intervention in the EEOC's suit. If the employee files suit first, the EEOC will participate, if at all, as an intervenor. In either case, the intervenor has the status of a party to the suit. Under the age statute, the EEOC has the whip hand. If the EEOC brings suit prior to the employee, the employee loses the right to file his or her own suit as well as the right to intervene in the EEOC's action. If the employee files first, the EEOC retains its right to bring its own suit. (If both the EEOC and the employee file lawsuits, the suits are often consolidated into one action.)

The fact that the EEOC can bring its own suit on an employee's charge leaves the employee with an important choice. The employee can, if he or she wishes, ride the coattails of the EEOC's action, letting the EEOC carry the ball. There are several advantages to this course of action. The employee does not have to pay for an attorney. The employee does not have to file his or her own legal action. If a court holds that the action is frivolous and imposes sanctions, it is the EEOC, not the employee, which suffers the consequences. On the other hand, should the EEOC prevail in its action and obtain monetary damages, the money all goes to the employee. If an employee does not have the resources to retain an attorney or is not prepared to act within the limitations period, the EEOC can be a great vehicle to ride. (It should be kept in mind, however, that the EEOC brings suit in a relatively small number of cases.)

The downside to this approach is that by allowing the EEOC to take over the litigation, the employee loses control over the way in which the suit is prosecuted and resolved. The EEOC's interest largely coincides with that of the employee. The EEOC usually acts in cooperation with the employee and in a way that is compatible with the employee's interest. Still, there is no legal requirement that the EEOC defer to the desires of the employee. That is because the EEOC *is not the employee's attorney or legal representative.* The EEOC does not sue just to vindicate the employee's interest. It sues to vindicate a broader public interest. The EEOC may believe that a proposed settlement serves that public interest even though it leaves the employee with very little in the way of monetary relief. When push comes to shove, the EEOC may well cut a deal that the employee perceives as undesirable. If the employee is prepared to do so, there are reasons to at least participate as an intervenor in any action brought by the EEOC to ensure that the employee's rights are fully protected.

When both the EEOC and the employee participate in the same proceeding, there is usually close cooperation. In some cases, the EEOC takes the lead role, with the employee's counsel serving in a backup capacity. In other cases, the employee's counsel takes the lead, with the EEOC's attorneys playing a more secondary role. Again, if any monetary relief is obtained in a case, that money goes to the employee.

A final factor that complicates the picture is that, apart from the role of the EEOC, not all discrimination suits are brought by a single employee acting alone. In the prototypical case, a single employee suffers an adverse employment action. That employee files a charge. The employee then files a lawsuit on that charge. In some cases, the scenario is different. The employer does not simply discriminate against a single employee. The employer engages in a pattern or practice of discrimination that affects a number of employees. In such a case, the EEOC could bring suit for the benefit of the employees who have been the victims of the employment practice at issue. Or, one or more of the affected employees could bring suit, perhaps seeking to represent a class of employees, all of whom were subject to the same discriminatory practice or policy.

The rules for cases of this nature differ. First, an employee can participate in a class-based action, even if the employee has not filed a charge, so long as there is at least one of the affected employees who has filed a charge that makes class-wide allegations of discrimination. The only limitation on such participation is that the employee's claim must otherwise be timely. In other words, the employee's claim must have arisen within (or continued into) the time frame covered by the charge filed by the other employee. There are also differences in the way in which cases involving class-wide allegations of discrimination are processed. Essentially, these cases focus initially on the issue of whether the employer has discriminated against an entire class of employees, with issues of individual relief arising only upon a finding of class-wide liability. Obviously, these cases can be huge enterprises, given the number of claimants involved. It is beyond the purview of this book to address fully the issues that arise in cases involving class-wide allegations of discrimination. Suffice it to say that where multiple employees are asserting claims of discrimination in a single lawsuit, the procedural issues can be highly complex.

Discovery and Pretrial Motions

Once the lawsuit is initiated, the first major stage of the litigation process will be discovery. Discovery is the means by which the parties uncover evidence that can be used at trial. The major discovery device is the deposition. A deposition is the sworn testimony of a witness, taken usually at the offices of the one of the party's attorneys. The deposition is not unlike the examination of a witness that occurs at trial, although the questions tend to have a broader reach, since the attorney asking the questions is fishing for relevant information of any kind. In addition to depositions, a party can ask questions through written interrogatories. A party can also request and compel the production of documents that may have relevance to the case.

In some respects, a form of discovery has already taken place in many discrimination cases, at least those in which the EEOC has fully investigated the employee's charge of discrimination. That is, the EEOC has built an evidentiary record of sorts through its investigation of the charge. The parties have access to the EEOC's investigative file and, thus, can use the information contained in that file in the lawsuit. Nevertheless, the information gathered during the investigation of a charge tends to be somewhat sketchy. It is rarely as detailed as the evidence that is developed during the pretrial phase of litigation. Thus, both parties (including the EEOC, if it has brought suit) can be expected to engage in substantial discovery efforts once a lawsuit is filed.

For the employee, the critical thing to understand about the discovery process is that the employee will be at the center of it. Almost invariably, the employer will want to depose the employee. The deposition will be taken under oath, with the attorney for the employer asking the questions. The employee will be asked questions about performance on the job and the events surrounding the claim of discrimination. The employee might be asked to explain why the employee thinks discrimination has occurred. The employee may be asked to explain away apparent inconsistencies in the employee's conduct or in prior statements that the employee has made about the incidents giving rise to the lawsuit. Because the deposition is taken under oath, what the employee says "can and will be used against him." Any false statements will be seized upon by the employer and used against the employee at trial (should the case ever get to trial). At least theoretically, false statements made under oath in a civil deposition can provide the basis for a perjury prosecution (although prosecutions for perjury stemming from testimony in a civil case are rare). In short, a deposition is serious business and should be treated as such by the employee.

It is important that the employee be well prepared for a deposition. Of course, the employee must answer all questions honestly. There is more than one honest way to answer a question, however, and the employee should be prepared to provide the honest answer that puts the employee's case in the best possible light. For example, an employee may be asked whether the employee has any evidence of discrimination. The answer is likely to be no if what the questioner means is whether the employee has any smoking gun evidence of discrimination. The problem is that if the employee answers no, the employer will treat the answer as an admission that the case has no merit and use it against the employee. An employee should be prepared to point to evidence from which discrimination can be inferred. The employee could respond by saying that the employer's explanation appears to be a fabrication. The employee could point to statements made by individuals at the company that are suggestive of a discriminatory bias. The employee (in a discharge case) could note that a younger individual or an individual of a different race or gender, as the case may be, replaced the employee following the discharge. The employee needs to sound confident in the employee's case and respond forcefully (but without anger) to the employer's questions.

Apart from his or her own deposition, the employee's role in the discovery process is to assist his or her attorney and bide time. The discovery stage of the case can drag on for several months (at the very least). Disputes often arise as to what material must be turned over to the other side. The court may have to intervene to resolve these disputes, thus creating delays. The parties may want to depose several witnesses and to even repeat depositions, in some cases, where new information is gathered that requires additional questions to be asked of a previously deposed witness. Even in the simplest case of employment discrimination, involving one employee and one employment decision, the discovery generated by the parties can be substantial.

When discovery is complete, many employers will file a motion for summary judgment. Summary judgment is a procedural device that allows the judge to throw out the employee's case without the employee having the opportunity to present the case to a jury. The judge does so by reviewing the written record that has been compiled in the discovery process. (That record includes depositions, affidavits, and exhibits.) Technically, the judge is authorized to grant a motion for summary judgment only if the judge determines that the employee's case is deficient as a matter of law. The judge may not decide issues of credibility (i.e., may not rule on whether the employer's witnesses are more believable than the employee's). The judge must view the evidence in the light most favorable to the employee and grant the employee the benefit of all reasonable inferences. The judge must be sensitive to the fact that proving a case of intentional discrimination is a difficult task, given the elusive nature of the factual issue in dispute (the employer's mental state), and should permit the employee to take the case to a jury when there is reasonable support in the record for the employee's position. In theory, summary judgment should be granted in only the rare case in which no reasonable inference of discrimination can be drawn from the evidence generated by the employee during the discovery phase of the case.

While this is the theory of summary judgment, summary judgment, in practice, is something far different. Many courts have a huge backlog of cases. A high percentage of these cases involve claims of employment discrimination. Summary judgment becomes an attractive way to reduce a court's docket by summarily dismissing claims of employment discrimination and avoiding the time and expense of a trial. On the surface, the judge will be careful to say that he or she is not weighing the evidence or making credibility determinations. In truth, the judge will be conducting a mini-trial on the merits, performing a role that is properly reserved for the jury. The dirty little secret of federal practice, as it pertains to claims of employment discrimination, is that many claims that would fare quite well before a jury never get that far. It is not a jury of the employee's peers but a life-tenured judge, reviewing a cold written record, who decides the employee's fate.

Not all judges, of course, are so eager to grant summary judgment. In many cases, employees survive summary judgment, try their cases before a jury, and prevail. An employee, moreover, is not without recourse should a trial judge dismiss a case on a motion for summary judgment. The employee can take an immediate appeal to the federal court of appeals in that region of the country. It is not uncommon for a grant of summary judgment to be reversed by a court of appeals, putting the case back in the trial court and leaving the employee free to pursue the claim before a jury. Still, it cannot be denied that a significant number of discrimination suits are dismissed on summary judgment. An employee must be prepared for the possibility that, no matter how strong the case may seem, the employee will never be able to tell his or her story to a jury.

For obvious reasons, summary judgment is the critical event in the pretrial stage. Other procedural issues, however, can crop up. There may be disputes, for example, over what evidence is admissible at trial. Issues might also arise with respect to the legal standards that govern the case or the employee's entitlement to the items of relief sought by the employee. These are the kinds of issues that are handled by the attorneys for each side, with little input from the parties themselves. On occasion, the court will intercede, at the eleventh hour, in one last attempt to achieve a settlement of the litigation. Indeed, many courts now have mediation programs designed to encourage settlement even as the case approaches trial. The chance for settlement increases if the judge has denied a motion for summary judgment by the employer, since the employer now knows that it faces a jury trial and the real possibility of a damage award. Assuming that no settlement is reached (and summary judgment has not been granted), the pretrial phase will eventually come to a close. At that point, there will be nothing left to do but try the case.

The Trial (and Beyond)

By the time a case is ready for trial, several years may have elapsed from the date of the adverse employment action giving rise to the lawsuit. The employee may have waited six months or more to file a charge. The charge may have sat with the EEOC for months. The lawsuit, while promptly filed, may have pended for months or even years as the case matriculated its way through the pretrial stage. The employee who testifies at trial may be far removed from the employee who was cashiered (or mistreated) several years before. The employee is likely to have a new job and maybe even a new outlook on life. One thing, however, is likely to have stayed the same—the employee's desire to have his or her day in court and to see the employer punished for its wrongdoing.

The trial of a typical discrimination case (involving a single claimant) may take no more than a few days to a week. The first step in most trials is to empanel a jury. Historically, many claims of employment discrimination were tried, not to a jury, but to a federal judge. When Congress passed the Civil Rights Act of 1964, Congress was concerned that juries would be unsympathetic to claims of discrimination. This was particularly true in the South, where a system of all-white juries left minorities with little chance to prevail on a claim of race discrimination. To avoid this problem, Congress vested federal courts with the authority to enforce Title VII, declining to provide the types of damages that would implicate the constitutional right to a jury trial (a right that could be exercised by either the employer or the employee). This system changed in 1991, when Congress provided a right to a jury trial for claims of compensatory and punitive damages under Title VII and expanded the scope of the Civil War–era statute that outlaws race discrimination in contracting. As it now stands, most discrimination claims are tried to juries.

Trials, in practice, are far removed from the dramatic affairs that one sees depicted *on Perry Mason, Matlock, LA Law* or *Law and Order*. They are much more like the real-world trials that are shown on Court TV—tedious and only occasionally of interest to an outsider. The employee, of course, is no outsider. The employee is at the center of the case. The employee will testify, under oath, in support of his or her case and be subjected to vigorous cross-examination by the attorney for the employer.

Once a jury is empaneled, the trial begins in earnest. The employee, as the party complaining of discrimination, will put on his or her case first. The employee's attorney will make an opening statement to the jury. The attorney will then call a series of witnesses who will testify on the employee's behalf. One of those witnesses will be the employee. When called, the employee will have an opportunity to explain his or her version of the events, assisted by the sympathetic questions of the employee's attorney.

The employee will then be subjected to cross-examination by the employer's counsel.

The employee should expect a vigorous cross-examination. In some ways, testimony at trial is a reprise of the employee's deposition. The difference is that the employee is now testifying in open court. The employer's counsel, moreover, will have learned something from the deposition (and the other pretrial discovery). Counsel will hone in on the weaknesses and inconsistencies in the employee's testimony, exploiting them to attack the employee's credibility. The experience of testifying in court can be jarring. This is particularly true where the employee is being attacked as a bad worker, a wrongdoer, or a liar. Again, the employee must testify honestly. The employee must believe in the case and exude that confidence (not arrogance) before the jury. The jury will be carefully watching the employee and gauging both the employee's verbal responses and body language. Cases of this nature often turn on whom the jury believes.

After the employee puts on his or her case, the employer will almost invariably file a motion for judgment as a matter of law. This is a technical step, designed to protect the employer's right to file a post-judgment motion (should the jury find in the employee's favor). Typically, the motion will be denied and the employer will put on its case. The employer is likely to call as witnesses those involved in the employment decision at issue. These individuals will, of course, tell a different story than the employee. They will also be subject to vigorous cross-examination, in this case by the employee's counsel.

Finally, the employee will be given a chance to put on rebuttal evidence. The employee might be called back to the witness stand to clarify some aspect of the employee's testimony. Or, other witnesses could be called to refute specific statements made by the employer's witnesses. After both sides make their closing statements, the case will be submitted to a jury.

The jury's verdict is critical, of course, but not the end of the process. If the jury returns a verdict in favor of the employee, the employer is likely to file a motion for judgment as a matter of law, or in the alternative, a new trial. These motions are sometimes granted. If the court grants judgment as a matter of law, the case ends in the trial court, leaving the employee nothing to do but appeal. If the court orders a new trial, the parties return to square one and retry the case. Should the judge deny the employer's motions, final judgment is entered against the employer.

It is possible, of course, that the jury will find in favor of the employer. At that point, the employee can file his or her own post-judgment motions, seeking to have the jury verdict overturned or to receive a new trial. The chances of any of this occurring are slim. The employee has the burden of proving unlawful discrimination. If the employee cannot persuade a jury that discrimination occurred, few judges will be willing to bounce the jury's verdict unless the employee can point to something fundamentally unfair in the way in which the trial was conducted. For all intents and purposes, a jury verdict in the employer's favor puts an end to the employee's case in the trial court.

Appeals are a commonplace feature of most discrimination cases. If the employee prevails in the trial court, there is a good chance that the employer will appeal. Along with an appeal, the employer is likely to seek a stay of the trial court judgment. A stay ensures that the employer is not required to pay money on the judgment until the appeals process ends. Stays of this nature are routinely granted, leaving the employee without the benefit of the favorable judgment, pending the resolution of the appeal.

If the employee loses in the trial court, the employee must consider whether to take on the additional time and expense of an appeal. An employee who loses a case at the pretrial stage— on summary judgment, for example—has a fair chance of having that decision overturned by an appeals court. An employee who has had his or her day in court, and lost before a jury, faces a severe uphill battle. The appeals court will not second-guess the jury. The appeals court will not reweigh the evidence. There might be an argument that the trial committed a legal error in excluding evidence or in instructing the jury on the governing law. Even then, however, the court of appeals might be inclined to see the error as harmless, letting the jury verdict stand. Unless there was some fundamental unfairness in the way the case was tried, the employee will have little chance of prevailing in an appeal. If the employee wants to make an appeal, the employee needs to act quickly. The time for appealing is 30 days from the date of the final decision in the trial court, except in cases in which an agency of the U.S. government (the EEOC, for example) is a party, in which case the time is extended to 60 days.

In the federal system, an appeal is taken to the court of appeals in that region of the country. There are twelve courts of appeals. While it varies from court to court, it typically takes some three to four months for the parties to file their legal briefs in the appellate court. It may take another several months for oral arguments to be scheduled. Eventually, the case will be argued to a three-judge panel. After the argument, the panel will take the case under advisement. Another several months may pass. Finally, the panel will issue a decision. The panel's decision is final unless a party is able to convince the full court to rehear the case. Such requests for rehearing are rarely granted.

As the above discussion suggests, the appeals process can drag out for some time. The game, however, is still not over. The last resort for the losing party is the U.S. Supreme Court. It may be the dream of every litigant (or at least the litigant's lawyer) to have a case heard by the Supreme Court. Unfortunately, it is a dream deferred in the vast majority of cases. The Supreme Court votes to hear only a tiny percentage of cases for which Supreme Court review is sought. The Court almost never hears a case unless the case raises significant legal issues and there is a disagreement among the lower courts as to how those issues should be resolved. Realistically, there is very little chance of having an adverse decision of the court of appeals overturned in the Supreme Court.

None of this, of course, will deter the party who feels wronged by an adverse decision. Employers may be the worst offenders. Unwilling to accept defeat, many plod onward, exhausting every avenue of appeal up to and including the

Supreme Court. In some cases, an employee may wait months, even years, for the appeals process to play out. The one thing that sweetens the pot for the employee is that the employee can recover the interest on the amount of money due (but not yet paid) to the employee.

Eventually, the process will come to an end (believe it or not). If the employee has a won a verdict in the trial court and the verdict has withstood the appeals process, the employee will finally collect on the favorable judgment. But even then the law has one last trick up its sleeve. Should the employee recover monetary damages, the employee must report those damages as taxable income. Even in victory, the employee must pay.

The Outlook for Al

It is impossible to say how Al would fare should he file suit and litigate one or more of his claims. We know that, at the very least, he has a solid claim of age discrimination. Additional discovery might provide more support for Al's case. If Al goes to trial, he would be wise to drop the weaker of his two claims (the race claim), unless he has uncovered, through discovery, some compelling evidence of racial bias. (This assumes that Al would have brought the race claim to begin with.) A party litigating a discrimination claim needs to come up with a coherent theory of the case. Arguing that the employment decision may have stemmed from age or race or both is likely to confuse and turn off a jury.

There is no guarantee, of course, that Al will ever make it to trial. As noted previously, summary judgment is a commonplace feature of federal court practice. Age cases seem particularly vulnerable to dismissal at the summary judgment stage. In truth, whether Al makes it to trial may well depend upon which judge is assigned to Al's case. A judge with some sympathy to claims of employment discrimination is likely to deny any motion for summary judgment, thereby giving Al his day in court. A judge with a different view of discrimination claims, or with a burning desire to reduce the size of his or her docket (i.e., the number of cases pending in the judge's court), could send Al packing.

If Al reaches a jury, his prospects for winning are good. Al is likely to be a sympathetic plaintiff. The company's explanations for the decision appear shaky. The company may well have difficulty making the performance-based explanation stick. Its claim that Al's job was eliminated is undermined by its own actions (e.g., hiring somebody to fill the position). If the jury disbelieves the company's explanations for the decision and has anything to hang its hat on in the way of a discriminatory bias (in this case, there are the age-biased comments of the company president), the jury is likely to return a verdict in Al's favor.

Will it be worth it to Al to have litigated (and perhaps won) his claim? This is for Al to say. To some, the prospect of protracted litigation may be daunting—too daunting perhaps to justify the time, effort, and cost (emotional, if not financial). To others, there may be no choice but to go forward. The desire to punish the employer for its wrongful conduct will be too great. The important thing is that an employee knows what awaits should the case end up in litigation. The process can be grueling, but the reward, in more ways than just financial, may well be worth the struggle.

Part III

Some Major
Workplace Issues

Part III of this book focuses on three areas of employment law that are significant enough, in their own right, to be addressed in separate chapters. The first of these is sexual harassment. Perhaps no issue involving the workplace has captured the public's attention more than sexual harassment. For obvious reasons (the word *sex* is involved, after all), the issue has dominated public discourse, providing the fodder for opinion columns and talk radio debate. To working women, in particular, the issue is not simply academic—it affects their day-to-day existence in the workplace. The main thing to understand about sexual harassment is that the law has its own definition of actionable harassment, one that may differ from the commonly held views of the general public. Some people, for example, may view any sexual advance in the workplace as a form of sexual harassment. Yet the law requires that the harassment be severe or pervasive. A single pass or sexual advance is unlikely to meet the standard of severe or pervasive harassment, although repeated advances, in the face of an employee's rejection of those advances, could be enough. Plainly, if an employee is terminated or demoted because she has refused a supervisor's sexual advances, the employee has a claim under the law. Fortunately, in several recent cases, the Supreme Court has provided guidance on the legal standards for determining when conduct rises to the level of actionable harassment and when an employer is responsible for the harassment. Those decisions provide the basis for understanding the law of sexual harassment, as it now stands.

The second issue discussed in this part is the phenomenon of corporate downsizing. Again, this is an issue that has often grabbed the headlines. It is in the headlines because it occurs so often and has such profound consequences for the affected employees. As a legal matter, downsizing raises several questions. First, in many cases, the law requires that advance notice be given to the affected employees. Second, the decision to terminate an employee, as part of a reduction-in-force, may well be an unlawful act. In carrying out a reduction-in-force, for example, an employer may not select an older employee for dismissal because of the age of the employee (assuming the employee is over the age of 40 and, thus, covered under the federal age discrimination statute). Next, a downsized employee is often presented with a severance agreement that requires the employee to waive rights under such statutes as the federal age discrimination statute. The law regulates these agreements carefully to ensure that any waiver is made in a knowing and voluntary fashion. Finally, once downsized, many employees will be forced to reenter the job market. Often, an older applicant for a job will be met with the objection that he or she is overqualified. In some cases, the use of this label will support a claim of age discrimination.

The last issue concerns the dilemma of an employee who suffers an injury that impairs the employee's ability to perform a job. Historically, an employee in this circumstance could apply for workers' compensation benefits (if the injury occurred on the job). The employee could also apply for Social Security disability benefits if the injury was so disabling that the employee was unable to work. These options are still available to an employee. The law, however, now recognizes that many individuals with disabilities can work. The law, in fact, requires employers to provide reasonable accommodations to disabled employees to assist those employees in performing the job. This development helps the disabled employee but also places the employee in an awkward position. What if an employee becomes disabled but is denied a reasonable accommodation, leaving the employee without a job? Can the employee apply for workers' compensation or disability benefits if the employee believes that he or she could have performed the job with a reasonable accommodation? And if the employee applies for such compensation or benefits, claiming to be totally disabled or unable to work, can he or she still sue the employer under the Americans With Disabilities Act (for the failure to accommodate), claiming to be an individual who can work (with accommodation)? If an employee is not careful, he or she may be caught between the law's traditional assumption—that a disabled individual is unable to work—and the assumptions of the new paradigm—that many individuals with disabilities can work and should be assisted in their efforts to obtain (and retain) employment.

CHAPTER 15

Sexual Harassment

There is no federal statute that makes sexual harassment, as such, unlawful. Sexual harassment is unlawful because it is a form of sex discrimination within the meaning of Title VII of the Civil Rights Act of 1964. To be actionable under Title VII, harassment must be sex- or gender-based and must be severe or pervasive enough to affect the terms or conditions of an individual's employment. Even if the conduct in question rises to the level of severe or pervasive harassment, the employer is not automatically liable. If the perpetrator of the harassment is a co-worker, the employer is liable only if the employer knew or should have known about the harassment and failed to take effective steps to redress the harassment. If the perpetrator is a high-ranking company official, the company is directly liable, since the high-ranking official is, in effect, a stand-in for the company. If the perpetrator is the employee's supervisor, the employer may be liable under a theory of vicarious liability, although a defense is available, in some cases, to an employer that adopts an effective sexual harassment policy.

In practical terms, the situation faced by a victim of workplace harassment can be a difficult one. When confronted with harassment, the employee has a choice to make. Do I complain about the harassment? Do I let a single incident pass? Do I make my objections clear to the harasser but hold back on any formal complaint? Do I continue to tolerate the harassment, and, if so, at what point do I step forward and complain? In some respects, the answers to these questions are informed by the law itself, which requires employees, in some circumstances, to complain about harassment before the employer is held liable. In large part, however, the choices flow from the real-world circumstances confronting the employee. The employee does not want to endure a gauntlet of sexual abuse. Nor does the employee, however, want to be known as thin-skinned, a whiner, or one of "those" women (in the case of a female employee). An employee, moreover, faces the real possibility that if he or she complains, the perpetrator (if a decision maker) will retaliate against the employee by firing the employee, demoting the employee, or generally making the employee's life miserable. No doubt, if the perpetrator pursues such a course, the law protects the employee. But that protection may be a long time in coming if the employee is forced to litigate a claim. In the meantime, the employee may be out of a job and tainted in the eyes of some because of his or her complaints. The law is designed to protect an employee who suffers sexual harassment in the workplace. But, in some respects, the employee must act with an eye toward the practical realities of the situation at hand, the legal protections notwithstanding.

Sex-Based Harassment

The first point to make about sexual harassment is the most basic. When people think about workplace harassment, they often focus on the prototypical case—a male supervisor harasses a female subordinate either by making sexual advances or threatening to take action against the female if she does not grant sexual favors. This scenario is, unfortunately, far too common. It does not, however, define the extent of the law's protection. First, the law prohibits harassment on the basis of any protected trait. This includes race, national origin, religion, age, or disability. (Racial harassment is discussed in Chapter 1.) More to the point, sexual harassment itself can take many forms. To be actionable, sexual harassment must be sex-based. Sex-based, however, does not mean that the harassment must be sexual in nature in the carnal sense. Nor does it mean that the perpetrator must always be male and the victim female. To the contrary, the law broadly reaches any conduct that results in different working conditions for men and women (so long as the conduct is sufficiently severe or pervasive to affect the terms or conditions of the individual's employment).

Take, for example, the case of a male supervisor who oversees the work of twenty subordinates. The supervisor works in a trade that is male-dominated. In this case, nineteen of the twenty individuals working for the supervisor are male. The supervisor decides that he wants to get rid of the one female worker and embarks on a campaign of harassment. The supervisor does not proposition the woman, touch her body in a sexual way, or make crude jokes of a sexual nature. Instead, the supervisor constantly yells at the female worker, gives her the more difficult work assignments, and, in general, treats her more harshly than any of the male employees. This is classic sex or gender discrimination. The supervisor has singled out a female employee for different treatment and made her working conditions far more onerous. Title VII reaches the supervisor's conduct.

Notably, the fact that the harasser is of a different gender than the victim is not decisive. Assume the same workplace as above, except in this case the supervisor is a woman. The supervisor is the first woman to occupy that position. She wants to prove her mettle with her male subordinates and decides to do so by subjecting the female subordinate to harsh treatment. The supervisor makes crude comments about the woman's appearance, touches her in an offensive way, and constantly criticizes her work without justification. Again, the supervisor has made the female employee a target of the harassment. As a result, the employee's working conditions are far less desirable than those of her male co-workers. Such conduct constitutes sex-based discrimination within the meaning of the antidiscrimination statutes.

In a recent decision, the U.S. Supreme Court confirmed that same-sex harassment of this nature is covered under Title VII. The Court explained that Title VII prohibits conduct that subjects members of one sex to disadvantageous terms or conditions of employment to which members of the other sex are not subjected. If there is evidence that a man or woman has suffered harassment that a member of the opposite sex did not suffer (or would not have suffered), the harassment can be viewed as sex-based. That is true regardless of the sexual identity of the harasser or victim. Thus, if a male supervisor makes repeated sexual advances in his dealings with a male subordinate, but makes no such advances with respect to any female employee, the male employee has a claim of sexual harassment. Similarly, if a group of male employees target a male co-worker for some form of physical abuse—of a kind not visited upon female employees—the victim of the abuse has a claim that he has been subjected to different working conditions because of his sex or gender.

In holding that the law reaches same-sex harassment, the Supreme Court made clear that the claimant must still *prove* that the harassment is sex-based. This can be a difficult task. Where a male harasses a female in a sexual way, it is obvious, in most cases, that the harassment is sex-based. It may be equally obvious where the harassment is male-on-male and involves sexual conduct of some kind, since it is fair to assume, absent evidence to the contrary, that the harasser is targeting the victim of the harassment because of his sex. The harasser, in other words, is a homosexual who is seeking sexual favors from another male (rather than a woman). But what about the case of same-sex harassment that does not involve sexual conduct or verbiage, as such? Males, in particular, frequently engage in horseplay among themselves. At times, this horseplay can lead to injurious conduct of some kind. Is this a form of sex-based harassment? Is it truly the gender of the victim that is causing the harassment? Is it not possible that women, if they were included in the horseplay, would be treated the same? These questions are not easily answered. In many cases, a claim of same-sex harassment will fail, not because Title VII does not cover such harassment, but because the claimant will not be able to show that the harassment is sex-based.

In the more typical case, the requirement of sex-based harassment is readily met. If a member of one sex harasses a member of the opposite sex and uses sexual conduct or banter in carrying out the harassment, it is hard to dispute the contention that the harassment is sex-based. Actionable harassment can include physical touching, comments of a sexual nature, requests for sexual favors, and sex-based threats ("either have sex with me or else"). It should be stressed that these activities are not covered under federal law because they are sexual (i.e., carnal) in nature. They are covered because the law assumes that, in most cases, sexual conduct implicates gender and, thus, triggers the law's prohibition against sex or gender discrimination.

On occasion, disputes arise as to whether a particular comment is sex- or gender-based. In the racial context, there are derogatory words that have an obvious connection to race. The word *nigger*, for example, is plainly racist, plainly offensive, and plainly out-of-bounds, at least when used by a white manager or worker in reference to an African American employee. Its use in the workplace can readily support a claim of racial harassment. Are there comparable terms or epithets of a sexual nature? Several come to mind, with the term *bitch* being, perhaps, the most tame example. Seemingly, the use of such a derogatory term, with an obvious connection to gender, would be enough to earn the sex-based label. On occasion, however, courts have found terms (such as bitch) to be ambiguous in their reference to gender. (In one case, a court held that a male co-worker's statement, "You cold northern bitch. Why don't you give us southern boys a break and say yes once in a while?" was not sexual harassment because it "was not necessarily meant in a sexual way.") As in most cases of sexual harassment, context will be key. If a male manager uses sexually coarse language in criticizing his female subordinates (referring to them as bitches or ugly cows), it is likely that a court will find the verbal barrage to be sex-based.

There are times when the sexual conduct or verbiage is not directed at a particular employee. In some companies, the workplace is sexually charged. There are posters of naked women and a daily barrage of derogatory jokes and comments about women and sex. One might argue that this conduct is not sex-based in the sense that it is not designed to single out a particular woman or group of women for harsher treatment. Indeed, one might argue that the conduct is equally offensive to men and women alike and, thus, not discriminatory. For the most part, courts have resisted the temptation to permit the sheer breadth of the sexual conduct or material to excuse the employer. The very point of the law is to ensure that working women, in particular, do not enter a working environment that is rife with sexual intimidation, ridicule, and insult. To argue that generalized portrayals of sex do not discriminate against women in their working conditions is to miss the essential assumption of sexual harassment law—that the depiction of sex almost invariably differentiates along gender lines, given the extent to which American society has objectified women in a sexual way. At least where the sexual conduct or material is gender-specific (i.e., there are not an equal number of pictures of naked men in the workplace), the conduct or material will be viewed as sex-based.

In most cases, the requirement of sex-based harassment is noncontroversial. If a male supervisor targets a female subordinate for sexual touching or propositions, it is clear that the harassment is sex-based. Even where the harassment is not sexual in nature or the perpetrator and victim are of the same sex, the law can reach the conduct. Conduct is sex-based and, thus, actionable if there is evidence that an individual is exposed to adverse working conditions to which a member of the opposite sex is not exposed.

Unwelcomeness Requirement

There are important reasons for making sexual harassment in the workplace unlawful. It must also be recognized, however, that extending the law to matters of a sexual nature carries with it some risk. Sexual conduct, when carried out in a coercive way, can be highly detrimental to an employee. Men, in particular, use sex as a way of exercising power over women, who may be in no position to resist the harassment. On the other hand, for many, a certain degree of sexual banter (even crude sexual banter) is a part of the courting ritual. Men and women have been interacting in a sexual way since the beginning of time. (So, too, one suspects, have men and men and women and women.) The law wants to ensure that the working conditions of one gender are not made more onerous because of coercive sexual behavior. It does not, however, want to outlaw the normal give-and-take of the sexual dynamic.

To guard against this concern, the law imposes a requirement that the sex-based conduct be unwelcome. Unwelcome means precisely what the word implies. If an employee willingly participates in (even instigates) the sexual conduct, the employee may have difficulty arguing that the conduct is unwelcome. If, however, the employee signals by his or her words or conduct that the sexual conduct is unwanted, the law will deem the harassing behavior to be unwelcome.

There are two critical points to make about the unwelcomeness requirement. First, compliance with this requirement is largely in the hands of the employee. When a manager solicits sex from a subordinate employee, the employee can simply say no. No, in this context, means no and will be taken as such by the law. If other workers engage in a daily barrage of sexual banter, the employee can tell fellow workers that he or she does not find the comments funny or appropriate. Or, the employee can signal disapproval of the comments by not participating in the banter or by removing herself (if possible) from the locus of the banter. As long as an employee makes clear that a sexual advance or comment is not welcome, there is no question that any ensuing conduct of a similar kind will be viewed as unwelcome.

This is not to say that an employee is required, in all cases, to make known her opposition to the sexual conduct. Sexual harassment is unlawful precisely because of its coercive nature. An employee confronted with unwelcome sexual conduct in the workplace may well be reluctant to express her disapproval of the conduct, fearing that it will lead to retaliation. An employee, in fact, may participate in sexual banter, to a degree, as a way of defending herself or signaling to her co-workers that she is "one of the guys." If it appears that an employee has gone along with the harassment, as a defensive measure, the law will not bar her claim. The standard for unwelcomeness, moreover, is not the same as the standard for legal consent. For example, an employee can consent to sex in a legal sense, thus vitiating any criminal prosecution for rape, and still claim that the conduct is unwelcome (i.e, that she granted the sexual favors because of the threat that she would lose her job or be demoted if she did not). The purpose of the unwelcomeness requirement is to ensure that an employee who willingly participates in sexual conduct in the workplace cannot turn around and unfairly accuse the employer of sexual harassment. It is not to trap the unwary employee who finds herself in a position where she cannot voice her objection to the harassment.

The second point to make about the unwelcomeness requirement is that an employee does not welcome sexual harassment by her dress or general sexual demeanor. What a person wears to work is a matter of taste. A woman does not forfeit her right to be free from sexual harassment by wearing a tight dress or deporting herself in a way that exudes a certain sexuality. A woman may choose to deemphasize her sexuality as a way of enhancing her professional credibility. A woman, however, is not required to make that choice to merit the protection of the law. A woman welcomes sexual conduct when she engages in specific behavior that signals her willingness to participate in a game of sexual repartee with a fellow worker. She does not do so simply by wearing clothes that may be viewed as sexually provocative.

By and large, issues concerning the unwelcomeness of sexual conduct blend into the nature of the conduct itself. If the alleged harassment is marginal or ambiguous in nature, the fact that the claimant appeared to go along with the harassment would tend to confirm that the harassment was not offensive. Where, however, the harassing behavior is severe in nature, the law assumes that the employee acquiesced in the conduct, if at all, only because the employee felt coerced into doing so. In most cases, severe incidents of sexual harassment will be viewed as unwelcome, absent compelling evidence that the employee was a willing participant in the conduct at issue.

Severe or Pervasive Harassment

The critical factor that distinguishes sexual harassment, as commonly understood, from sexual harassment, as legally defined, is the requirement that the harassment be sufficiently severe or pervasive to trigger the protections of the law. The law does not prohibit sexual harassment because it is a bad thing. It prohibits sexual harassment because it is a form of sex discrimination that adversely affects the terms or conditions of an individual's employment. To be unlawful, unwelcome sex-based harassment must be severe or pervasive enough to create an abusive working environment.

There are two components to the requirement of severe or pervasive harassment. First, the employee must perceive the working environment to be abusive. Typically, this is easy enough to show, at least in those cases where the employee has complained about the harassment. The more difficult requirement is that the harassment creates a working environment that a reasonable person would find hostile or abusive. This imports an element of objectivity into the standard. It ensures that the delicate sensibilities of a particular employee not dictate the threshold for unlawful harassment.

The Supreme Court has made clear that there is no one factor that determines the existence of a hostile working environment. The Court has stated that all of the surrounding circumstances must be examined, including the frequency of the conduct, its severity, whether it is physically threatening or humiliating, and whether it unreasonably interferes with an employee's work performance. The Court has rejected the view that harassment must cause psychological harm to give rise to a legal claim. Thus, an employee is not required to run a gauntlet of sexual abuse before the law steps in to provide protection.

By the same token, the law does not reach every petty slight or offensive comment. Some assume that any comment or action of a sexual nature in the workplace is legally out-of-bounds. This is simply not the case. The law does not police every workplace infraction, nor does it reach every sexually charged encounter among employees. A single off-color joke made around the water cooler is not likely by itself to trigger the protection of the law. Nor is an off-hand comment about a worker's appearance or a simple request for a date.

Plainly, a critical factor bearing upon the lawfulness of sexual conduct is the number of incidents of harassing behavior. In the typical case, unlawful harassment results from a series of offensive acts. Take, for example, the case of a male supervisor who is attracted to a female subordinate. The supervisor approaches the employee in the workplace and propositions her. Is this enough to implicate the protections of the law? Probably not. While rude and inappropriate, the single proposition is not enough to alter the terms or conditions of the individual's employment. Say, however, that in response to the proposition, the female employee says no in no uncertain terms. The supervisor does not take no for an answer. The supervisor continues to proposition the employee and to make crude sexual comments. At some point (very soon), the supervisor's conduct implicates the protections of the law.

There are cases where the law does not demand more than one or two incidents of harassing behavior. As noted previously, harassment must be severe *or* pervasive. This implies that if the conduct is severe enough, it need not be pervasive (i.e., carried out on a number of occasions). The most obvious example would be a sexual assault. Plainly, one sexual assault is enough to create an abusive working environment. A single proposition might be enough to alter the working conditions of a reasonable employee if the proposition carries with it a physical threat or involves more than simply the request for a sexual favor (e.g., is accompanied by physical groping of the employee being propositioned). For the most part, the law demands some degree of repetition before conduct reaches the legal threshold for unlawful harassment. This is certainly true with respect to jokes or comments of a sexual nature. In some cases, however, particularly those involving an act of physical touching, an isolated incident of harassment might be enough to bring the employee within the protection of the law.

Employer Liability

In one critical respect, harassment is unlike any other form of discrimination. Where a company official fires or demotes an employee, there is no doubt that the company is responsible for the official's action. Having bestowed decision-making authority upon the official, the company must pay the price for the official's discriminatory decisions. Harassment is different. Harassment does not involve an employment decision in the traditional sense. Often, the harassers are simply co-workers, with no authority to act on the company's behalf in employment-related matters. Even where the perpetrator of the harassment is a supervisor or company official, it is unlikely that the company has authorized the supervisor or official to engage in acts of sexual harassment against other employees. No doubt, the employer bears substantial responsibility for what takes place in its workplace. It seems clear, however, that the employer cannot be held strictly liable for every act of sexual harassment perpetrated by an employee.

Over the years, courts have struggled with formulating standards for imposing liability in sexual harassment cases. In two recent cases, the Supreme Court clarified the state of the law in this area. The Court, in essence, adopted separate legal standards for three different categories of harassment: (1) harassment that results in a tangible job detriment; (2) harassment that does not result in a tangible job detriment but which is perpetrated by an immediate supervisor or somebody higher up in the chain of command; and (3) harassment that is perpetrated by a nonman-agerial co-worker.

The first category of harassment focuses on the classic quid pro quo form of sexual harassment discrimination. The sexual harassment theory grew out of cases in which a company official, usually the employee's supervisor, would use his or her position of authority to coerce sexual favors out of the employee. The supervisor would pose a quid pro quo to the employee—either put out or suffer the employment consequences. If the employee refused to submit to the sexual advance or proposition, the employee would be fired or suffer some other tangible job detriment. It is now clear that if a supervisor poses a quid pro quo to an employee, which the employee rebuffs, the employer is liable if the supervisor responds by taking some adverse employment action against the employee (e.g., firing the employee, demoting the employee, assigning the employee to a less desirable job, refusing to promote the employee, or reducing the pay of the employee).

In some cases, a supervisor will pose the quid pro quo to the employee but not carry through on the threat. Historically, many courts took the position that this was per se unlawful, no different than if the supervisor had acted on the threat. This is no longer the law. If the supervisor threatens to take a tangible job action against an employee and then carries through on the threat when the employee rebuffs the supervisor's sexual advance, there is strict liability for the employer. If, however, the supervisor merely threatens the employee with a tangible job detriment but no such detriment ensues, the employer is not automatically liable. The employer can be held responsible for the supervisor's threats, but only if the threats meet the liability standard for actions taken by a supervisor that do not result in a tangible job detriment.

The second category of harassment concerns conduct that does not result in a tangible job detriment but which carries the imprimatur of the company because it is undertaken by a supervisor with immediate (or successively higher) authority over the employee. In some cases, a supervisor will take action against an employee who refuses to acquiesce in the supervisor's sexual demands. In others, the supervisor will simply engage in harassing behavior. The supervisor might subject the employee to a barrage of verbal harassment. The supervisor might proposition the employee but not threaten explicitly to take any action against the employee. Or (as noted previously), the supervisor might threaten the employee with some tangible job detriment but not carry through on the threat. In these cases, the supervisor is not acting as the decision-making arm of the company in carrying out the harassment (unless the employer has authorized the harassment, which is unlikely). Thus, it may not be fair, in all cases, to hold the employer directly responsible for the supervisor's actions. On the other hand, the supervisor is a manager (not a mere employee) who may well be using supervisory authority to carry out the harassment. The employer cannot simply bury its head in the sand, acting as if it has no responsibility for the unlawful actions of its management-level officials.

In cases of this nature, the law adopts two standards for employer liability. In cases in which the harasser is a high-ranking official, the employer will be strictly liable for the harassment. Strict liability is appropriate in such a case because the harasser, due to rank, is a virtual stand-in or proxy for the company. The classic example of the proxy harasser would be the president of a small company who is an alter ego of the company. The president *is* the company, and his harassment is the company's harassment.

In the more typical case, where the harasser is an immediate supervisor (or some other low-level manager with authority over the employee), the law presumes that the employer is responsible for the supervisor's harassment, given the supervisor's role as the employer's agent in employment-related matters. The law, however, provides the employer with the opportunity to demonstrate that it is not responsible for the supervisor's actions. The employer can do so by meeting a two-part affirmative defense. The employer must first prove that it exercised reasonable care to prevent and promptly correct any sexually harassing behavior. The employer must also show that the employee failed to take advantage of any preventive or corrective opportunities provided by the employer.

It is unclear how the affirmative defense (recently adopted by the Supreme Court) will play out in actual cases. There are, however, some observations that can be made. First, the defense provided to employers does not appear to be an absolute defense. As discussed previously, there are cases where the harassment is so severe that a single occurrence of the harassment is enough to create an abusive or hostile working environment. If such a severe incident occurs and is perpetrated by the employer's supervisor, the employer is directly liable for the supervisor's harassment. The reason for this is simple. Employees should be encouraged to complain about harassment in the workplace in order to provide employers with the opportunity to correct the harassment and to prevent future incidents of harassment. Where, however, a severe incident of harassment has already occurred, the bell cannot be unrung. No matter how vigorously the employer responds to the harassment, the employee has already suffered an injury for which the law provides a remedy. If the employee fails to complain about the initial harassment and more incidents of harassment occur, the employer might have an argument that it is not responsible for the damages resulting from those subsequent acts of harassment. The failure to complain, however, would not preclude a claim for the initial harassment, assuming that the initial harassment is sufficiently severe, by itself, to create an abusive or hostile working environment.

The second point to make about the affirmative defense is that it requires more than a written sexual harassment policy. Many employers have sexual harassment policies of some kind. The existence of such a policy will assist the employer in arguing that it had mechanisms in place to prevent or correct harassment, thus undercutting the claim of an employee who fails to utilize the employer's complaint procedures. The mere fact, however, that the employer has committed to an antiharassment policy, on paper, is not enough. There must be evidence that the policy, in practice, is effective. This could include evidence that the policy is widely disseminated and discussed (in training or work sessions), that the policy permits complaints to be made to individuals outside the employee's chain of command (e.g., human resources personnel), that complaints of harassment are taken seriously, that complaints of harassment are fully and conscientiously investigated, and that the company takes appropriate corrective action in response to complaints that are deemed to have merit.

Further, even if the employer has an effective sexual harassment policy, an employee might still have reasonable grounds for not complaining about the harassment. By definition, the harasser, in these cases, will have decision-making authority of some kind over the employee. The harasser might tell the employee that there will be retribution if he or she complains about the harassment. Confronted with such a threat, an employee might reasonably forgo any complaint, even given the existence of an effective sexual harassment policy. In other cases, the harasser might have close connections to the individuals who run the company. This is particularly true in a small company, where the harasser could be a relative or close friend of the owner or company president. The employee may rightly feel that any complaint of harassment will be ignored or, worse, that he or she will be persecuted for having made the complaint (and, thus, will be twice victimized). If it is reasonable for the employee not to take advantage of the preventive or corrective opportunities made available by the employer, the employee can assert a claim for unlawful discrimination stemming from a pattern of harassing behavior, even where no complaint about the harassment has been lodged.

Plainly, the affirmative defense is designed to ensure, as much as possible, that harassment is dealt with effectively in the workplace, thus reducing its occurrence (and recurrence). The defense provides an incentive for the employer to establish effective mechanisms for preventing and correcting unlawful harassment. Indeed, an employer that fails to do so will be per se liable for sexual harassment perpetrated by supervisors and low-level managers with decision-making authority over the employee. By the same token, an employee has an incentive to invoke the employer's complaint mechanisms. An employee who promptly complains about harassment preserves his or her legal rights,

assuming that the employer fails to take effective action to prevent the harassment, thus resulting in more incidents of harassment. An employee who fails to complain is not barred in all cases
from maintaining a claim. The employee, however, is at risk of
losing the claim (or having damages reduced) if it is later determined that it was unreasonable for the employee not to invoke
the employer's complaint mechanisms.

The final category of harassment may be the most common—harassment perpetrated by co-workers who are not in a
position of authority over the victim. In this context, there is no
basis for holding the employer directly responsible for the harassment. The co-worker is not the employer's agent with respect to
employment decision making. The co-worker stands on equal
footing with the victim in the corporate hierarchy, and is not
using any authority ceded by the company to carry out the
harassment. Nevertheless, the harassment is taking place in the
employer's workplace. Surely there is some basis for holding the
employer accountable for the impermissible actions of its employees in the workplace.

To deal with this scenario, the law has adopted what
amounts to a negligence standard. That standard requires the
employee complaining about harassment to make two showings.
First, the employee must show that the employer knew or should
have known about the harassment. Second, the employee must
show that the employer, upon learning of the harassment, failed
to take prompt remedial action that prevented the harassment
from recurring. In essence, the employee must prove that the
employer had notice of the harassment and failed to redress it
effectively.

In most cases, the "knew" or "should-have-known" standard
is met by the employee complaining about the harassment. The
phrase *should have known* implies that there are circumstances
where the employer can be charged with notice of the harassment even where the harassment has not been brought to the
specific attention of the employer (by, for example, an employee
complaint). This is true in cases in which the harassment so per-

vades the workplace that the employer's failure to know about the harassment is itself negligent. The employer can also be charged with notice if the company, through its management officials, learns about the harassment, even though no complaint about the harassment has been lodged. Despite these forms of constructive or third-party notice, the law has tended to require some complaint from the victim, at least where the company has in place a sexual harassment policy that provides a mechanism for reporting harassment. To be absolutely protected, the employee may need to lodge a complaint about the harassment to ensure that the employer is held legally responsible for any ensuing acts of harassment.

The second component of the liability standard focuses on the employer's response to the harassment once the matter is brought to the employer's attention. The initial step for the employer is to investigate any complaint of harassment. The employer's investigation must be thorough and conscientious. An employer may have a written antiharassment policy. That policy may provide a mechanism for reporting or complaining about harassment. The employer, however, must do more than write a policy. It must act and act decisively once an employee invokes the policy. An employer is not required to believe the complainant's story. Nor can the employer, however, bury its head in the sand or conduct a cursory inquiry that concludes in no action being taken on the complaint. An ineffective investigation amounts to an ineffective remedial response, thereby exposing the employer to liability if the harassment does not cease.

The second part of the employer's duty is to take appropriate remedial action once it determines that harassment has occurred. There are a number of remedial measures available to the employer. The employer can issue a stern reprimand to the offending employee. The employer can discipline the harasser by docking the harasser's pay or suspending the harasser for a certain number of days without pay. If the harassment is severe and appears likely to recur, the employer can (and should) take steps to ensure that the harasser does not work in close proximity to the victim. This can be accomplished by transferring the harasser to a different job or work shift. The employer should not separate the victim and the harasser by moving the victim out of a job unless the victim expresses a desire to work elsewhere in the company.

The effectiveness of the employer's response is judged, in part, by what occurs after the employer takes its remedial response. If the harassment ceases, the response has been effective and the employer avoids any legal liability. If, however, the harassment continues, the employer is exposed to liability for the subsequent acts of harassment. The mere fact that a remedial response is ineffective does not, in all cases, subject the employer to liability. An employer does not have a crystal ball and cannot always predict what level of response is necessary to eliminate the harassment. Nevertheless, at some point, the employer must take whatever remedial steps are necessary to make the harassment stop or else pay the consequences. Certainly, the employer will find itself in hot water if it fails on multiple occasions in its attempt to put an end to the offensive conduct.

The employer's ultimate weapon, of course, is to fire the harasser. This can be a dangerous course for the employer. The employer is charged with the responsibility of protecting the victim of the harassment. If, however, the employer takes the drastic step of terminating the harasser's employment, the employer implicates the employment rights of the harasser. If the employee is a member of a union, the employee can grieve the termination under the collective bargaining agreement. (Grievances of this nature are often successful.) The employee (whether a union member or not) can also bring a lawsuit, alleging wrongful discharge. In several high-profile cases, employees have prevailed in these suits, having established that the termination was unjustified under the circumstances. With results like these, many employers feel that they are caught between a rock and a hard place—damned if they do take action against the harasser and damned if they don't.

As it turns out, the employer's plight is not so precarious. The law does not require the employer to discharge the harasser.

The law simply requires the employer to take prompt and appropriate remedial action. After an initial complaint of harassment, the employer is typically safe in taking some action short of discharging the harasser (unless the harassment involves something as serious as a sexual assault, in which case the loss of a job is the least of the harasser's problems). The employer, for example, can reprimand or suspend the harasser, making it clear that more serious consequences will ensue if the harasser repeats the behavior. If the harassment persists, it may reach the point that the employer is left with no option but to terminate the harasser's employment (or else face liability for the harassment). At that point, however, the harasser is unlikely to have a legal leg to stand on. The employer has warned the harasser that he or she needed to cease the harassment or risk the loss of his or her job. The employer has engaged in progressive discipline in an attempt to put an end to the harassment. Only after these attempts failed did the employer pull the trigger and fire the harasser. Of course, disgruntled employees can always sue, and, by firing the harasser, the employer may well have bought a lawsuit for wrongful discharge. Having, however, laid the groundwork for its decision, the employer will be on solid ground in arguing that the discharge was justified.

One final point. The standards discussed above are used in determining the liability of the employer (or company). That is, they provide the basis for determining when a company can be made to pay for the harassment of one of its employees or managers. Under federal law, the harasser himself or herself cannot be sued for damages in his or her individual capacity (at least where the harasser works for a private company). Any claim for damages is against the company, not the perpetrator of the harassment.

That is not to say that the harasser gets away scot-free. First, some states may permit individual managers to be sued in their individual capacities. In addition, most states recognize actions in tort for intentional infliction of emotional distress. These actions, by their very nature, are brought against the individual who has engaged in the improper conduct. Proving a claim of intentional infliction is no easy task. Nonetheless, in egregious cases, such a claim provides a way for making the truly guilty party pay for the harassment.

The Real World

Enough of the law. It is important for an employee to know what legal protection exists in theory. The central issue for the employee, however, is how to react in the real world when confronted with workplace harassment. The law helps inform the employee's decisions, but it cannot be the sole guide. Harassment is an intensely personal experience. Each employee will react differently. The workplace, moreover, is a complex web of social interaction. In a particular circumstance, it may make sense for the employee, as a nonlegal matter, to let an incident of harassment pass. In others, the employee may be left with no choice but to complain. It is often the practical considerations, more so than the legal, that drive the employee's actions.

To illustrate the point, let us pose a hypothetical example. You are a female employee. You have just been hired to work as an administrative assistant for a company official. The official has the title of vice president but is not the kind of high-ranking official who can be viewed as the alter ego of the company. During your first week on the job, you notice that the official is looking at you in what appears to be a flirtatious way. The official makes comments that might be construed as sexually provocative, although they are ambiguous enough to be written off as tasteless, but inoffensive, asides. You are concerned, but you let it pass. Eventually, the official calls you into his office. The official makes some small talk and then drops a bomb; he wants to have a sexual relationship with you. The official does not touch you or threaten you in a physical way. Nor does he say explicitly that you will lose your job if you do not give in to his sexual demands. He does suggest, however, that if you want to get ahead, you would be wise to play along. You walk out of the office reeling, wondering what to do next.

This scenario is not atypical. Sexual harassment is no longer the deep dark secret of the American workplace. It is now out in the open more so than ever, due, in part, to well-publicized incidents involving the military and some high-profile public figures. Still, even as society receives a well-needed education in the legalities (or illegalities) of harassment, there is still a surprising amount of blatant harassment that persists in the American workplace. Many managers, even bigoted ones, are sophisticated enough not to make an explicitly racist remark. Yet, these same managers will openly harass women (in particular), touching them, propositioning them, and making crude sexual jokes at their expense. Given the amount of harassment that still pervades many workplaces, employees are forced to develop practical strategies for dealing with the harassing conduct of co-workers and supervisors.

The first thing for the employee to consider is whether the harassment at issue is unlawful. In our hypothetical case, the employee has been propositioned on a single occasion. The proposition occurred without any physical threat or touching, although it carried the implication that the employee's job prospects might depend upon her submitting to the sexual advance. Under these circumstances, the single proposition is not enough to violate the law. That is, the proposition, while the kind of thing that could support a legal claim of sexual harassment, is not severe or pervasive enough to affect the terms or conditions of a reasonable person's employment. If repeated, the official's conduct could give rise to a legal claim. Standing alone, it is not enough.

This is not to say that the proposition does not have legal consequences. As noted earlier, the liability standard in cases of supervisory harassment encourages employees to utilize the employer's complaint procedures. If an employee fails to complain about the harassment and then brings a lawsuit alleging unlawful harassment, a court may find that the suit is without merit because the employer was not given the opportunity to redress the harassment. There are circumstances, moreover, where a decision not to complain of harassment can come back to haunt the employee. The law requires that individuals file a charge of discrimination with the EEOC within a certain number of days from the employment action. (This procedural require-ment is discussed in Chapter 13.) In cases involving sexual harass-ment, the incidents of harassment are often strung together in a tight series, allowing the employee to challenge all of the inci-dents in a single charge. If, however, the incidents are separated out over a long period of time, a charge of discrimination, filed after the last of the incidents, might be viewed as untimely as to some of the previous incidents of harassment.

In the circumstance at hand, there appears to be little risk to the employee. The single proposition is not itself unlawful. If the official repeats his behavior on a number of occasions, over the employee's objections, the employee would be in a position to complain about the harassment. The employee would not have lost anything by waiting until the conduct rises to the level of actionable harassment. Nor is there much risk that the employee will file a charge of discrimination that is viewed as untimely. If nothing else, it appears almost certain that if the offi-cial wants to persist in his boorish behavior, he will strike while the iron is hot (in his mind anyway), giving the employee ample time in which to file a charge that covers all of the incidents of harassment. The bottom line is that the employee could let the incident pass without filing an internal complaint or an EEOC charge, with little risk that she would forfeit any of the law's pro-tections.

The law, however, does not provide the only answer to the employee's conundrum. Even if the proposition is not unlawful, an employee does not have to wait until the conduct becomes unlawful to complain to the employer. Presumably, it is in the employee's interest to nip the harassment in the bud before it blossoms into something far worse. The employer has the same interest, since it faces the risk of legal liability if the harassment repeats itself. The legal considerations aside, the employee has a choice to make. How do I respond to what I take as an offensive and unwanted sexual advance, with an implicit quid pro quo of good things happening if I assent?

There appear to be several possible responses to the harassment. At one extreme is the decision to quit the job and file a charge of discrimination with the EEOC, with the intention of bringing a lawsuit against the company. This would appear to be a poor choice under the circumstances. The single proposition does not give rise to a viable legal claim. The law, moreover, will not look kindly on an employee who has preempted the employer's opportunity to redress the harassment by initiating legal proceedings. This is particularly true if the employer has an effective sexual harassment policy that could provide a defense to a legal claim. Of course, the employee has every right to quit her job if she so desires. The employee, however, should not do so with the expectation that the law will support her harassment claim.

At the other extreme is the decision to play the official's game. The employee could agree to grant sexual favors to the official. Or, the employee could say no, with a wink, and play a flirtatious game of cat and mouse with the official, which, in the end, may be all that the official truly desires. Many, of course, would find such conduct to be demeaning, even objectionable. Women, however, have been forced to pursue such strategies for years, given the lack of any other meaningful opportunity for advancement. Legally speaking, this course imperils any subsequent claim of harassment, since the employee's conduct invites an argument that she welcomed the sexual attention. The employee can argue that she was coerced into accepting the implicit quid pro quo, but if her contemporaneous actions suggest that she was a more calculating and willing participant, her claim may be doomed. Still, as distasteful as it may be to many, this is a real-world option for some employees.

We will assume that our hypothetical employee chooses neither of the extreme courses of action. Instead, the employee opts for the middle ground. There appear to be two middle-ground choices. First, the employee could make clear to the official that she finds the proposition unwelcome but take no other action. In other words, the employee would not file a complaint under the employer's antiharassment policy. This approach would allow the employee to make clear that she finds the sexual proposition objectionable, while solidifying any legal claim that the harassment was unwelcome. It would also, however, give the official a way out, since the company would not be aware of the harassment at that point. The world is full of professional women who have endured harassment from male superiors. Depending on the context, they have managed the situation, without resort to legal process, by dealing directly with the harasser in ways that head off future misconduct. In some cases (where the harasser seems particularly aggressive), the employee's response may be a stern rebuke. In others (where the harasser seems more hapless than hurtful), it may be a polite no, calculated to head off any further harassment without upsetting an individual who may well wield influence over the employee's advancement at the company. At least in some cases, these strategies are successful; the harassment stops and the employee goes on with her job.

The second middle-ground choice is for the employee to make clear to the official that the sexual advance is unwelcome and to complain about the harassment to the appropriate company official or officials. The advantage of this approach is that it sends a strong message to the harasser that such behavior will not be tolerated. It also defuses any argument that because the employee did not act promptly in complaining about the harassment, the harassment did not occur or was not truly offensive to the employee (an unfair charge to be sure, but one that is frequently made). This approach seems most desirable in a company that has an effective sexual harassment policy. By invoking the company's own procedures for complaining about harassment, the employee may well put the company on her side. It may turn out, in fact, that the official has a history of harassing his female subordinates. Perhaps this will be the straw that breaks the camel's back, leading the company to take action against the harasser. The result could be good for both the employee and, in the long run, the company itself (and its other employees).

There are, of course, potential downsides to this approach. Suppose the harasser is a vice president, and the company is not supportive of the employee. The employee may then find herself exposed in the workplace. The harasser could turn up the harassment even more or take actions against the employee in retaliation for her complaint. At the very least, the complaint could taint the employee in the eyes of other company officials, who could view the employee as being weak or too thin-skinned. No doubt, the law makes it unlawful for an employer to retaliate against an individual who has complained about harassment. But there is often a gap between what the law guarantees in theory and what it protects in practice. The employee has every right to complain about sexual conduct that she finds objectionable. She is particularly justified in complaining if she senses that the sexual overtures are a prelude to more aggressive or violent behavior. The employee must understand, however, that these actions do not come without some real-world price, at least in those workplaces where sexual harassment is not taken seriously.

Let us assume that the employee in our hypothetical example chooses the first middle-ground approach. She informs the official that the sexual attention is unwanted but does not lodge a complaint with the company. Unfortunately, in this case, this strategy fails. The official continues to harass the employee, repeatedly asking for sexual favors and lacing his comments with sexual innuendo that is no longer ambiguous, judged in the context of the sexual advances. The official has made the employee's working life difficult at best, intolerable at worst.

The employee's options are now more clear. Legally speaking, the harassment may have risen to the level of being sufficiently severe or pervasive to trigger the protections of the law. The employee must now decide whether she wants to pursue a legal claim. To do so, she would be well advised to first file an internal complaint with the company. This would give the company an opportunity to put an end to the harassment but would also ensure that the employee has preserved her legal rights to hold the company responsible for the harassment. The company may indeed act promptly and effectively in ending the harassment. If it does not, the employee would be justified in pursuing a legal claim. The employee could file a charge with the EEOC while retaining her job (assuming that she can stomach the ongoing harassment). Or, she could quit her job and file a charge. In either case, the employee would have a strong claim that the company should be forced to pay for the unlawful behavior of the harassing official.

Again, there are practical issues to consider. The employee has a viable claim of unlawful discrimination. That does not mean, however, that she necessarily wants to assert that claim. In our hypothetical case, the harassment may have reached the point of no return (where it is too oppressive to be tolerated). The employee has nothing to lose in lodging a complaint with the employer or filing a charge with the EEOC. In other cases, however, the employee may feel that she can manage the situation. Invoking the law can have its rewards, but it also entails risk and sacrifice. An employee should not be naïve in embarking upon a strategy of legal intervention to combat workplace harassment.

All of this suggests that the decisions of the employee, confronted with harassment, are quite pragmatic. The law is now, more than ever, on the side of the employee on issues of sexual harassment. Ultimately, however, the law can only do so much. The employer can act promptly and decisively in redressing workplace harassment, which is reason enough to invoke the assistance of the employer when confronted with the harassment. But where the employer defaults in its obligation, the protection of the law can be slow in coming (if it comes at all). So long as harassment persists in its current form, the role of fending off the harassment will continue to lie largely with those on the front line, using their wits and guile, as much as the law, as their guide.

CHAPTER 16

Down(Sized) but Not Out

I n 1967, Congress enacted the Age Discrimination in Employment Act (ADEA). At the time, the American economy was in full gear. Companies were prospering, the standard of living was high, and the annual rate of growth was still at post–WW II levels. The ADEA was passed to combat societal stereotypes concerning the capabilities of older workers. It was passed on the assumption that companies had jobs available in large numbers that could be given to qualified older Americans. That a company would make massive cuts in its personnel, as a cost-cutting measure, was a foreign concept. The ADEA was seen as a vehicle for ensuring the full employment of those older individuals who desired to work.

What a difference three decades makes. In the intervening years, the American economy has stagnated. There have been periods of high growth, but, overall, the rate of growth has flattened out. Citing this economic trend and the specter of global competition, American companies have made substantial reductions in their workforces, resulting in the downsizing phenomenon. Downsizing is pervasive. It has entered our vocabulary, our culture, and our economy. It is no longer strange to think that a company would make massive reductions in its workforce as a way of cutting costs. What seems strange (almost quaint) is the assumption that those who perform their jobs well will keep those jobs until retirement.

For the employee, downsizing has obvious real-world implications. In the past, an employee had a reasonable expectation that if the employee made a commitment to a company and performed his or her job up to the employer's standards, the employer in return would reward the employee with a secure job. This expectation has been swept away. Thousands of American workers have lost their jobs as a result of a reduction-in-force or plant closing. These workers are not fired because of poor performance on the job. They are fired because of economic efficiencies—efficiencies that are sometimes driven by the dictates of Wall Street more so than any fair assessment of worker productivity.

The law's response to this phenomenon has been less than adequate. Congress has passed a smattering of laws designed to give some protection to the downsized worker. Congress, for example, has required employers to extend health benefits for a certain period following an individual's termination of employment. Congress has required advance notice in certain cases in which massive layoffs are going to occur. For the most part, however, Congress has relied upon existing statutes. These include the ADEA and the Employee Retirement Income Security Act of 1974 (ERISA). The ADEA, in particular, has proven to be less protective of employees in this situation than one might have hoped. As noted above, the ADEA was passed in a different economic climate. Congress envisioned the statute as a tool for achieving full employment for older workers on the assumption that most companies would be in need of additional employees. Using the ADEA as a bulwark against company downsizing is like fitting a square peg into a round hole. Nevertheless, the ADEA provides much of the legal protection that exists for those subjected to a reduction-in-force, at least for those over the age of 40 (who are the most likely victims of a downsizing). There is no comprehensive statutory framework that provides protection for those employees who are victimized by a reduction-in-force. But in bits and pieces, the law provides some assistance to the discarded employee.

The Initial Decision

Let us begin with a hypothetical example. An employee has worked for a manufacturing company for over twenty years. The employee started working for the company when she was twenty-three years old. The employee has been a successful worker, receiving pay increases and promotions along the way. Now, the climate has changed. For months, there has been speculation that the company is going to lay off a significant number of workers. The company claims to be losing money. The company, moreover, has been talking about moving some of its operations overseas. Finally, it happens. The company announces that there will be a significant reduction-in-force. The company cites a figure of approximately 1,000 workers. Within a few days, a list of the targeted workers is disseminated in the workplace. Our employee's name is on the list.

The initial concern for the employee is whether she is going to retain any of her employee benefits. As a longtime employee, the employee is likely to be receiving benefits under some kind of employee plan. These could include valuable health insurance benefits for herself and her family. They might also include pension benefits under a defined benefit plan that guarantees the employee a certain amount of retirement income once the employee vests in the plan.

In Chapter 8, I discussed some of the benefit protections available to an employee who is terminated from his or her job. First, the employee is entitled (in many cases) to an extension of any health insurance benefits that he or she is receiving under a group health plan maintained by the employer. Specifically, the employee is entitled to have such benefits continued for a period of eighteen months (or more in some cases) following termination. This helps to ensure that the employee and his or her family are not left without any health insurance coverage while the employee searches for a new job. In addition, the employee is entitled to retain any pension benefits that have vested under a benefit plan that is covered by ERISA, the federal statute that regulates employee benefit plans. Under no circumstances can an employer fire an employee for the simple purpose of cutting off benefits under an ERISA-covered plan. An employer can, however, terminate an employee for some other legitimate reason, thereby eliminating the employee's right to receive benefits under an employer-sponsored benefit plan. The exception to this rule is for pension benefits. Once those benefits have vested, they cannot be taken away from the employee. This is true even if the employee is terminated from a job for reasons that are entirely legitimate (i.e., have nothing to do with a desire on the employer's part to strip the individual of pension benefits).

In this case, the manufacturing company may have an employee benefit plan of some kind that provides for pension benefits. If so, the employee, a twenty-year veteran of the company, is likely to be vested in the plan, since ERISA requires vesting to occur after either five or seven years of service (depending upon the vesting method chosen by the employer). With a vested interest in the plan, the employee is entitled to the accrued benefits under the plan. The employee is not entitled, however, to have those benefits paid out at the time of separation from employment (unless the plan provides for such a contingency). The pension benefits are a source of future income security for the employee, but in all likelihood they will not provide the employee with an immediate cushion for the economic blow of the termination.

Often, an employer will make additional benefits available to an employee who is terminated as part of a downsizing or reduction-in-force. The employer, for example, will provide severance benefits of some kind to the employee. Or, the employer will permit the employee to have immediate access to an accrued pension benefit in a lump sum payment. Increasingly, the employer will provide these benefits as part of a waiver agreement. The employer agrees to sweeten the pot for the employee, with some additional severance benefit or perk, and, in return, the employee waives any claim of unlawful discrimination that he or she may have stemming from the reduction-in-force. The validity of these agreements has been the subject of much debate (and is discussed in more detail in a later section of this chapter). Suffice it to say here that agreeing to such a waiver requires careful consideration on the employee's part.

The other concern for the employee is one of notice. No employee likes to be fired. The trauma of a discharge is exacerbated, however, when the employee is dismissed with little or no notice. In such a case, the employee is literally thrown out in the street. The employee has had no opportunity to search for another job and is without an immediate stream of income (assuming that the employer has not provided the employee with a significant severance benefit of some kind).

In our case, the employee has worked for the company for over twenty years. The rumors of a downsizing may have prompted the employee to make inquiries about other job opportunities. It is likely, however, that until she was actually notified that she was targeted for termination under the reduction-in-force, the employee did not engage in a significant job search. If the employee is immediately cut loose from the company, she will be forced to hit the pavement running, having been given no opportunity to pursue job leads or make alternative transition plans for herself and her family.

There is one federal statute that provides the employee with some degree of protection. That statute is the Worker Adjustment and Retraining Notification Act (WARN). The WARN Act applies to companies with 100 or more employees. The Act requires that, in certain circumstances, the company provide notification to employees who will be adversely affected by a plant closing or a mass layoff. The notification must be made within 60 calendar days of the plant closing or layoff. Those entitled to notice include hourly and salaried workers, as well as managerial and supervisory employees. A mass layoff is subject to the terms of the act when the layoff is for six months or longer and affects 500 or more workers or 33% of the company's workforce (in cases in which the number of affected workers is between 50 and 499). An employer that fails to comply with the notification requirement is liable for back pay and benefits for the period of the violation, up to 60 days.

The WARN Act would apply in our hypothetical case. It would ensure that the employee is given at least 60 days' notice before the plug is pulled on her employment. This may provide small comfort to the employee, but it affords the employee the opportunity to adjust to the loss of employment. The employee is given a reasonable period of time to procure alternative employment or to enter a job training or retraining program that will enable the employee to compete in the job market. (In addition to requiring notice to the affected employee, the WARN Act provides for notice to state dislocated worker units. This allows these units to provide dislocated worker assistance in a prompt fashion.)

As always, federal protection is not "the end all and be all." Some states have their own laws dealing with worker notification. These laws may establish additional protections beyond those provided under the WARN Act.

Challenging the Discharge

After the employee gets over the initial shock of the announced reduction-in-force, the employee's attention may turn to the legality of the employer's actions. The employee is likely to feel that she has been treated unfairly. The employee may intuit that for such an unjust act, there must be a legal remedy. Unfortunately, the law provides no easy answer for the employee. There is no federal law that makes it unlawful for an employer to terminate employees for economic reasons. The employer is the master of the workplace. The employer can choose to make massive reductions in its workforce no matter how unfair that decision may seem. Out of deference to the free market and employer prerogative, the law has largely removed itself from the downsizing phenomenon, permitting employers to achieve their financial goals at the expense of their workers.

One exception to this scenario is the principle of nondiscrimination that pervades employment law. An employer can choose to lay off employees for economic reasons. It cannot, however, act in a discriminatory fashion in choosing which employees to let go. The federal statute that has the closest connection to the downsizing phenomenon is the ADEA. By its very nature, a downsizing affects individuals who are current employees. In many cases, these employees have worked for the company for years, meaning that many are over the age of 40 and, thus, in the ADEA's protected age group. If there is evidence that the employer has picked on older workers in carrying out a reduction-in-force, a claim of discrimination lies under the ADEA.

Reductions-in-force have been a fertile source of litigation under the ADEA. In some cases, employees have prevailed, demonstrating the requisite age bias to support a claim. By and large, however, prevailing in cases of this nature has been difficult. One reason, to be sure, is that age is not a significant factor behind many reductions-in-force. Obviously, few employers are going to engineer something as drastic as a mass layoff of their workforce as a mere pretext for getting rid of their older workers. The reasons for the layoff will be economic (just as the employer contends). Even so, the employer can be held liable if, in carrying out the layoff, it unfairly targets older workers for discharge. And there is the rub. An employer will be motivated by a desire to reduce the number of its employees. The employer, however, may have little concern about the relative ages of those who are dismissed. No doubt, a number of employees affected by the reduction will be in the protected age group. It is likely, however, that a significant number of employees under the age of 40 will also be subject to termination under the criteria established by the employer. When the dust clears, a number of workers (many over the age of 40) will no longer hold jobs with the company. Age, however, will not be the decisive factor behind the layoffs.

While there are legitimate reasons why the ADEA has not been an effective bulwark against the downsizing onslaught, it is also fair to say that courts have not applied the statute as aggressively as they might. In carrying out a workforce reduction, an employer may not be acting out of an invidious age-based stereotype (e.g., older workers are unproductive or incompetent). It is entirely possible, however, that the employer is relying upon a factor that correlates very closely with age. An employer, for example, may have a desire to get rid of the employees with the highest salaries. The employees with the highest salaries tend to be the older employees. Or, the employer may want to purge the workforce of those employees with the most seniority, a factor that has an obvious correlation with age. The Supreme Court has instructed the lower courts that reliance upon an age-related factor (e.g., seniority) is not necessarily reliance upon age. Fair enough. But surely an employer's reliance upon a factor that correlates closely with age is suspicious enough to provide the evidentiary basis for a claim of age discrimination. If nothing else, it could support a claim that the criteria used by the employer in carrying out the reduction-in-force have had an adverse impact upon older workers. In practice, many courts have shied away from these evidentiary theories, leaving employers free to make massive cuts in their workforce, cuts that fall hard on those in the protected age group.

At bottom, the ADEA's relative impotence in the face of the downsizing phenomenon is emblematic of the point made at the beginning of this chapter. The ADEA was enacted in 1967 at a time when downsizing was virtually unknown. The law was passed to encourage the full employment of older workers on the assumption that there were plenty of jobs to go around for everyone. It was not designed to preserve the jobs of older workers in an economic context in which jobs are a scarce commodity. The awkward fit between the original aims of the ADEA and the modern realities of the American economy has stymied courts in their attempt to apply the statute to workforce reductions. One can question whether courts could have been more creative in fashioning ways to adapt the ADEA's goals to the changing economic landscape. What is certain is that the ADEA has not been the impenetrable obstacle to downsizing initiatives that it could have been.

This is not to say that the ADEA can never be used to combat a reduction-in-force. In some cases, an employer will target older workers, in particular, for termination. If the employer does so (in a statistically significant way), the numbers will bear that out and the discharged employees will be able to mount a viable challenge to the workforce reduction. Further, many cases involving reductions-in-force are made out at the micro level. An employer may have legitimate economic reasons for downsizing its workforce. The employer, overall, may act in a nondiscriminatory fashion in carrying out the reduction-in-force. Yet, in making certain individual decisions with respect to which employees to retain, the company (or one of its decision makers) might take age into account. The employer, for example, might retain a younger employee in one division, in lieu of an older worker, under circumstances that are suggestive of an age bias.

Take, for example, the case of a company that decides to engage in a workforce reduction. The company has seven managers who work in Division A. One of these managers must be let go as part of the reduction-in-force. The oldest of the seven managers is 55. Another manager is 45. The rest are all under age 40. The company discharges the 55-year-old manager. The company claims that it applied a neutral, performance-based criterion in choosing which manager to let go. The evidence shows, however, that the 55-year-old was a solid performer. By contrast, at least one of the managers under the age of 40 had received a number of negative performance evaluations. The 55-year-old can mount a viable age discrimination claim. The employee can make out a prima facie case of discrimination based on the fact that the managers retained by the company were substantially younger. The employee can also point to evidence that calls into serious question the employer's performance-based explanation for the decision.

In the case of our hypothetical employee, it is unclear whether the employee would have a viable age discrimination claim. The company is laying off some 1,000 employees. A statistical run may reveal that the company has disproportionately targeted older workers for termination. Again, it is not enough to show that substantial numbers of older workers were let go as part of the workforce reduction. One must show that, as a comparative matter (given the relative numbers of older and younger employees in the workforce), a much higher percentage of older employees were singled out for termination. Many employers are sophisticated enough to crunch the numbers in advance of the workforce reduction, thereby giving them an accurate accounting of how many older employees can be let go without creating a statistically significant disparity. Based on those numbers, the employer will target workers in a way that makes it difficult to prove an overall pattern of age bias in the reduction-in-force. This still leaves the employee with an argument that, at the micro level, the company has relied upon age in terminating the employee as opposed to other younger workers in the same division or unit. Whether this argument can be made, in a particular case, will depend upon the circumstances surrounding the individual decision (e.g., whether younger individuals are retained in similar positions or whether there are reasons to question the employer's selection criteria for the workforce reduction).

The other federal law that has a connection to the downsizing phenomenon is the ERISA. ERISA makes it unlawful for an employer to discharge an individual for the purpose of interfering with an individual's employee benefits. In theory, the Act could serve as a substantial barrier to downsizing initiatives. Many workforce reductions are calculated to save the company money by cutting personnel costs. In many cases, employee benefits comprise a substantial percentage of those costs. The case could be made that by cashiering employees out of a desire to save on personnel costs (including the costs of employee benefits), the employer runs afoul of ERISA's prohibitions. The problem is in the proof required to make out a case of benefit discrimination under ERISA. It may be true that a company has achieved substantial savings by dismissing a number of its existing employees. It is not enough, however, that a number of employees have been stripped of their benefits by virtue of being terminated from their jobs. A claimant must show that the principal motivation behind the workforce reduction was the elimination of employee benefits. This is difficult to show in cases involving large workforce reductions, since courts tend to defer to the employer's claim that there were legitimate economic reasons for the layoffs, reasons that extend beyond the issue of employee benefits. Saving money on employee benefits may have been a by-product of the reduction-in-force, but it was not the chief motivating factor behind the reduction.

ERISA is not unlike the ADEA in its failure to provide a legal barrier to unrestrained downsizing. ERISA was passed in 1974 to provide benefit protection for employees. It is fair to say that the downsizing phenomenon was not a principal focus of the legislative debates leading to the passage of the Act. Many courts are reluctant to extend the Act to downsizing decisions, even if the decisions are in part motivated by a desire to save costs on employee benefits. Employers can run afoul of the Act when they engage in actions that are obviously calculated to strip employees of their benefits (e.g., reorganizing the workforce in a way that leaves employees with their jobs intact but without the benefits that they had under an employee benefit plan). In general, however, ERISA has proven to be ineffectual as a bar to large-scale reductions-in-force.

The Severance Agreement

It would seem that employers have the upper hand in carrying out workforce reductions. This is true to a point, but there are factors that tip the scales the other way, at least to a degree. First, there are cases in which workforce reductions are successfully challenged on legal grounds. This is something that the employer wants to avoid at all costs, even if it occurs in a relatively small percentage of cases. Further, regardless of the success rate, legal challenges to workforce reductions are commonplace. In many cases, an employer will prevail in defending against the challenge. The employer, however, will do so only after years of protracted litigation. The employer will have expended substantial time and money in defending its actions, making the victory hollow, if not Pyrrhic.

In order to head off such litigation, many employers seek what amounts to an insurance policy against future litigation stemming from a reduction-in-force. Specifically, the employer will ask the employee, targeted for dismissal under a workforce reduction, to sign a severance agreement. From the employer's perspective, the purpose of the agreement is to head off a lawsuit. Thus, the agreement will typically state that the employee waives any legal claim that the employee may have resulting from the reduction-in-force. In return, the employer will provide the employee with a severance benefit. The employer might agree to pay an additional amount of money to the employee in exchange for the employee's promise to forgo a suit. Or, the employer might make available in a lump sum payment amounts to which the employee is entitled (in the future) under a benefit plan. If the employee executes the agreement (and the agreement is upheld as valid), the employer will have a defense to any subsequent lawsuit brought by the employee. The employee, in turn, will have the monetary benefit provided under the agreement.

On the face of it, a severance agreement of this nature seems fair enough. Both the employer and the employee give up something in return for a benefit (money in the employee's case, and a defense to suit in the employer's case). The problem is that many employees are left with no choice but to sign the severance agreement. The employee is being terminated from his or her job. The employee is likely to be in need of an immediate infusion of cash. The employee, moreover, is in no position, at that point, to judge the lawfulness of the employer's actions. The employee may assume that there is no basis for challenging the termination. As it turns out, there could be compelling evidence of discrimination in the reduction-in-force. The employee will agree to the severance package, but it will not be a knowing and voluntary waiver of the employee's legal rights.

In response to these concerns, Congress took action in 1990, enacting the Older Workers Benefit Protection Act (OWBPA). The OWBPA applies to the waiver of rights or claims under the ADEA. The Act provides that an employee may not enter into an agreement to waive any right or claim under the ADEA unless the agreement is knowing and voluntary. To be knowing and voluntary, the agreement must, at a minimum, meet certain statutory requirements. The agreement must specifically state that the employee is waiving rights or claims under the ADEA. The agreement must achieve the waiver of any right or claim only in exchange for consideration in addition to anything of value to which the employee already is entitled. Finally, the agreement must provide the employee with sufficient time in which to consider the agreement. In a case in which the employee is *not* being terminated in connection with an exit incentive or other group termination program, the employee must be given twenty-one days. In the case of a group termination (or exit incentive), the period is forty-five days. In the latter case, the employer must also provide the employee with information concerning the class, unit, or group of employees targeted under the exit incentive or group termination. This includes information with respect to the job titles and ages of those individuals who are subject to the exit incentive or group termination, as well as the ages of all employees in the same job classification or unit who are not subject to the exit incentive or group termination. In all cases, the employee must be given a period of seven days following the execution of the agreement in which to revoke the agreement.

There are several points to make about the OWBPA. First, an important requirement of the Act is that any waiver of rights or claims be made in exchange for additional consideration to which the employee is not otherwise entitled. This means, quite simply, that the agreement must provide the employee with a new or additional benefit of some kind. An employer can condition the receipt of some additional benefit (e.g., a higher severance benefit) on the employee's willingness to forgo a claim. It cannot, however, browbeat the employee into waiving rights or claims with the threat that the employee will lose out on an existing benefit if the employee does not execute the severance (or waiver) agreement. Thus, if the employee is already entitled to a severance benefit of a certain amount under a benefit plan maintained by the employer, the employee cannot be told that in order to receive that benefit (at that amount), the employee must be willing to forgo a lawsuit stemming from the reduction-in-force. If the agreement conditions receipt of an existing benefit on the employee's willingness to waive rights or claims under the ADEA, the agreement is not valid.

The agreement, moreover, cannot achieve what amounts to a prospective waiver of the employee's rights or claims. In cases of this nature, the waiver agreement is being tendered in the context of an employee's separation from employment. The employer is entitled, in that context, to demand a waiver of rights or claims arising in the context of the termination decision in exchange for valuable consideration of some kind. The employer, however, is not entitled to use the severance agreement as a way of securing a waiver of any future claim of discrimination that may arise. At some point, the employee may reapply to work for the employer. Or, the employer might take some action in the future that affects the employee's job benefits. The employer can obtain a waiver of rights or claims arising from the employee's separation from employment, but it cannot buy itself a complete defense to any and all claims of discrimination.

The OWBPA's informational requirements have the closest connection to the downsizing phenomenon. When Congress enacted the OWBPA, the specter of mass layoffs and reductions-in-force was very much on its mind. Congress did not confront the issue head-on, by restricting an employer's ability to engage in group terminations, but sought to ensure that employees would not be coerced into signing away their statutory protections. In the case of a group termination, the employer must provide the employee with information concerning the ages and job titles of those individuals being retained and let go under the reduction-in-force. The purpose of this requirement is to provide the employee with some basis for assessing the legality of the workforce reduction, thus informing the employee's decision whether to sign the waiver agreement. The requirement might also have the indirect effect of discouraging employers from targeting older workers under a reduction-in-force, since the employer knows that any pattern of age discrimination may well be revealed to the employee as part of the information provided under the OWBPA.

It should be stressed that the OWBPA, by its terms, applies only to rights or claims that arise under the ADEA. Thus, the specific requirements of the OWBPA do not apply to the waiver of rights or claims under other federal statutes. Nonetheless, in a mass layoff or workforce reduction, the employer is likely to use a standard form agreement. The employer knows that a number of the employees targeted for dismissal will be over the age of 40. This means that the agreement, to achieve its purpose, will have to cover claims under the ADEA, which, in turn, necessitates compliance with the waiver requirements of the OWBPA. Often, the employer will include within a single waiver provision a reference to all of the statutory rights and claims being forfeited under the agreement. The employer will subject the waiver provision to the specific requirements of the OWBPA, effectively extending the protections of the OWBPA to the waiver of rights or claims under other federal statutes.

The OWBPA is plainly designed to protect employees from being coerced out of their statutory rights. The Act achieves this goal, to a degree, by imposing certain preconditions upon the waiver of rights or claims under the ADEA. There is, however, one way in which the OWBPA encourages the very thing that it seeks to regulate. The OWBPA contains a laundry list of specific requirements that must be met for a waiver to be considered knowing and voluntary. What is missing from the list is any specific provision that deals with the core problem—the economic coercion that is inherent in an agreement that is foisted upon the employee precisely at the point at which the employee is most vulnerable. Althouth the OWBPA leaves open the possibility that an employee can challenge a particular waiver agreement as being unduly coercive, it largely vacates the field on this critical point. The bottom line for many employees is that the offer of a severance benefit or lump sum payment will be too tempting to pass up, regardless of how well informed they are about their statutory rights. By placing its imprimatur on waiver agreements that comply with the technical requirements of the OWBPA, Congress may have encouraged a practice that undermines the enforcement of the ADEA by permitting employers to obtain waiver agreements under potentially coercive circumstances. The one check against this is that a waiver agreement cannot be used to impair the ability of the Equal Employment Opportunity Commission (EEOC) to enforce the statute. An agreement can achieve a waiver of the employee's right to bring an action in court. It cannot preclude an employee from filing a charge with the EEOC.

The last point to make about the OWBPA may be the most critical. On its face, the OWBPA is easy enough to comply with. Many employers, however, have decided to push the envelope by drawing up agreements that are not in technical compliance with the Act. This leads to cases in which the employer tenders a noncompliant agreement to the employee. An agreement that does not comply with the OWBPA is unenforceable. The problem is that the employee may have executed the agreement, in any event, and pocketed the additional money provided under the agreement. Armed with the knowledge that the agreement is not in compliance with the OWBPA, the employee may later decide to bring suit under the ADEA. The employer will object, arguing that the employee has received the benefit of the agreement and, thus, cannot renege on the employee's promise to forgo suit. From the employer's perspective, the employee must either tender back the money to the employer, as a condition of bringing a lawsuit, or else live with the agreement as is.

The Supreme Court has addressed this very issue. The Court has sided with the employee, holding that the OWBPA rejects the application of a tender-back rule. If the agreement does not comply with the OWBPA, the agreement is unenforceable. If the agreement is unenforceable, it cannot be used in any way, shape, or form to preclude the employee from bringing suit. The employee, in other words, can proceed with a legal action without having to tender back the proceeds of the agreement. It is possible that the employer will be given an opportunity to recoup the money, perhaps as an offset against any recovery that the employee has in his or her lawsuit. At least as an initial matter, however, the employee can proceed with his or her suit without having to tender back any money paid under the defective agreement.

Let us return to our hypothetical downsized employee. In this scenario, the employee is part of a massive reduction-in-force. It is likely, in this context, that the company will proffer severance agreements that call for the waiver of any claim arising from the termination. If the employer does so, the agreements will undoubtedly apply to the waiver of rights or claims under the ADEA, bringing the requirements of the OWBPA into play. If so, the agreements will be subject to the provisions of the OWBPA dealing with group terminations. Thus, the employee would have forty-five days in which to consider the agreement. The employee, moreover, would be entitled to information concerning the ages of those individuals who are being let go as compared to those who are being retained. That information would have to be broken down by organizational unit, giving the employee a decent sense of whether the workforce reduction is skewed against those in the protected age group. The employee would have time enough to consult a lawyer and time enough to assess whether there is possible merit to a claim of age discrimination. A lawyer, moreover, could advise the employee as to whether the agreement is in compliance with the requirements of the OWBPA. If the agreement does not comply with the OWBPA, the choice is made easier for the employee. The employee can sign the agreement and accept the proceeds of the agreement without forgoing any right to later bring suit under the ADEA.

The legalities aside, the real choice for the employee is one grounded in the real world. As noted earlier, many employees are left with no choice but to sign the agreement, given their economic circumstances. There is, however, a countervailing tendency, at least among those who have the means to withstand the economic pressure. Many employees will feel that the employer is treating them unfairly. Many will find it difficult, as a matter of principle, to sign away their legal rights for what amounts to "thirty pieces of silver." This is an understandable reaction. The employee, however, must take a deep breath, step back from the situation, and take a hard, dispassionate look at the circumstances. Proving a claim of discrimination, in the context of a reduction-in-force, is no easy task. The employee faces protracted litigation with an employer that, in all likelihood, will be disinclined to settle, given the employee's rejection of the initial severance or waiver agreement. If the employee is truly concerned with the legalities of the employer's action, the employee can file a charge with the EEOC, providing that agency with the opportunity to investigate the workforce reduction and eradicate discrimination that might be taking place. If, however, the employee simply wants to blow off some steam by taking on the employer, the employee should think twice. The central question for the employee is whether, on balance, the money being tendered by the employer as part of the severance package seems fair and reasonable. In many cases, it will be in the employee's best interest to swallow his or her pride, accept the waiver agreement, and move on.

The Overqualified Employee

For many employees, the above scenario is all too familiar. The employee has worked for a company for years, performing his or her job well. The employee is targeted for a reduction-in-force. The employee is presented with a severance agreement that requires the employee to waive rights in order to receive an additional severance benefit. The employee considers the options and decides, reluctantly, to sign the agreement. The employee executes the agreement, takes the money, and leaves what may be the only career-oriented job that he or she has ever had.

The next step for the employee is to find another job. Some employees may be at the age where they would prefer to retire rather than start over. Others, however, will need or want to obtain another job. In a perfect world, the employee would have no difficulty in making the transition into alternative employment.

After all, the employee has substantial work experience. The employee was fired for economic reasons, not for poor performance. The employee, moreover, may well receive a letter of recommendation from his or her former employer. Despite these factors, many older workers have difficulty in becoming reemployed once they are let go as part of a workforce reduction. In part, the difficulty stems from the demands of the market. The employee is likely to have substantial job skills. But those skills may not match up with the kinds of skills that are needed in a changing economy. The employee, in fact, may need to enter a retraining program of some kind to acquire more marketable skills. Many long-time employees have learned to do one thing well; that one thing, however, may no longer be in demand.

While there are free market factors that hamper the reemployment prospects of some older employees, there is one obstacle faced by older workers that does have its roots in an age-related factor. An older worker, displaced from a job, faces a whipsaw effect in his or her attempt to become reemployed. On the one hand, the employee is told that he or she lacks the qualifications for certain jobs because the employee's skills are too limited or job-specific. On the other hand, the employee is told that he or she is overqualified for certain jobs because the employee has too much work experience to compete for the kind of entry-level position at issue. The effect of this whipsaw can be devastating. The use of the label *overqualified* is particularly hard to swallow, since the employee is being shown the door while being told, in effect, that he or she is too good for the job.

For our purposes, the critical question is whether an employer's rejection of an older worker's employment, on the grounds of overqualifications, gives rise to a claim of discrimination under the ADEA. The answer is—it depends. Clearly, reliance upon this factor does not constitute per se age discrimination. One can be overqualified for a job for reasons that have nothing to do with age, as such. Nonetheless, there is an obvious correlation between being overqualified, based on years of experience on a job, and age. Because of this correlation, an employer exposes itself to liability under the ADEA when it purports to rely upon a factor such as overqualifications in making an employment decision. There are two circumstances, in fact, where reliance upon this factor can support an ADEA claim.

First, a claim can be asserted for disparate treatment discrimination when the employer vaguely invokes the label of overqualified in rejecting the employment of an older applicant. The theory here is that the employer is using the overqualified label as a mask for age discrimination. Of course, the employer is not precluded from considering the relative qualifications and experience of a job applicant, since the employer may have valid concerns, in a particular case, about the ability or willingness of an experienced worker to adapt to an entry-level position. Where, however, the employer simply uses the buzzword *overqualified* in rejecting an older applicant, the employer's explanation is sufficiently suspicious to support an inference of an age bias in the decision.

A simple example illustrates the point. A company announces an opening for the position of insurance adjuster, an entry-level job. A 60-year-old individual, John, applies for the job. John worked for years in the insurance industry, reaching management-level status, but was recently let go as part of a reduction-in-force. John has impeccable credentials and interviews well for the job. He says nothing in the interview that would suggest an unwillingness to work for a younger supervisor in the entry-level job. To the contrary, he expresses enthusiasm for the job. The company does not hire John. It hires, instead, a much younger candidate whose credentials seem barely to measure up, if at all, to the minimum requirements set forth in the job announcement. The company informs John that he was rejected for the position because he was overqualified. The company explains that, due to the length of John's experience in the field, John is not the right fit for an entry-level job. There is a strong argument that the company is using the overqualified label as a code word for age discrimination. The company has no objective basis for believing that John would have difficulty in adapting to the entry-level job. The company hired, in lieu of John, a much younger applicant with weak credentials. Under these circumstances, John has a viable claim that the company has made an age-based decision in rejecting John's bid for employment.

The second type of claim that can be asserted in this context focuses on the adverse impact of an employer's qualifications standard. In the previous example, the employer vaguely alluded to the issue of overqualifications, suggesting that the employer was using that factor as a mask for age discrimination. In other cases, the employer will adopt a more explicit hiring policy. The employer will state flat out that it will not hire an individual with more than a certain number of years of experience. Or, the employer will seek applicants that are one or two years out of college. In this case, it cannot be said that the employer is using the qualifications factor as a cover for age itself, since the employer has defined the criterion in a way that is analytically distinct from age. On the other hand, a policy of this nature may well have the effect of screening out a disproportionate number of older applicants. At least in those courts that recognize the disparate impact theory under the ADEA (a point discussed in more detail in Chapter 5), an employee might be able to argue that the employer's policy impermissibly screens older workers out of the hiring process.

Of course, the overqualifications theory is just one piece of the puzzle. An employer is prohibited from relying upon age in refusing to hire an applicant for employment. If there is evidence that the employer has taken age into account in rejecting an older applicant, the rejected applicant has a claim of age discrimination. An older worker who is victimized by a workforce reduction will face a number of obstacles in seeking to become reemployed. One of those obstacles may well be a bias against hiring older individuals for certain types or classes of jobs. The worker has some legal tools at his or her disposal and should use those tools, where necessary, to break down the barriers of employment.

CHAPTER 17

The Disability Dilemma

F or years, the law's approach to the plight of the disabled was munificent, if condescending. The law assumed that disabled individuals, by and large, could not work. It created programs designed to provide the disabled with a stream of income that would ensure a degree of economic security. The law did little to assist the disabled in obtaining employment. In fact, it created a disincentive to work by establishing a social welfare system that guaranteed benefit protection (e.g., health insurance coverage) only if the disabled individual remained on the disability rolls. With little encouragement from the law to work, many disabled individuals threw up their hands, gave up on work, and locked themselves into permanent benefit status.

The law's approach to the disabled population changed dramatically in 1990 with the enactment of the Americans With Disabilities Act (ADA). Suddenly, the focus shifted from providing maintenance income to disabled individuals to assisting disabled individuals to work by requiring employers to accommodate their needs. With minimal assistance or accommodation, many disabled individuals can work. Those who are wheelchair-bound need only have access to the workplace (at least where the job is sedentary in nature). Those who are visually- or hearing-impaired can perform a wide variety of clerical or professional jobs so long as they are provided with assistive devices that enable them to process information. Those who are limited in their ability to lift or bend or grab can still work if relatively minor modifications are made in the way in which their jobs are performed. As a result of the ADA, thousands of disabled individuals are now productive members of the workforce, thus providing a benefit to employers and easing the burden on the public fisc by reducing payments for social welfare benefits.

Although the ADA ushered in a new era in the law's approach to disability issues, the act did not abolish the old social welfare regime. To the contrary, that regime exists largely intact. Thus, individuals who are injured on the job can receive benefits under the various workers' compensation statutes that most states have in place. Individuals who are unable to work because of a disabling condition can receive Social Security disability benefits. Disability benefits are also available under private insurance plans maintained or funded by employers. Many disabled individuals have made the transition from the disability rolls to employment, but many others still need benefit protection.

As it turns out, there is a built-in tension between these two legal regimes. To assert a claim under the ADA, an employee must be able to show (in most cases) that he or she is capable of performing the essential functions of the job at issue. But to obtain Social Security disability benefits, an individual must certify a total disability or inability to work; a similar standard applies to claims under the workers' compensation statutes, at least where the employee is seeking benefits for an injury that is total and permanent in nature. On the face of it, these assertions appear to be irreconcilable. An individual cannot have it both ways (so the argument goes). Either the individual can or cannot work. For the disabled individual who wants to work but who needs disability benefits during those periods in which work is not possible, this presents a difficult dilemma. If the individual applies for disability benefits (or workers' compensation), he or she could be viewed as having forfeited any claim of being able to perform the essential functions of a job within the meaning of the ADA. If, on the other hand, the individual swears off any disability benefits, he or she may go for months, even years, without obtaining a job, notwithstanding the support provided by the ADA. As the law makes the transition from one approach to the treatment of the disabled to another, many individuals find themselves caught on the horns of a dilemma (of the law's own making). How to work through that dilemma is an issue of substantial importance for the millions of disabled individuals who desire to work but who face substantial real-world barriers to employment.

The Dilemma

Sam has worked for years as a laborer in a manufacturing plant. His job entails a certain amount of heaving lifting, and for years he has never had a problem performing his job. One day, while at work, he feels a sharp pain in his right arm and neck. The pain subsides in a few minutes, but his neck and arm are numb. He is taken to a hospital, where he is diagnosed and treated for a rare nerve disorder. He is released from the hospital and put on a regimen of physical therapy.

As a result of his injury, Sam is severely restricted in his ability to lift, grab, and reach. In particular, his right arm is affected. He can move it, but he is unable to lift any object weighing more than five pounds (with that arm). He also has difficulty reaching with his right arm and grabbing objects with his right hand. While physical therapy has been somewhat helpful, it is clear that Sam's condition is permanent and that any improvement in the condition is likely to be marginal at best.

Despite his severe injuries, Sam has a strong desire to continue working. He knows that he can no longer perform his job, as currently configured, so he proposes two alternative accommodations to his employer. One is that his job be restructured. His job involves some heavy lifting, which Sam can no longer perform. The heavy lifting, however, is sporadic. In large part, the job involves manual tasks that Sam is still able to perform, even given his condition. He believes that he could do the job if the employer assigned the heavy lifting functions to other workers on the line, who often pitch in, in any event, when the heavy lifting has to be performed. The other alternative is that he be reassigned to some other vacant position at the company. There are a number of vacant positions at the company that do not require significant lifting, positions for which Sam appears to be qualified and which are classified at the same level as his existing job.

His employer is not receptive to Sam's proposed accommodations. The employer tells him that his existing job cannot be restructured and also dismisses Sam's request to be reassigned to another job, claiming that the company has a policy of accommodating employees only in their existing jobs. The employer informs Sam that he has sixty days of company leave remaining. If Sam's condition does not improve by the end of that period, making it possible for Sam to perform his job as currently structured, he will be terminated.

Sam's condition does not improve. True to its word, the employer terminates his employment at the end of the sixty-day period. He is left without a job, saddled with a condition that substantially impairs his employability.

Left without an immediate source of income, Sam feels desperate. He wants to work. The problem is that he has limited job prospects. He has worked as a laborer his entire adult life. He has no college degree nor does he have the necessary skills to compete for most jobs of a purely sedentary nature. Sam's condition precludes him from doing the type of work he has always done unless the employer is willing to make accommodations of some kind. Sam's experience with his own employer makes him skeptical that such accommodations will be forthcoming—skepticism borne out by actual experience, as several employers have rejected Sam's application for employment.

With nowhere else to turn, Sam seeks to obtain statutory benefits. He first applies for workers' compensation benefits. He claims that he has a total and permanent disability that renders him unable to work. The compensation board determines that his condition was not the product of an on-the-job injury, but was caused by an underlying impairment (the nerve disorder) that could have surfaced at any time, and denies his claim for workers' compensation.

Sam also applies for disability benefits under the federal Social Security Act. On his application, he claims that he is totally disabled. He accurately describes his physical condition and explains the circumstances surrounding his discharge from his prior job. Using the language provided on the form application, Sam states that he is unable to work. When Sam's application is initially denied, he requests a hearing before an administrative law judge. The judge rules in Sam's favor and awards disability benefits to him, retroactive to the date that he was discharged from his prior job.

Sam is relieved that he has obtained the disability benefits and, thus, will have a stream of income of some kind. His real goal, however, is to work. He believes he was mistreated by his former employer. He consults a lawyer, who explains the workings of the ADA, and Sam files suit under the ADA, alleging that his former employer violated the statute in refusing to accommodate his disability and in firing him because of his disability.

Sam's ADA claim has substantial merit. First, there is a strong argument that he has a disability within the meaning of the ADA. Sam has a physical impairment that significantly restricts him in his ability to lift, reach, and grab. His impairment is permanent, and the effects of the impairment appear to be sufficiently severe to meet the ADA's definition of a covered disability. On the merits, Sam has a compelling argument that the company violated the ADA in failing to accommodate his disability. It is arguable whether the company could have restructured Sam's existing job without eliminating or reassigning an essential job function (something that an employer is not required to do under the ADA). Sam, however, also sought a reassignment to another vacant position. The ADA requires this as a reasonable accommodation where there are vacant positions for which the disabled employee is qualified. In this case, there were. The company's refusal to even consider the possibility of a reassignment puts the company in a difficult legal position.

As it turns out, Sam's case may be in trouble for reasons that have nothing to do with the merits of his claim. In suing under the ADA, Sam is claiming that he was fully capable of performing the essential functions of his prior job, with reasonable accommodation, or some other job to which he could have been reassigned. Sam has also claimed, however, that he is totally disabled and unable to work in applying for workers' compensation and Social Security benefits. Sam was awarded Social Security disability benefits for a period that dates back to his last date of employment with his former employer, covering, in effect, the very time frame at issue in his ADA case. On the surface, it appears that Sam has taken inconsistent positions. On the one hand, he has claimed that he is able to work in his ADA action; on the other, he has represented that he is unable to work in applying for disability benefits.

Seizing upon the apparent inconsistency, the company pushes to have Sam's case dismissed. The company does not argue that its actions are justified under the ADA. The company argues, instead, that Sam's ADA claim should be barred because Sam has taken inconsistent positions. The company cites a legal doctrine known as judicial estoppel, which prohibits a party from taking inconsistent positions in legal proceedings. The company argues that the employee has done just that, claiming an inability to work in applying for disability benefits, and now claiming the polar opposite in prosecuting a claim under the ADA.

The Law's Response

The above hypothetical case does not come out of thin air. This scenario has played out repeatedly, in one form or another, since the enactment of the ADA. An employee is fired from his or her job. The employee applies for post-termination disability benefits. The employer argues that the employee has taken inconsistent positions, thus barring the employee's claim under the ADA. The question is whether the employer is entitled to invoke the supposed inconsistency as an absolute defense to the ADA claim.

Initially, courts responded with favor to the employer's argument. Courts accepted the view that the positions being taken in these two statutory contexts were inconsistent. Based on that premise, they held that an individual who certifies a total disability in applying for disability benefits of some kind is barred from maintaining an action under the ADA (claiming to be an individual who can perform the essential functions of the job at issue). Courts dismissed employees' claims even where there was evidence to support a finding that the employer acted unlawfully in terminating the employees.

The initial court decisions on this issue drew a swift rebuke from two government agencies. The Equal Employment Opportunity Commission (EEOC) issued a lengthy policy guidance that argued against these case law developments. The EEOC was joined by the Social Security Administration (SSA), which clarified that the positions being taken in these statutory contexts are not in fact inconsistent, given the different legal standards involved. The SSA first pointed out that it does not take into account the issue of reasonable accommodation in determining eligibility for disability benefits. (Nor, as it turns out, do most private insurance plans or workers' compensation statutes.) In other words, an individual can be considered totally disabled or unable to work, within the meaning of the legal standards applied by the SSA, even if the individual can perform the essential functions of his or her prior job (or some other job) with a reasonable accommodation. The SSA also noted that many individuals are awarded disability benefits on a presumptive basis. The SSA maintains a list of presumptive disabilities. If an individual has a disability that falls on the list, he or she is eligible to receive benefits without regard to whether the disabling condition does, in fact, limit the individual's ability to work. Finally, the SSA has a number of work incentive programs designed to encourage those on the disability rolls to search for work. Most notably, the SSA maintains a trial work period under which beneficiaries can work for a period of up to nine months, while retaining their disability benefits. The SSA recognizes that for many individuals in the disabled population, it is not an either-or proposition (either you can work or you cannot). Many individuals have disabilities that present real-world barriers to employment, even though there may be jobs that these individuals could perform with some assistance or accommodation. The SSA does all it can to assist its beneficiaries in finding those jobs, thus helping them make the transition into permanent employment.

Based on these representations (particularly those of the SSA), the judicial tide quickly turned the other way. Courts began to recognize that the positions being taken in these different statutory contexts were not inherently inconsistent. Courts focused, in particular, on the reasonable accommodation issue. In awarding disability benefits, the SSA does not ask whether the individual could perform a job with a reasonable accommodation. (Again, this is also true of most private disability insurance plans and workers' compensation statutes.) Reasonable accommodation, however, is the linchpin of the ADA. The very purpose of the ADA is to deem, as qualified, individuals who can perform a job if provided with a reasonable accommodation. Plainly, an individual can assert claims, with consistency, under these various statutory schemes. An individual, in other words, can be totally disabled or unable to work, within the meaning of the disability benefit statutes, and still be someone who, with reasonable accommodation, can perform the essential functions of a job. Because of these legal distinctions, most courts ended the practice of barring ADA claims based merely on the fact that the claimant had applied for or received disability benefits. Courts permitted ADA claims to go forward if there was evidence to support a finding that the employee could perform the essential functions of a job with reasonable accommodation, notwithstanding the fact that the employee had certified a total disability in applying for disability benefits or workers' compensation.

The legal debate surrounding this issue has not been fully resolved. Most courts have moved away from the pro-employer position, but there are still some holdouts (at least as this book is being written). It is possible that at some point, the Supreme

Court will step in to resolve the broader legal question. However the issue ultimately plays out, it seems likely that the law will no longer take the per se view that an ADA claim is barred merely by the fact that the employee asserting the claim has also asserted a claim for disability benefits.

While most courts have adopted a more flexible approach to this issue, they have not taken the position that statements made in the disability benefit context have no relevance to an ADA claim. To the contrary, specific representations made in support of a benefit claim can be relevant to the issue of qualifications in an ADA case. This is particularly true where the applicant makes very specific factual assertions with respect to his or her physical or mental condition. The mere fact that an individual certifies a total disability, in applying for disability benefits, means very little, given the different legal standards applied under the respective statutory schemes. In some cases, however, the individual will not merely invoke the generic language of the benefit form. The individual will describe in some detail the way in which the physical or mental condition limits his or her functional capacities. These detailed factual narratives, made under oath, can and will be used against the individual should he or she attempt to reverse field and set forth a different set of facts in support of an ADA claim.

Consider an example. An employee suffers a severe injury to his back. The employer determines that the employee can no longer perform his job and dispenses with the employee's services. The employee applies for Social Security disability benefits. On his application, the employee provides the standard certification of a total disability. The employee, however, says much more. The employee states that as a result of his back condition, he cannot lift any object weighing more than five pounds and is virtually precluded from doing any repetitive lifting. The employee claims that he has been impaired to this degree since the date of his injury. Based upon these representations, the employee is awarded disability benefits. Subsequently, the employee brings suit under the ADA. The employee claims that he was fully capable of performing his prior job even without reasonable accommodation. That job required the employee, on a regular basis, to lift objects weighing as much as 50 to 100 pounds. Obviously, there are specific factual contradictions in the two stories. At the very least, the employee can be impeached in his ADA action with his prior inconsistent statements. The inconsistency may in fact lead to the dismissal of the employee's suit, since a court may hold the employee to his prior sworn statements, which, in turn, may make it impossible for the employee to claim that he was capable of performing the essential functions of his prior job. The employee's ADA claim may well be defeated by what the employee has said in applying for Social Security disability benefits.

The Employee's Way Out

Given the above example, it is clear that an ADA claimant can be trapped by prior statements made in support of a benefit application. The claimant's suit will not be barred simply because the claimant has applied for or received disability benefits (or workers' compensation). The law understands that the positions at issue are reconcilable and that disabled individuals, attempting to make the transition from benefit status to permanent employment, may need to obtain subsistence benefits in the interim while they attempt to use a statute such as the ADA to break down the barriers to employment. An employee, however, may make specific statements in applying for disability benefits that could come back to haunt the employee in a subsequent ADA action. The question for the employee is how to avoid this potential trap.

There are two things that an employee can do to ensure that prior statements made in support of an application for disability benefits do not impale a subsequent ADA action. First, in applying for disability benefits, the employee can provide a completely honest account of the underlying facts. This may seem an obvious point, particularly since statements contained in benefit applications are often made under oath, thus subjecting the employee to a possible prosecution for perjury for any false statements. We all know, however, that the truth can be shaded in ways that do not support a charge of perjury. When an individual applies for disability benefits, the individual will want to characterize the facts in the most favorable light. To do so, the individual will make the condition sound as debilitating as possible. This is fine if the employee's only interest is in obtaining disability benefits. If, however, the employee has a desire to pursue a claim under the ADA, the employee must be more guarded in what is said in applying for disability benefits. The employee should stick to the facts, truthfully stated, without the kind of spin that might create a problem for the employee in a subsequent ADA action.

The second thing that an employee can do to avoid being boxed in by the prior statements is to say precisely what the employee needs to say to obtain the benefits and no more. In applying for disability benefits, there is a tendency to support the claim with a detailed factual narrative. In part, this is due to the applications themselves, which often ask for such information. In many cases, there is no need for such an amplification of the facts. The SSA, for example, awards benefits, in some cases, on the basis of presumptive disabilities. In doing so, the SSA acknowledges that an individual can obtain benefits even if the individual is able to work. If the individual has an impairment that falls clearly within the list of presumptive disabilities, the individual does not need to "gild the lily" by providing a detailed factual description of the debilitating nature of the condition. It is these detailed narratives, gratuitous in many cases, that come back to haunt the individual when the individual brings suit under the ADA.

The most obvious thing that an employee can do, in this regard, is to make clear that any representation about the employee's inability to perform his or her prior job does not take into account the issue of reasonable accommodation. The SSA has made clear that it awards disability benefits without regard to the availability of reasonable accommodations. Thus, the fact that an employee could have performed his or her prior job with a reasonable accommodation does not defeat the employee's claim for disability benefits. That being the case, there is no reason for the employee to make representations that imply a complete inability to work, even with reasonable accommodations. There is every reason, in fact, for the employee to say the opposite—that the employee could have performed his or her prior job with a reasonable accommodation, an accommodation that the employer refused to provide. By taking that simple step, the employee can avoid any collision with his or her ADA claim without compromising the employee's ability to obtain what may be necessary subsistence benefits.

The one thing that will undoubtedly ensnare an employee is inconsistency on discrete factual points involving the employee's functional capacities. An employee, for example, cannot say that he or she is unable to walk, in applying for disability benefits, and then state, in an ADA action, that he or she is fully ambulatory unless there is some explanation for the inconsistency (e.g., that the employee's condition deteriorated between the time in which he or she worked for the employer and the time in which he or she applied for disability benefits). Courts are tolerant of individuals who are trapped between the unfair demands of two legal regimes. Courts are not tolerant of individuals who blatantly make false statements in applying for public benefits.

How does all of this affect Sam, our hypothetical employee? In applying for disability benefits, Sam used the terms appropriate to that context, stating that he was totally disabled and unable to work. This should not present a problem for Sam for the reasons discussed previously. In all other respects, Sam gave an entirely honest account of the state of his physical condition. Sam could do so, without compromising his ADA claim, because his ADA claim is premised on the availability of a reasonable accommodation. Sam is in a particularly good position because one of his proposed accommodations is reassignment to another position. Thus, even if Sam's application were viewed as an admission that he was unable to perform his prior job (even with accommodation), Sam could still argue that there was another job, involving little or no lifting, that he could perform. Sam would appear to be on solid ground in arguing that he has a viable ADA claim, notwithstanding his receipt of Social Security disability benefits.

The importance of allowing Sam's claim to go forward should be obvious. Sam is a disabled individual. Sam has a strong claim that his former employer violated the ADA by invoking a hardheaded policy of not attempting to accommodate disabled individuals in other positions. If Sam's claim is dismissed, the employer gets away with the discrimination and is left free to continue applying its suspect policy to other disabled workers. The ADA, moreover, may provide Sam with his only realistic opportunity for obtaining employment. Sam has a severe physical impairment. Sam may have difficulty finding meaningful employment, given the nature of his condition and his relatively limited educational attainment and job skills. If Sam is not able to use the ADA to achieve reinstatement to his former job (or some other vacant position to which he could be reassigned), Sam may end up as a disability beneficiary for life. This is not good for Sam and certainly not good for the public, which is forced to foot the bill for Sam's benefits.

Over time, the disability dilemma described in this chapter should subside. The law is in a period of transition. Eventually, things will shake out, providing a clear separation between those in the disabled population who will have difficulty working under any circumstance, those who can work with little or no difficulty, and those stuck in the middle, moving from benefit status to employment and back again. In the latter case, the law will do all that it can to ensure that the disabled individual has a safety net of benefit protection while being encouraged to search for (and obtain) employment. Through the help of such statutes as the ADA, many of these individuals will cross the bridge into permanent employment. In the meantime, individuals need to approach the existing legal framework with a certain degree of sophistication, careful to avoid the trap of committing to inconsistent positions in working through that framework.

In many ways, the ADA is symbolic of the changes that have occurred in the law over the past several decades. Employers once controlled the workplace, unhampered by any outside interference. The ADA is the latest example of the law's rejection of unfettered employer prerogative. The ADA, in fact, may take the law to a new level. The ADA potentially covers millions of Americans. The ADA imposes affirmative obligations upon employers, placing the onus on the employer to provide accommodations that will enable those with disabilities to work. It is debatable whether the ADA has been fully successful in achieving its objectives. The larger point, however, is that the ADA illustrates the changing legal climate. Still clinging to the employment-at-will model, America's lawmakers seem unwilling to play the ultimate trump card, imposing a regime in which workers can be terminated only for just cause. The day may not be far off, however, where such a regime is effectively achieved, if not directly so, by the sheer volume of legal regulation. As it now stands, employers still retain the upper hand. Employees, however, are not without weapons of their own. Those weapons, used judiciously, can provide a level of fairness to the employment relationship, leaving intact the essential dominance of the employer but providing the employee with a bulwark against certain kinds of unfair treatment.

INDEX

ADA, *see* Americans with Disabilities Act of 1990
ADEA, *see* Age Discrimination in Employment Act
ADR, *see* alternative dispute resolution
affirmative action, 6–7
affirmative defense, 270–272
age discrimination, 68–83, 128–129
  and age 40 cutoff, 69–72
  and age proxies, 72–78
  and bona fide benefit plan defense, 78–81
  and bona fide occupational qualification defense, 81–83
  prohibition against, 69
  and replacement issue, 69–70
Age Discrimination in Employment Act (ADEA), 1, 143, 283–284, 289–291, 297–299, 301–303
age proxies, 72–78
alternative dispute resolution (ADR), 231–235
Americans with Disabilities Act of 1990 (ADA), 1, 84–106, 228, 308–317
  asserting claims under, 305–306
  definition of disability in, 85–93
  and FMLA, 157–159
  impact of, 304–305
  and pre-employment inquiries, 98–101

  qualifications standard of, 93–98
  and reasonable accommodation principle, 101–106
  rights of EEOC under, 239
  and right-to-sue letter, 238
antiretaliation provisions, 197–205
arbitration, 231–235

benefits, *see* employee benefits
BFOQ defense, *see* bona fide occupational qualification defense
bona fide benefit plan defense, 78–81
bona fide occupational qualification (BFOQ) defense
  in age discrimination cases, 81–83
  in sex discrimination cases, 26–30, 42
business necessity, 11–12

Catholic Church, 58–60
charges
  filing, 214–221
  processing, 221–226
child labor, 108
Civil Rights Act of 1964, 1, 25, 212, 246,
  see also Title VII
Civil Rights Act of 1991, 229

319

claim(s), *xiv–xv*
  arbitration of, 231–235
  employer's explanation in,
    177–182
  evaluating feasibility of pursuing,
    191–196, 205–211
  hypothetical events leading to,
    175–177
  relevant context in, 186–191
  and retaliation by employer,
    196–205
  risks of pursuing, 195
  settlement of, 226–227
  and specific evidence of
    discriminatory bias, 183–186
  statutory relief of, 227–231
  see also litigation
"cliff" plans, 142
COBRA, *see* Consolidated
    Omnibus Budget Reconciliation
    Act of 1985
collective bargaining agreements,
    162
common law doctrines, 160–161
compensable time, 117–121
conciliation agreements,
    225–226
Consolidated Omnibus Budget
    Reconciliation Act of 1985
    (COBRA), 130–133
context, relevant, 186–191

damages, 228–231
deferral requirement, 213
Department of Labor (DOL), 111
depositions, 241–243
disability benefits, 305
disability discrimination, 84–106
  and definition of disability, 85–93
  and pre-employment inquiries,
    98–101
  qualifications standard for, 93–98

and reasonable accommodation
    principle, 101–106
discovery, 241–243
discriminatory statements, 23–24,
    184–186, 261
disparate impact, 7, 10–12, 16,
    76–78
disparate treatment, 7–10
DOL (Department of Labor), 111
downsizing, 283–303
  challenges to, 288–293
  hypothetical example of, 285–288
  of overqualified employees,
    300–303
  and severance agreements,
    293–300
duties test (exempt employees),
    111, 114–116
dyslexia, 102–103

EEOC, *see* U.S. Equal Employment
    Opportunity Commission
employee benefit(s), 126–143
  basic protections related to,
    137–143
  coverage issues related to,
    133–137
  health insurance as, 129–133
  as privilege, 126–127
  reasons for providing, 127
  scope of regulation of, 127–129
employee discounts, 122
Employee Retirement Income
    Security Act (ERISA), 134–143,
    284–287, 292–293
employer-employee relationship,
    historical changes in, *xi–xii*
employment-at-will, *xi,* 160–161,
    166–170
employment disputes, *xiv*
Employment Retirement Security
    Act, 2

English language fluency, 51–54
Equal Pay Act, 30
ERISA, *see* Employee Retirement Income Security Act
essential job functions, 94–95
ethnic discrimination, *see* national origin discrimination; race discrimination
exempt employees, 110–117

Fair Labor Standards Act (FLSA), 2, 107–125
  calculating pay under, 121–125
  compensable time under, 117–121
  employees exempt from, 110–117
Family and Medical Leave Act (FMLA), 144–159
  and ADA, 157–159
  employer's obligations under, 152–157
  limitations of, 145–146
  medical certification requirement of, 149–152
  notice requirements of, 146–149
  provisions of, 145
Family and Medical Leave Act of 1993, 2
FLSA, *see* Fair Labor Standards Act
fluctuating workweek, 124–125
FMLA, *see* Family and Medical Leave Act
"for cause," termination, 164–165

gender discrimiation, *see* sex discrimination

harassment
  racial, 13–15
  religious, 65–67
  see also sexual harassment
health insurance benefits, 129–133
Health Insurance Portability and Accountability Act of 1996 (HIPAA), 130, 132, 133
hostile environment, 13–15

Immigration Reform and Control Act, 47
implied contract theory, 161–166
intragroup discrimination, 60

litigation, *xiv–xv*, 236–251
  arbitration as alternative to, 231–235
  discovery in, 241–243
  and filing of suit, 237–241
  and pre-suit procedures, 212–226
  pretrial motions in, 243–245
  and statutory relief, 227–231
  trial as component of, 245–250
lunch, time off for, 119

major life activities, 87–88, 91–92
McDonnell Douglas standard, 16–18, 20, 21, 23, 69, 178
medical leave, *see* Family and Medical Leave Act
Medicare, 131–132
minimum wage, 108, 122
monetary damages, 228–231

national origin discrimination, 45–54
  and definition of discrimination, 49–51
  and definition of national origin, 46–49
  and English fluency, 51–54
  race discrimination vs., 45

Older Workers Benefit Protection
   Act (OWBPA), 78–81, 294–299
on-call periods, 120–121
opposition activity, 197–198
overqualified employees,
   downsizing of, 300–303
overtime pay, 108, 123–124
OWBPA, *see* Older Workers Benefit
   Protection Act

paramour preference, 34–37
pension plans, 134–143
pre-employment inquiries, 98–101
pregnancy discrimination, 41–44
pre-suit procedure(s), 212–226
   filing charges as, 214–221
   processing charges as, 221–226
pretext proof (pretext evidence),
   18–22, 178
pretrial motions, 243–245
prima facia cases, 16–17, 20
probative evidence, 22–24,
   183–185
protected employee activities, 197
public policy exception (to at-will
   employment), 166–170
punitive damages, 229–230

race discrimination, 3–24
   and definition of discrimination,
      7–13
   and definition of race, 3–7
   national origin discrimination vs.,
      45
   pretext evidence of, 18–22
   probative evidence of, 22–24
   prohibition against, 3
   proof of, 15–24
   sex discrimination vs., 25–26
   and terms/conditions of
      employment, 13–15
   and timeliness requirements, 238

racial/ethnic minorities, 5–6
racial harassment, 13–15
reasonable accommodation,
   60–65, 95, 101–106
reduction-in-force (RIF), 70–71
refusals to hire, 16–17
refusal-to-hire cases, 187
Rehabilitation Act of 1973, 1,
   84–85
relevant context, 186–191
religious discrimination, 55–67
   and exemption for religious
      organizations, 56–60
   harassment as, 65–67
   prohibition against, 55
   and reasonable accommodation
      principle, 60–65
retaliation by employer, 196–205
retirement plans, 134–143
RIF, *see* reduction-in-force
right-to-sue letter, 237–238

salary test (exempt employees),
   111–113
same-sex harassment, 259–261
seniority, 73
settlements, 226–227
severance agreements, 293–300
sex discrimination, 25–44
   and bona fide occupational
      qualification defense, 26–30
   in paramour preference cases,
      34–37
   and pregnancy discrimination,
      41–44
   and privacy concerns, 29–30
   prohibition against, 25
   race discrimination vs., 25–26
   and stereotyping, 37–41
   and wage discrimination, 30–34
   see also sexual harassment
sexual assault, 266

sexual harassment, 13, 257–282
  employer liability in cases of,
    267–276
  practical aspects of, 276–282
  severity/persuasiveness
    requirement for, 265–267
  sex-based requirement for,
    258–262
  unwelcomeness requirement for,
    262–265
smoking gun evidence, 183
Social Security, 305, 308
Social Security Administration
  (SSA), 310–3
state laws, 2
statements, discrim   –24,
  184–186, 261
stereotyping
  racial, 97
  sex, 37–41
subminimum wage, 108
substantially limiting impairments,
  88–91
suits, see litigation
summary judgment, 243–245

tender-back rule, 298–299
terms and conditions of
  employment, 13–15
tips, 122–123
Title VII (of Civil Rights Act of
  1964), 1, 2, 30, 56, 58, 224,
  227, 228, 237–239, 257, 260
training programs, 119–120
trials, 245–250

unwelcomeness requirement
  (sexual harassment), 262–265

U.S. Constitution, 55
U.S. Equal Employment
  Opportunity Commission
  (EEOC), xiv, 196, 206–207,
  212–216, 218–225, 232, 235,
  236, 238–242, 298, 310
U.S. Supreme Court, 249
  and age discrimination, 69–70, 78
  and charge-filing process,
    217–218
  and disiability discrimination, 87
  and race discrimination, 5–7, 12,
    16, 20–21
  and sexual harassment, 260,
    265–268
  and tender-back rule, 298–299

vesting, pension plan, 140–141
vicarious liability, 14

wage discrimination, 30–34
WARN Act, see Worker Adjustment
  and Retraining Notification Act
welfare plans, 140–142
Worker Adjustment and Retraining
  Notification Act (WARN Act),
  287–288
workers' compensation, 307–308
workplace discrimination, federal
  laws prohibiting, 1–2
wrongful discharge, 17,
  160–171
  and employment-at-will doctrine,
    160–161
  and implied contract, 161–166
  and public policy exception,
    166–170
  recent trends in, 170–171